The Compleat
Gentleman

The Compleat Gentleman

Five Centuries of Aristocratic Life

GEOFFREY BEARD

RIZZOLI
NEW YORK

First published in the United States of America by
Rizzoli International Publications, Inc.
300 Park Avenue South. New York, NY 10010

copyright © 1993 by Geoffrey Beard

Beard, Geoffrey
The compleat gentleman: five centuries of aristocratic life/by Geoffrey Beard.
p. cm.
Includes index.
ISBN 0-8478-1629-X:
1. Nobility—England—History.
2. Men—England—Conduct of life—History.
3. England—Social life and customs. I. Title. HT653.G7B415 1992
305.5'223'081—dc20   92-14418
CIP

*Jacket front: John Singer Sargent. "Sir Frank Swettingham" (detail). 1904. Oil on canvas, 50 x 40".
The National Portrait Gallery, London*

*Jacket back: Benjamin West. "Portrait of Mr. and Mrs. John Custance." 1778. Oil on canvas, 60 5/16 x 84".
The Nelson Atkins Museum, Kansas City, Missouri. (Nelson Fund) 34-77*

*Title page: François-Xavier Fabre. "Allen Smith Contemplating Florence across the Arno." 1797. Oil on canvas, 28 x 36".
Fitzwilliam Museum, Cambridge*

Jacket and book design by Pamela Fogg
Printed in Singapore

Photo credits: Art Resource, New York: pgs. 16 (top), 32, 123, 143, 167; Bruce Bailey: p. 210; Bridgeman Art
Library, London: pgs. 96, 103, 104, 146; Richard Caspole: pgs. 27, 68, 76-77, 107, 112, 124, 130, 134, 149, 152, 155,
156, 157; Graham Challifour: p. 82; Country Life Library, London: pgs. 100, 101, 201; Mark Fiennes: p. 20;
Fotomas Index, London: p. 25; Angelo Hornak: pgs. 41, 93; Anthony Kersting: pgs. 36, 78, 204, 205; Horst Kolo:
p. 81; Micheal Marsland: pgs. 29, 128, 158, 161, 163; Alan North: p. 98 (bottom); Pilgrim Press, Ltd., London:
p. 70; Joseph Szaszfai: pgs. 111, 150; Thomas-Photos, Oxford: p. 108 (bottom); Three's Company: p. 84; Andreas
Von Einsiedel: p. 98; John Webb: p. 69; Jeremy Whitaker: pgs. 30, 74, 89, 207; R. A. Wilsher: p. 57.

Contents

Preface

This book is based on the six Kathy and F. G. Summit Distinguished Scholar Lectures that I gave at Colonial Williamsburg in February–March 1987. Lectures do not easily become books, having as they do a superfluity of illustrations, some five hundred in this case, and many irrelevant, if amusing, asides. The theme and overall balance have been maintained, but four further chapters have been added. Very few words from the original starting point remain, but the title, suggested by knowledge of Henry Peacham's influential book *The Compleat Gentleman*, published in 1622, was retained. My subject was also explored by Daniel Defoe in 1729 (*The Complete English Gentleman*). However, in the present age, when the role of women is recognized, justly, as an equal one, I have been mindful that it was they who gave birth to the new life and saw to its early continuance, albeit with the aid of wet and dry nurses. In all years there was not only room for a "mother's boy," but also for the care and attention given to household life and living by mothers, wives, and sisters. They have an honored place in this story.

In the writing of books there are those who help by their energy, advice, or sympathetic support, or even a combination of all three. I would not have got far in my initial labors without the support of Kathy and F. G. Summit and Graham Hood, Chief Curator at Colonial Williamsburg. The subjects were refined over several years with the percipient help of my students at Lancaster University and those on the Attingham Summer School (a course devoted to study of the country house in Britain). In particular, I have long benefited in many ventures from the encouragement of Helena Hayward, John Lewis, Annabel Westman, Sybil Bruel, Robyn Asleson, the Earl of Scarbrough, the late Lord Howard, Sir Nicholas and Lady Goodison, Wendell and Betsy Garrett, and not least, my wife, Margaret, and daughter, Helen.

The illustrations are an integral part of this book in that they have their own important contribution to make,

independently of a necessarily limited text. I thought about each one, and the contribution it could confer, for a long time. Gathering them, against my lists, has been accomplished with great dedication by Cynthia Horowitz. Much specific help in this respect was also given by Jeremy Whitaker, Angelo Hornak, Mark Fiennes, Anthony Kersting, Clive Aslet, Jane Hirschowitz, Duncan Thomson, and Ian Ward. My handwritten text, old-fashioned but efficient enough as a means of producing at least my books, was carried on to the word processor, with patient care, by Joanne Ford. Maureen Barton did additional typing with her customary efficiency.

An author's text is always improved by a good editor, and I have been fortunate in the skill and good humor Charles Miers has bestowed on the book—and on me. I turned to an American, rather than an English publisher, in a year when those in England seemed depressed and cautious over a title dealing with a conspicuously English subject. As I become older it seems more important to strive for the personal pleasure given by a good, well-designed book. This was fostered in me in earlier years by handling all the wondrous productions of the great private presses in the collections of the Birmingham Reference Library. Rizzoli excels at providing good design, and I am much indebted to its senior designer Pamela Fogg for her considerable efforts on this title. Technical expertise was also provided by Rizzoli's computer-typesetting specialist Michael Bertrand and production and editorial manager Elizabeth White. I have chosen to give this book no dedication other than to all those friends, on both sides of the Atlantic, who satisfy in me Robert Southey's statement:

My never failing friends are they,
With whom I converse day by day.

Geoffrey Beard
Bath, October 1991

Hans Holbein the Younger (1497–1543). "Thomas Howard, 3rd Duke of Norfolk." 1539–1540.
Oil on wood panel, 31 x 24". By gracious permission of Her Majesty, Queen Elizabeth II

Introduction

Although the early seventeenth-century writer Philip Massinger wrote in his *Parliament of Love* (1624), "There are a thousand doors to let out life," I want, in this short study, to open but one. Yet as the door creaks wide, one sees many vistas leading to some aspects of the ideal life here created. The role of the gentleman in English life and letters and, where relevant, of such life in America, needs at least ten sections: birth and early life; schooling, university, and the Grand Tour; marriage; the building of a suitable house; seeking a profession; pursuits in the town and country; activities within the home; a glance at life in the present century; and finally, as it thus comes to everyone, the sad panoply of death.

The idea of "the Compleat Gentleman," complex in its ethos, developed in classical Greece and had achieved finely balanced attitudes by the time of the Renaissance. It is said that the Emperor Charles V kept three books at his bedside: the Bible, Niccolò Machiavelli's *The Prince* (1513), and Baldassare Castiglione's *Il Cortegiano* (c. 1508–1518)— "The Courtier." Castiglione's treatise, which had great influence, stressed the human values consistent with the attitude of any gentleman: of not hurting the feelings of others, of not making them feel inferior, of behaving with ease and grace, and of experiencing proper joy in the wonders of true love and service, one to the other. When these books began to circulate widely in England, and as travel increasingly familiarized Englishmen with the land of their origin, it was a short step to accepting the values they advocated.

In England, the poet John Milton (1608–1674) dismissed the Middle Ages, at least the fourteenth and early fifteenth centuries, as a dreary tale of battle between kites and crows. Yet an age that gave us the triumphs of soaring Perpendicular Gothic architecture, the lively writings of Geoffrey Chaucer and Sir Thomas Malory, and the great carols and ballads was also one in which "gentlemanly" ideas of chivalry were already active. Expressed in the feats of heroism, usually in single combat, or in jousts and tour-

naments, courtly love and the feudal forms of loyalty were developed and sharpened. Codes of courtesy and etiquette were invested with strictness and increasing elaboration. The orders of knighthood advanced those in families of established rank and strengthened an *élite*. The similar sophistications of Renaissance behavior, of concern with rank, precedent, and possessions, were discovered by those on adventurous travels in Italy and elsewhere. Their transfer to England mingled with what was inherent and enriched attitudes already fertile. By the late fifteenth century the seemingly wondrous and chivalric exploits of the Crusades (the military expeditions by European Christians in the eleventh to thirteenth centuries to recover the Holy Land from the Mohammedans) were long forgotten, but the ideals of selfless commitment to a cause were not. It was this dedication that overrode all other considerations in the activities of the gentry. They were secure in a long lineage, often as the descendants of families originating at the time of the Norman Conquest in 1066.

Loyalty to family, ancient house, and estate has manifested itself uniquely in England. In France and Italy so many *châteaux* and *palazzi* lie empty, with the bustle and noise of family life long gone. But an English country house, each "the hub of the landlord's existence," is often still inhabited and cherished by those best able to care, the families who saw to its origin. For our purposes it is sixteenth-century courtiers who start the story, by their beggaring attempts at raising houses grand enough to attract Queen Elizabeth I on one of her summer progresses. Families group and regroup across the succeeding years, always parrying the insistent sacrifices imposed, in order that each house and its often fabled contents can go forward as completely as possible to the succeeding generations.

By the nineteenth century, due to the rich diet of the novels of Sir Walter Scott and others, it was fashionable to look back to these earlier years with nostalgia for their imagined goodness and steady progress. If beyond the clois-

Sir Joshua Reynolds, PRA (1723–1792). "General Sir Bannastre Tarleton." 1782. Oil on canvas, 93 x 57". The Trustees, The National Gallery, London

*Currier and Ives. "The Celebrated Trotting Mares Maud S. and Aldine driven by William Vanderbilt,
June 15, 1883." Colored lithograph. Museum of the City of New York. The J. Clarence Davies Collection*

tered stretches of a rolling Repton landscape and behind sentinel-like stone lodges, life was advancing inexorably to a technology-ridden future, an archaic security of tenure still persisted—even though passage had been given to the new railway to cross the distant reaches (out of earshot and preferably out of sight of those in the south-facing drawing room).

It is difficult for any except those involved to grasp the full relevance of a family's continuity over many long centuries. Few of us can now recite the names of the Plantagenet kings or know the classical orders as our forebears (usually) did. There are no longer formal letters of instruction on how to behave, such as those issued by Lord Burghley in the sixteenth century and (copying him) by Lord Chesterfield in the eighteenth. We are also distanced from those in the past by wider opportunities and facili-

ties and by better regimens of diet and exercise, with their controlled intakes of vitamins and rigorous specifications of movement. Whilst our health is not given too much thought by us, that of any Elizabethan nobleman did concern him, almost daily. There is effective modern treatment to help in alleviating illness and now a readier access, across the social spectrum, to education, travel, comfort, and leisure. Yet, given the past's shortcomings, there was an urgent desire to achieve and succeed—the brilliant career of Sir Christopher Wren (1632–1723), astronomer and scientist, and—seemingly by accident—architect, is but one example. Succeeding well has always been a paramount accomplishment among England's and America's ruling classes. Given the opportunity, as they were, to study at the great public schools, boarding there, away from home, and able to study and play in an over-intensive milieu of learning in near one-to-one encounters with a tutor, they were a privileged minority, and were, for the most part, male. Emancipation of women, of course, was tardy in acceptance, and while great progress in women's status has been made, it is in many ways still insufficient.

The pattern of a gentleman's development has always been bound in some way to that of his land. Landed income was the basic criterion of title, for as Richard Brome (d. 1652), servant to the writer Ben Jonson, wrote in *The Damoiselle*:

> . . . your fair titles
> Are but shadows of your ancestry;
> And you walk in 'em, when your land is gone,
> Like the pale ghosts of dead nobility.

The possession and careful management of land was of prime importance in providing money in more than ordinary quantity. The story of the English country house would be different without the surrounding and revenue-producing landscaped park. There was space there for cattle and sheep and for growing timber. Good enough reasons to appreciate, with some amusement, Lady Bracknell's questioning of Jack Worthing, a prospective suitor for her daughter Gwendolen's hand, in Oscar Wilde's novel *The Importance of Being Earnest* (1895):

> "What is your income?"
> "Between seven and eight thousand a year."
> "In land, or in investments?"
> "In investments, chiefly."
> "That is satisfactory. What between the duties expected of one during one's lifetime, and the duties exacted from one after one's death, land has ceased to be either a profit or a pleasure. It gives one position, and prevents one from keeping it up. That's all that need be said about land."

With the vital stretching reaches of land, the nervous stag-antlered silhouettes, and the plunging carp in distant silvered lakes went the rearing pile of the ancestral house itself. While its internal arrangement may have been sacrificed in convenience to the dictates of some arcane woodcut design in the vellum-bound treatises by the leading Renaissance architects, Sebastiano Serlio, Vincenzo Scamozzi, or Andrea Palladio, it was still destined to be the physical expression of the standing of the family. As Roger North wrote in the "Premise" to his tract "Of Building" (c.1695–1696):[1]

> The prime and most exalted spirits, have bin declared
> lovers of building. And the greatest Statesmen,
> and favorites of fortune, after proof of all the envyed
> grandure upon earth, have chosen, either upon dis-
> grace or voluntary retirement, to imploy their time,
> in designing fabricks and executing them.

The matrimonial alliance, however, was of greater moment to a family. Its terms were a matter of close and hard bargaining, pointed up by William Hogarth's *The Marriage Settlement* (plate 40). Marriages had to be so arranged as to bring more land, greater wealth, or further influence to a family. The rights of the heir must be restricted, so that what had been carefully nurtured across countless generations could go forward unencumbered. But there was no escape from the amount of the dowry or the burden of the jointure (the portion paid to a widow after her husband's death). The bargaining was protracted and conducted as adroitly as each side's lawyers could manage. Yet in the late sixteenth century, Lord Burghley told his son, Robert Cecil, to avoid choosing a wife only for her wealth, "For it will cause contempt in others and loathing in thee." Robert was instructed also to avoid dwarfs or fools, which "beget a race of pigmies" or give weariness "to hear her talk." The way to be pursued was by sensible disposition, the support of parents, a respectable income—"For a man can buy nothing in the market with gentility"—and avoidance of those whose religion gave rise to persecution. The legal ramifications of the strict settlement ensured that the family estates, cared for in detail by successive stewards, should be in the hand of a life-tenant only, entailed so that he could not do what he liked with his patrimony. And there was also a long time in which if all the factors of an arranged marriage (in which love or even faint affection came a poor second) could not be arranged to the satisfaction of a tetchy father, he could seek another suitor for his daughter's hand, and his own enrichment, with the minimum of consultation.

It had become fashionable in England from the sixteenth century on to increase income—additional to that gained from the land—by seeking a profession. The elder son might have duties enough about his estate but younger sons could seek out a career in the law or look for the rewards of office in the church, the army, or the navy. More resources could be garnered for daily living and expenditure on houses, paintings, furniture, horses, gaming, and even whores by activity in trade. If commerce could be managed "distantly" enough, without daily attendance or undue haggling over money, it was a befitting enough role for gentlemen. They had capital assets to deploy, which their bankers could use as security, and they could, if as astute as Lionel Cranfield, Earl of Middlesex, or Sir Arthur Ingram in the early seventeenth century, make a fortune by obtaining licenses and monopolies. There were resources on or under their estates, such as lead, copper, or standing timber, and provided the ravages of obtaining and felling were contained out of sight of the house-roof viewers of the trumpeting hunt, all was satisfactory. There may not have been Lady Bracknell's taint of commerce on Jack Worthing's father:

> He was evidently a man of some wealth. Was he born in what the Radical papers call the purple of commerce, or did he rise from the ranks of the aristocracy?

"Commerce" was best left as an unheralded contributor to conspicuous aristocratic wealth, although from the Elizabethan period on there were always those whose wealth was known to be derived chiefly from exploiting the mineral resources of estates as adroitly as any later American entrepreneurs such as Henry Clay Frick or Henry E. Huntington. But what wealth, from whatever source, provided was a country house and a town house to give further status, a "bought" seat in Parliament—by bribing the electorate—or the first start in a profession,

as well as the advantage and convenience of many material possessions. These might be useful, as in a handsome coach and four, or aesthetically pleasing too, as in a silver toilet service by Paul de Lamerie.

In 1665 Edward Waterhouse noted in *The Gentleman's Monitor* that everyone prepared a full table, kept horses, wore rich clothes, retained many servants, built magnificently, and had other "costly diversions," but that it all pinched the "paunch of an estate"; and in a deliciously convoluted phrase, "the succulency [is] sussurated from its amassation." Crippling expenditure was the due result of satisfying such consumption. Between 1738 and 1786 a family trust paid off over 200,000 pounds of debts for the Duke of Newcastle, but 79,350 pounds was still outstanding at his death.[2] Many families rose clear—the dukes of Westminster and of Portland—on the sizes of their London property, but as late as 1870 the Duke of Newcastle was before the bankruptcy courts with increasing debts. In 1839 these debts stood at 158,000 pounds,[3] but were minuscule by comparison to those of the first and second dukes of Buckingham. Successful marriages throughout the eighteenth century had given the Grenvilles, dukes of Buckingham, a large landholding with an income of 69,000 pounds. The first duke (d.1839) was more than profligate but was easily overtaken by his son. By 1844 there was a massive debt, standing at about 1 million pounds. The complicated story must have seriously disturbed any silver-mustached aristocrat of the time, especially those who did not live to see the third duke "rescue a good deal from the ruins"[4] and see off the moneylenders and mortgage bankers.

In any account such as this, the various ways in which family life was carried on, in town or in country, are of abiding interest. A peer might argue, unconvincingly to those engaged in lesser matters, that visiting Parliament, attending political parties, sitting for portraits, playing at the gaming tables, buying antiques at Mr. Christie's rooms, or peering, anxiously, at the full folios in his bank ledger was tedious, and even dull. But for some men of action, quietly fishing, painting, reading, and attending to the country estate was dull. Many strained constantly to be away on travels to unknown parts of the world, active as explorers or soldiers. The later exemplars of this traveled in strange, allegedly cool clothes on hot safaris or served in diplomatic or religious missions as "soldiers" of the Crown or of the Lord.

It was left often for wives to worry alone about life in the home. With every minor ailment a threat to life itself, every housewife had her book of remedies. Some were harsher than the rigors of the complaint itself, and in their purging, vituperative way they were outdone only by the attentions of many physicians, complete with a jar of leeches and, to us, strange ideas of treatment and little knowledge of prevention. But on happier days both husband and wife could consider the advancement of their children or the intricacies of archery, croquet, golf, hunting, of flying kites with their sons, of bowling clicking wooden balls, cutting flowers, overseeing meals, attending to endless "calling" and "resident" relatives, and admiring their new-fangled coach-lacquered cars. They might win or lose at cards, or love, and hope to have resources still to pay for seeing that the exotic plants in the glazed conservatory survived the icy rigors of winter. But such conspicuous expenditure was often brought to a halt by many unforeseen factors: death, war, or the enormous expense caused by spiteful litigation over infidelity or divorce.

In this volume, I have included some remarks about gentlemanly life in America—the colony most influenced by England—for while there was not concern there with court life, Americans, fashioned from colonial stock and those daring entrepreneurs who opened lands to the west, were every bit as feudal-minded and patronizing as their English counterparts. William Byrd II of Westover, Virginia, declared in 1726:

Like one of the Patriarchs, I have my Flocks and my Herds, my Bond-men and Bond-women and every sort of trade amongst my own servants, so that I live in a kind of independence on everyone but Providence.

Settled in splendor in his new house on the James River, Byrd represented how Horace had been at his Sabine villa and how countless English milords saw themselves at their Palladian country houses: firm and benevolent patriarchs.

It has been argued "that the British aristocracy declined in status after 1919."[5] Admittedly in the war there was great carnage of bright-eyed sons, which the poet Rupert Brooke called "pouring out the red Sweet wine of youth."[6] And years have advanced, taking their toll in higher wages for labor, changing social attitudes, taxation, and structural decay: the powdering of magnesium limestone façades of great beauty before trickling acid rain, the long processions of curious house visitors—willing to pay, anxious to sniff the air for the smell of tobacco or of richer food and hopeful of seeing hastily abandoned *petit-point* lying on a red-lacquered chair, or an almost-ironed copy of *The Times*. But beyond all that, and admittedly from positions of often considerable privilege, the "Compleat Gentleman" and his family give out to many, offering wide public service and selfless dedication to every worthy endeavor and a willingness to think anew: computers in the estate office now abound. There is, in my view, little decline. Each house-owner will struggle to preserve what he has, to hand it on to the future, as best he can, with systems of taxation ever pressing and often self-defeating. There may no longer be need to gather up the unused food from the dining-room table to give to the needy at the park gates. But there will ever be a willingness to open up land to the local cricket match, to pay toward repairing the church roof and bells, to administer justice to the poachers of their game and salmon, and to catch the London train to see solicitors in Gray's Inn over granting the site for a new village hall. It was ever thus, in varying degrees and details, and betokens more good than ill.

As such my story here can be of no planned or unplanned oblivion. It is rather that of which Henry Howard, the poet earl of Surrey wrote as long ago as 1539, "the households of continuance." They transcend Death itself, with all its ritualistic and marbled commemoration, worthy of a noble house, but cheated by the wonder of each new birth-cry. Tiny fingers are already grasping at the coronet of life, of title, and of eventual unremitting commitment, to family, and, as Sir John Vanbrugh had it of Castle Howard, to "a great fine house."

CHAPTER I

Born of Great Lineage

Of gentlemen, the first and chief are the king, the prince, the duke, marquesses, earls, viscounts, barons, and these are called the nobility, and all these are called lords and noblemen: next to these be knights, esquires and simple gentlemen.

Sir Thomas Smith, "De Republica Anglorum," 1583

The subject matter of this short study is arranged under the headings most common to the conduct of human affairs: birth, education, marriage and family life, engagement in a profession, activity in town and country, and, lightly enough I hope, the finality of death. At least I start with a contradiction: whilst people are certainly born, and as certainly, if reluctantly, die, they may choose not to marry. But for the considerations of securing a family and its house to some permanence, marriage—the alliance of great names—was certainly most important, and enough pursued its uncertain state for some conclusions to be made as to its dominant role.

From medieval times many writers have tried to establish, with limited success, "what a gentlemen is." I have adopted the embracing view of Sir Thomas Smith in 1583, quoted above, because it gives me the necessary freedom to regard anyone as a gentleman, from kings to "esquires and simple gentlemen." The view Guy Miege had in 1691[1] was that the title of gentleman was one commonly given in England to all those who distinguished themselves from the common sorts by "a genteel dress and carriage, good education, learning or an independent station." He neatly categorized that "all noblemen are gentlemen though all gentlemen are not noblemen." In 1729 Daniel Defoe wrote in his *The Complete English Gentleman* that a gentleman was one born "of some known or Ancient family; whose ancestors have at least for some time been raised above the class of mechanics." Dr. Johnson, concerned enough to give five definitions of "gentlemen" in his *Dictionary*, noted him first to be a "man of birth: a man of extraction though not noble."

It would be possible to raise a substantial essay on the

1. George Romney (1734–1802). "The Clavering Children." 1777. Oil on canvas, 60 x 48".
The Henry Huntington Art Gallery, San Marino, California

2. *David des Granges (1611/13–1675). "The Saltonstall Family."*
Oil on canvas, 78 x 107". Tate Gallery, London

Sir Richard Saltonstall (d. 1650) is seen approaching the bedside of his wife,
Elizabeth, who has just delivered a child. The baby is held in swaddling
clothes by a wet nurse.

3. *William Redmore Bigg, RA (1755–1828). "Christening of the Heir."*
c. 1799. Oil on canvas, 25 x 30". Yale Center for British Art,
Paul Mellon Collection

A baby lies docile in a clergyman's arms in this rare artistic
depiction of a father, mother, two daughters, and family friends
looking on at the auspicious event.

various definitions. What I have done further is to take the title of Henry Peacham's book *The Compleat Gentleman*, first published in 1622, as a convenience under which to examine the constants over five centuries of English (and American) aristocratic life. In his *Certaine Precepts* (1617), instructions that he wrote to his son, Lord Burghley noted that "Gentilitie is nothing but ancient Riches." What he characterized further was a land-owning group, not necessarily armigerous, who were "by birth or fortune" occupying a position directly above the rest of the community.[2] In the fevered circumstance of being born as the long-awaited heir to a title or estate, with both parents relieved at the avoidance of yet one more girl to put to the wet nurse, what did the future hold?

First, there was the right of succession to a title and estate that belonged to the firstborn son: the rule of primogeniture. In practice, however, family continuity was often in the hands of the younger sons, and, on rare occasions, daughters. In Elizabethan England, for example, only about 70 percent of inheritance cases were determined by primogeniture. Second, a knight had the right to bear arms: the heraldic distinctions recorded his family liaisons. Following approval by the Heralds of the College of Arms, these could be displayed on a "coat of arms"—a coat, vest, shield, or escutcheon, as appropriate.

Apart from the seigneurial rights given by land ownership, peers (members of the five hereditary degrees of nobility) could be representatives in a separate house of Parliament, the Lords; they could vote, when necessary, by proxy; enter protests in the *Lords Journal;* and, between 1499 and its abolition in 1948, claim the right to trial by fellow peers of the upper house of Parliament for all offenses except those occurring in the armed forces.

The peerage, baronetage, and knighthood were honors granted within the gift of the Crown. The terms "knight" and "esquire" were associated originally with battlefield awards and carried overtones of a chivalric nature. "Esquire" was limited to the younger sons of peers, the heirs of knights, and those who showed that their lineal ancestors were so styled. "Gentleman" appeared as a separate title in 1413, when the Statute of Additions required that in suits and indictments every defendant should give his "estate, degree and mystery." The lowest social position recognized by the Office of Arms as armigerous was

·VIII·OCTOB · M·D·LXIIII·   ·ÆTAT MENS·VI·

4. Anonymous. "John Thynne at the Age of Six, in 1564." Oil on panel, 30 x 20".
Inscribed: "VIII.OCTOB.M.D.LXIIII.ÆTAT.MENS.VI." The Marquess of Bath, Longleat

John Thynne, here with his coral rattle, succeeded his father in 1580 and like him became a passionate builder,
completing Longleat during the late sixteenth century.

that of gentleman. The office, however, lacked the authority to enforce its precepts, although for one hundred and fifty years, from 1530 until 1686, its heraldic officers, on visitations, tried to ensure correct claiming of titles. In the latter half of the seventeenth century no one could be a justice of the peace if below the rank of esquire or, under the terms of the 1671 Game Act, appoint a gamekeeper. The assessment of whether one was part of the aristocracy was more complex. Property qualifications and wealth were the determining factors in assessing such an important social position. A gentleman might become a member of the nobility "but not necessarily for what came to be recognised as the aristocracy."[3]

If it was assumed that the newly born heir would one day swell the ranks of the higher levels of society, would he enter a large burgeoning "club"? The numbers of the aristocracy are complicated to define[4] and only brief details are relevant here. A knight was a military follower, who had served as a page and squire, without title, and then been knighted for personal merit or service in battle. The highest orders of knighthood were the Garter, created in 1348; the Thistle, for Scottish peers (1687); and the St. Patrick (1783). From 1725 knighthoods were awarded also within the Order of the Bath and during the nineteenth

century there were many other points of entry, including the Royal Victorian Order, within the sole gift of the sovereign. In 1658 there were held to be 119 peers; by 1900 the figure had grown to over 520. The Tudor kings (1485–1603) had been sparing with peerage creations, the first two Stuart kings (1603–1649) lavish, and after 1660 there was a three-fold increase. Charles II (1660–1685) granted 43 peerages within a twenty-year period after his Restoration in 1660. There were 14 creations or revivals of dukedoms alone within his reign, compared with 2 between 1500 and 1658. George I created 28 new titles, but George II and George III set themselves against unduly expanding the peerage, and many of the "new" titles went to existing members. Within the nineteenth century this frugal attitude altered. From the 1780s to 1830 the numbers of peers rose: at Queen Victoria's accession in 1837, the House of Lords was about double the size it had been in 1783. The ease with which a peerage could be obtained through William Pitt the younger, prime minister from 1783–1801, was much derided.[5] At the end of the eighteenth century almost 10,000 families held the right to bear arms, and in the computations he made in 1883 for his *The Great Landowners of Great Britain and Ireland* John Bateman noted 14,000 owners of 300 acres or more

5. *Martha Chute. "The Nursery at The Vyne, Hampshire." c. 1857. Ink drawing, 9 x 14".*
The National Trust (The Vyne, Hampshire)

A formal paneled room a little too grand for robust use is the setting for afternoon tea,
an unusually tranquil moment.

6. Child's Dining Set and Flatware. c. 1893. Silver gilt, marked "Tiffany & Co.,"
engraved "From Grandpa, Christmas 1893." Museum of the City of New York, gift of Miss Isabel Shults

The overflowing use of flamboyantly decorated silver for those "born with a silver spoon in the mouth"
is as typical of the young gentleman's accoutrements in 1893 as it might have been in a Renaissance court setting.

of land. The compensations of being a member of such an *élite* were considerable.

There is a desire in most parents to have their children enjoy all the advantages denied, in many cases, to themselves, but from the latter half of the sixteenth century the capacity to reproduce children had been "affected by diet and disease, by inherited propensities, and by age and duration of marriage."[6]

Most children, in whatever age, try hard to lay their puny claim on life. Unfortunate perhaps were the two children of the sixth earl of Rutland, Henry and Francis, styled Lord Roos. On the earl's impressive monument in Bottesford Church, Lincolnshire, erected after 1623 (plate 143) it is stated that by his first wife "he had two sonnes, both of wych died in their infancy by wicked Practice and Sorcerye." Seven years after their death (in 1613), a woman called Joan Flower and her two daughters were executed at Lincoln in March 1620 for bewitching them. The 1619 pamphlet *The Wonderful Discovery of the Witchcraft of Margaret and Philippa Flower* was referred to by the county historian John Nichols as late as the 1790s.[7] If children managed to avoid being bewitched, they were still often a cause of concern. While parents believed their children to be precious, it was with sons that the future of the lineage rested. The uncertain chances of rearing children

meant that extra attention was lavished on the eldest son at the expense of younger sons and daughters.

One of the most attractive features of life in the seventeenth-century is that parents had a genuine love for their children. Portrait painters such as Sir Anthony Van Dyck and Gerard Van Honthorst delighted in rendering children; in almost every English country house there are many lesser examples. The children were painted as men and women in miniature, "the boys with hose and doublet like their fathers, the girls with their soft satin skirts just touching the ground, their hair looped back with ribbons on threaded pearls, round their slender necks wide falling collars of lace as rich as that which adorned their mothers, while with both the expression on their faces is as demure and dignified as their dress" (plate 1).[8]

The many other portraits that show, in stilted pose, gentlemen, their wives, and children offer perhaps further testimony to the ordered life in which affection had its part to play. Only a flicker of annoyance might be seen to be present on the face of the imperious nobleman if the portrait is filled with girls and no richly clad heir to the title. So many girls flit through accounts merely in the purchase of holland frocks, petticoats, and red wool coats. Boys, especially if heirs, were watched more anxiously as they strove to counter the purgatives, the cordial boluses, and

7. The Nostell Priory Doll's House. c. 1735. The National Trust (Nostell Priory, Yorkshire)

This splendid architectural model opens to show nine well-equipped rooms above a rusticated basement. With its blend of English and Dutch artefacts, including two canopied beds, the house has been attributed to the eighteenth century's leading cabinetmaker, Thomas Chippendale.

conserves destined to cure them of childish, but often dangerous ailments and to build up a precariously held strength. Even toothache could be stressful to a weak child. Toothbrushes were not known to Sir Ralph Verney in the 1640s, although he believed the French used them, and his doctor confessed in 1649 that he had never seen one "nor know of what use they may be."[9]

It is difficult for us, from a modern viewpoint, to realize that this affection for children in the seventeenth century was often sacrificed to the encouragement of a breeding designed to make them attractive, eventually, in the marriage market. So it was that the superstition that a wet

nurse's traits "could be given in the milk to a suckling child" made unattractive servants less desirable.

While still in the nursery children learned the alphabet from a hornbook, on which the letters were printed atop the page and the Lord's Prayer below. Not surprisingly, many children were advanced for their years. Richard Evelyn, at two and a half years old, "could read perfectly any of the English, Latin, French or Gothic letters, pronouncing the three first languages exactly," and at five was "making congruous syntax" and "had a strong passion for Greek." He died of "six fits of a quartan ague" in his fifth year.

Much of the early training of children was religious in character, for many agreed with John Milton that "the end of learning is to repair the ruins of our first parents by regaining to know God aright." So childish faults were rendered as grave sins, and the result was a precocity in children such as Richard Evelyn that was deplorable. One is not attracted to Mrs. Hutchinson's account[10] of herself as a child: "Play among other children I despised, and when I was forced to entertain such as came to visit me, I tired them with more grave instructions than their mothers." It is almost with relief one notices that she also pulled their dolls to pieces.

In the seventeenth century the great Puritan families followed the precept of William Gouge in his *Of Domesticall Duties* (1622) that "Pietie is the best thing that a parent can teach his child . . . learning, civilities, calling, portion are all nothing without pietie." There were many heads of households such as Sir Simonds D'Ewes who found it their duty to instruct their children, pray for them, supervise their reading of spiritual works, and regularly catechize them. Lady Anne Waller catechized both her servants and her children each week.[11]

There was a common practice of sending young children into another household to be reared. It has been variously suggested[12] that this was based not only on lack of parental concern, but on a willingness to let others administer the discipline parents wished to avoid; further, the use of a wet nurse reduced the personal difficulties presented by the high rate of infant mortality. The servants provided for a child's daily needs, care in frequent illness, and necessary amusements.

There was a belief, held widely enough, that the use of physical punishment in disciplining children had divine approval. John Brinsley assured his readers in 1612 that God had "sanctified the rod and cor-

rection to cure the evils of their conditions, to drive out that folly which is bound up in their hearts, to save their souls from hell and to give them wisdom. . . .To spare them in these cases is to hurt them." The Puritan Sir John Holland debarred his child from eating meat if she failed her catechism and made her write out the sermons if she did not remember; however, William Gouge, concerned to put his "Domesticall Duties" into practice, did not correct his children when they displeased

8. *Child's cradle. 1867. Oak with carved gilt and painted panels, designed by Norman Shaw.*
Trustees of the Victoria & Albert Museum, London

This charming, zodiacal cradle was made for Julian, privileged son of Shaw's wealthy architect friend, Alfred Waterhouse. The hood lifts, and there is a treadle motion for rocking.

him, instead showing his anger by his silence.

In Stuart-period literature children find as large a place as in its art. Their early deaths, lamentably common, are edged away by the compelling attraction many poets had for describing children. None exceeded Thomas Traherne (1637?–1674) in his study of the wonder of childhood:

All appeared new and strange at first, inexpressibly
rare and delightful and beautiful. I was a little
stranger, which at my entrance into the world was
saluted and surrounded with innumerable joys.
My knowledge was Divine.

Adam Winthrop, father of the first governor of Massachusetts, addressed verses[13] in the early seventeenth century to his newly born nephew, Henry Mildmay of Graces Hall, Essex. The texts underlined the concern for honoring and obeying one's parents:

And to they mother be deere
Obedient be and kinde
Give eare unto her loveing words
And print them in thy minde.

Thy father also love
And willingly obey
That thou mayst longe possesse those lands
Which he must leave one daye.

Sir Thomas Wentworth (1593–1641), first Earl of Strafford, the formidable Lord Deputy, or King's Minister in Ireland—but the most loving of fathers—was raptly devoted to his children, and when Nan and little Arabella were staying with their grandmother, he wrote delightful letters[14] about them: "Wherever they are, my Prayers shall attend them"; "Nan, they tell me, dances prettily, and Arabella is a small practitioner that way also," but he wished her French accent were better, and he hoped her grandmother would remedy this.

In 1647 loving parents Sir Ralph and Lady Verney hoped that a new French maid, if selected with care, could even teach their seven year old to read.[15] A few years earlier the Yorkshireman Sir Henry Slingsby began to teach his four-year-old son Latin in his enthusiasm to rear a

member of a governing class.[16] Another lovable father was Endymion Porter, one of the Gentlemen of the Bedchamber, or personal attendants, to Charles I. When he was with the Prince of Wales in Madrid he wrote constantly about his children, George, the eldest, and Charles:[17] "Send me word how the children do, and whether Charles be black or fair"; a little later he sent home "six little glass bottles with silver chains for little George, and I make no doubt he will keep a terrible stir with them," and asked: "I pray you send me word whether he hath ever a great tooth yet or no, and how many teeth little Charles hath." He further wrote to his wife about George: "I would have you. . . not beat him overmuch"— an indication of the way Stuart parents corrected children they undoubtedly loved. Schooling was a necessary second stage in disciplining the young mind.

Both Henry Peacham and John Locke[18] agreed that parents were often unwilling to spend money on securing men of good qualifications as tutors. Much was done by their mothers. School attendance did however bring the important, if limited, curriculum of study of the Bible, the speaking and writing of Latin—the continual repetition of William Lily's *Latin Grammar* or the newer method of Comenius of reciting simple dialogues relating to common objects—and study of rhetoric. Locke noted, "There can scarce be a greater defect in a gentlemen, not to express himself well either in speaking or writing." So declamations were recited at school prize days—the grammar schools rising in many cases from endowed chantries at which a priest recited a daily mass for the founder and also undertook additional duties of teaching in a free school. One has only to read the speeches of the average member of Parliament in the seventeenth century to realize that such schools succeeded in their aim.

Greek, Hebrew, mathematics, and science were given a due place in many curricula, but the study of English was somewhat neglected. In his *The Compleat Gentleman* (1622), Henry Peacham bade Mr. William Howard, "labour to get the habit of a good stile, in English as well as in Latin" and advised him to read Sir Thomas More's *Richard III*, Sidney's *Arcadia*, and the works of Francis Bacon and Richard Hooker. In noblemen's houses much stress was also laid on music, on singing, dancing, fencing, and riding, and on the inculcation of fine manners and a fine courtesy.

9. *Sir Anthony Van Dyck (1599–1641). "Thomas Howard, 2nd Earl of Arundel with His Grandson Thomas (later 5th Duke of Norfolk)."*
c. 1635–1636. Oil on canvas, 57 x 48". His Grace, the Duke of Norfolk

The earl is depicted in armor with the badge of the Garter, the most exclusive order of knighthood (founded in 1348),
and the Earl Marshal's baton in his right hand. A discerning patron and collector, the earl had the painting sent to Rome
to be translated into a marble bas-relief, possibly by Dieussart.

Locke also prescribed for children "plenty of open air exercise and sleep," advice with which many children presumably disagreed. Reverence for parents and fit courtesies were insisted on, as can be seen in Edward Coote's poem *The Schoole Master to his Scholler* (1627):

> First I commend thee God to serve,
> Then to thy parents duly yeeld,
> Unto all men be courteous
> And manerly in town and field.

> Your clothes unbuttoned do not use
> Let not your hose ungartered be
> Have handkerchief in readinesse
> Wash hands and face or see not me.

> Wherefore, my child, behave thyselfe,
> So decently in all assayes,
> That thou maist purchase parents' love,
> And eke obtaine thy master's praise.

With girls there was little hope of their desire for an education like that given their brothers. If some women, such as Elizabeth, Lady Falkland,[19] and Mrs. Hutchinson, had succeeded in learning several languages and in becoming well educated, the majority of girls, whether at home or at school, had their studies restricted to reading, writing, arithmetic, French, needlework, music, dancing, and drawing. Daniel Defoe, in his *Essay on Projects* (1697), was anxious to let women learn "that they might have had

10. Master of the Countess of Warwick. "William Brooke, 10th Lord Cobham, and His family." 1567.
Oil on panel, 38 x 49". The Marquess of Bath, Longleat

Lord Cobham is shown with his second wife, her sister, and six of his children. In this very rare panel, Maximilian
has a dog jumping onto his lap, William a bird on his hand, and Margaret a pet marmoset.

more wit." He was mindful of the strictures of Mary Astell in her *Defence of the Female Sex* (also of 1697) that men "had endeavoured to train us up altogether to Ease and Ignorance." Yet a mother's role should not be so underestimated: it was important in Stuart England and later.

If children survived their earliest years, complex situations could be still thrust upon them. James Brydges, later to be the first Duke of Chandos, was born in 1674. By October 1681, aged less than eight years, he went with his mother to join his father in Constantinople and was there for five years before joining his brothers at Westminster School in 1686 at the age of twelve. While there may have been eventual great rejoicing and the ringing of bells at the delivery in January 1709 of George

Lyttelton—he was a seven-months' child and at birth had been almost cast aside as dead—position was soon thrust upon him. As a seven-year-old boy, son of a younger son of a baronet, he assumed importance when his uncle died in 1712 followed by his grandfather in 1716, thereby bringing him the mastership of a large estate. He fought against his delicate constitution and almost constant ill-health at the first family house at Hagley in Worcestershire (which had sheltered some of the escaping Gunpowder Plot rebels in 1605) and described by Horace Walpole in 1753 as "immeasurably bad and old." His mother, preoccupied with her own poor health and the frequent early deaths of other offspring, was typical of many who were glad the eldest boy survived.

11. *John Michael Wright (1617–1695).* "*James Cecil, Viscount Cranborne, with His Sister, Lady Catherine Cecil.*" *c. 1669.*
Oil on canvas, 63 x 51". The Marquess of Salisbury, Hatfield House

In this sensitive, cool painting, both children wear frocks. The pomegranate and flowers are associated with Prosperine,
the nymph of Spring. Cupid, god of Love, appears in the cameo in the boy's feathered hat.

In a provocative history of childhood, Philippe Ariès[20] traced the changes in parental attitude toward child raising from the Middle Ages. He quoted a French report of 1766 (which was as true of England in the same period) of the nobility pampering their children:

The excessive delicacy of their physical education, especially in the early years of childhood and youth, has today made them the most wretched specimens of the human race. . . .They are carefully locked up in hermetically sealed apartments three fourths of the time where they are either lying down, sitting, or tenderly carried about. They are hardly permitted to spend a twentieth of their time on their own two feet and besides take nothing but light dishes and often useless, or even harmful medications. When they reach maturity you see them pale, spare, delicate and infirm.

The nineteenth-century child may too often have been "pale, spare, delicate and infirm"—the lives of the Brontë sisters are evidence enough of constant illness—but there were many exceptions. As Augustus Hare tells in *The Years with Mother*, published in 1896, more than sixty years after his birth in 1834:

In earliest childhood my dearest mother treated me completely as her companion, creating interests and amusements for me. . . and making me so far a sharer in her own spiritual thoughts that I have always felt a peculiar truthfulness in Wordsworth's line, "Heaven lies about us in our infancy."

Unusually, from the age of four Hare never had any playthings or companions, but he reveled in looking at books in his uncle's library. At the age of five he began his lessons: besides English reading, writing and spelling, history, arithmetic, and geography, he had to study German reading and writing and a little Latin. To this seemingly advanced curriculum he was made familiar with the topography of Jerusalem and the architecture of the Temple, although he was utterly ignorant of the topography of Rome or London and of the architecture of St. Peter's or St. Paul's. The young boy never recalled a moment of his "indoor childhood" when he was not undergoing education of some kind, and generally of an unwelcome kind. There was often a good deal of screaming and crying over the writing and arithmetic, and he recalls that he never got on satisfactorily with either subject until his grandmother or his aunt banged his knuckles with a ruler until his fingers went the right way.

The second Earl Grosvenor's eldest son, Viscount Belgrave, and his wife, Lady Elizabeth Leveson-Gower, had already had two girls born to them when their first boy died at the age of nine months. So it was with great rejoicing that another son was born to them in 1825. Attended by Dr. Harrison from Chester, who slept in the house for the last few nights prior to the birth, and attended also by a midwife from the Middlesex Hospital, Hugh Lupus Grosvenor, to be eventually first Duke of Westminster, was a "large healthy, handsome child." He was christened by the Bishop of Chester in the family church, his godparents being the Earl of Derby and Lord Gower, later the Duke of Sutherland. The large family party with their many guests drove to Eccleston in five carriages, to a church crowded with tenants and retainers. But even at this point in the nineteenth century Hugh was put out for rearing to a wet nurse, and he flourished from birth under the care of two nurses and the nursery maids in the Eaton nursery. The Westminster household, as so many others, knew nothing of the fact that in 1628 the Countess of Lincoln had written a book urging mothers to feed their own children. At the London house of the Westminsters in Grosvenor Square (plate 113) little time could be spared for him from the busy social and political life of his parents: his nurse, he said, was his "mother." But before Hugh Lupus was five his natural mother could note that he began to do his lessons, both in English and German, with a governess. He could then read a little, repeat the catechism, and had a good idea of drawing.[21]

What young boys and girls were always capable of, beyond the strictures of tutor, governess, and perhaps even a concerned parent, was to enjoy a playtime: to bowl wooden bowls, to bring a kite indoors to show to mother, to explore the doll's house (plate 7), or to be hoisted on horseback for the first ride. Was happiness an aristocratic perquisite? While it may have been present on many a childish excursion or indulgence, wealth did not guar-

12. Joseph Francis Nollekens (1702–1748). "Children Playing with a Hobby Horse." c. 1741–1748. Oil on canvas, 18 x 22". Yale Center for British Art, Paul Mellon Collection

Nollekens specialized in imitations of Watteau, especially painting genre scenes of affluent domestic interiors including children, often his own.

antee its exclusive presence in a titled household, or indeed an English one.

The normal practice for Scottish peers in educating their young children was to send them, at the age of five or six, to the local grammar school. The Marquis of Atholl sent his sons in the 1660s to Perth Academy, the Earl of Airlie's son was taught in Dundee, the Earl of Annandale's children in Haddington, and James, Earl of Arran, later fourth Duke of Hamilton, at the Hamilton Burgh School, founded by his ancestor. His companions in learning to read, write, and count were the sons of the palace servants and local farmers. The earl also had his own governor who taught him Latin and allowed him from the palace gardens in the summer to watch, beyond its walls, cockfighting and

puppet plays. At the age of eleven he could continue his education; taught by his governor at home or at grammar school—and by the age of thirteen, he was off to university, like the sons of most Scottish noblemen, often on the Continent, The Netherlands, France, or Italy.[22]

There were many too in England who wished to set up in a new world or to give their children what they felt to be a better chance in life. The great Puritan migration in the 1630s to North America—when perhaps some 20,000 people left England—was to the areas near Massachusetts Bay, as far north as Maine, and eventually as far south as South Carolina. The men, women, and children who immigrated had had close ties of "kinship, neighbourhood, church congregation, or parish association in England."

13. *John Michael Wright (1617–1695). "Randolph and John Corbet." c. 1685. Oil on canvas, 55 x 51".*
Virginia Museum of Fine Arts, gift of Mr. and Mrs. Seymour Waxman

Wright had a fine capacity for capturing the natural ways of aristocratic children. In his late portrait the boys impatiently clutch
their bowling balls and the frisky dog is set for disturbing their action, depicted again in the park landscape of the middle distance.
The painter was mindful to include statuary that evoked the educational process of the Grand Tour.

14. *Arthur Devis (1712–1787). "Children in an Interior," formerly called "The Chomondeley Children." c. 1742–1743.*
Oil on canvas, 39 x 49". Yale Center for British Art, Paul Mellon Collection

With the child's kite propped improbably at the right, the bright-eyed sitters are carefully positioned in an imposing
classical setting. Devis excelled at creating such images of a small world.

There is little doubt that schooling for a long period was rudimentary, at a mother's knee, and hardly able to cater to a growing population. New England's population rose from about 27,000 in 1650 to approximately 100,000 by 1700. This growth rate was due to two primary factors: the lower age of marriage for women "and the relatively low rate of infant, child, and adult mortality."[23]

The mother's role in teaching her young children was important in many cultures and continued actively. As late as 1818 Thomas Jefferson noted that his daughter Martha, the mother of twelve children, had "made their education the object of her life." It was often necessary to do so due to the absence of good and nearby schools.

Naturally, unless the mother was single-minded (and what mother can be so?), home education was at best a good substitute, often interrupted by pregnancy, children's illnesses, and the inadequate support given by servants.[24]

Throughout the seventeenth and eighteenth centuries in particular children were subjected, at least weekly, to church attendance. While they may not have understood the sonorous, declamatory reading of the Gospels they assimilated some of the phrases, although they were probably unable to write them down. In Virginia in the 1740s Devereux Jarratt, a young schoolmaster, eventually to become a clergyman, recalled how he felt that learning in gentlefolk towered authoritatively over him. He borrowed

15. *Sir Joshua Reynolds, PRA (1723–1792). "The 4th Duke of Marlborough and His Family." 1778.*
Oil on canvas, 86 x 64". His Grace, the Duke of Marlborough

The duke holds a sardonyx in his left hand while his heir, the Marquess of Blandford, carries one of the cases containing
the Marlborough family gems. It is said that the painter was anxious to catch Lady Anne Churchill's look of fear (she was four)
when she first saw him and cried out, "I won't be painted?" Hence the charade the child affects with a mask.

Burkett's commentary on the New Testament:

As I had no candle, my custom was, in an evening, to sit down flat on the hearth, erect the volume on the end of a chest, which stood near, and by the light of the fire, read till near midnight. . . .By these means. . . I soon became, what was called a good reader, and my relish for books and reading greatly increased.

Soon he was being employed as a tutor in the house of Mr. Thompson Swann at 40 pounds per annum.[25] The education of children by these means was widespread with the establishment of the College of William and Mary in 1695, backing up those who wished to acquire a "liberal education." However, a twentieth-century habit of taking it for granted that secular education was available to all obscures the progress Thomas Jefferson tried to make with his "Bill for the More General Diffusion of Knowledge." Since instruction would no longer be combined with reli-

16. John Singleton Copley, RA (1738–1815). "The Sitwell Children." 1786.
Oil on canvas, 61 x 71". Sir Reresby Sitwell, Bt.

The four children of Francis Hurt Sitwell of Renishaw are depicted in one of the American artist's most brilliant
conversation pieces. The first baronet Sir Sitwell Sitwell (1769–1811) has his sister Mary (1771–1791) at his right,
his brother Francis (d. 1813) at the left, and Hurt (d. 1803) in front.

gious duty, Jefferson, while mindful of the importance of Bible teaching, wished that "at every of these schools the books which shall be used. . . for instructing the children to read shall be such as will at the same time make them acquainted with Graecian, Roman, English and American history." Above the groupings of the local schools, where poor children could be given three years of free instruction toward a basic literacy, were to be set the grammar schools, for the sons of the gentry and for one poor boy (who was promising) per year from each of the elementary schools. From these categories one boy each year was to be chosen to proceed to the College of William and Mary.

But tax resistance set aside the bill destined to do so much.

School for some was not a happy boyhood experience. In nineteenth-century England, Lord Burlington, who succeeded as eighth Duke of Devonshire in 1858, had been unhappy at Eton and refused to send his own sons to school. They were taught in their earliest years by a governess, Miss Hastings, and later mainly by Lord Burlington himself, who had at Cambridge achieved the remarkable feat of being both second in the honors degree in mathematics and one of the top few men in the honors degree (or tripos) in classics. Teaching at home may have taught the boys more than if they had gone to Eton or Harrow,

17. William Holman Hunt (1827–1910). "The Children's Holiday
(Portrait of Mrs. Thomas Fairbairn and Her Children)."
1864–1865. Oil on canvas, 82 x 57".
Torbay Borough Council, Torquay

This painting, commissioned to hang at the top of the impressive
staircase at Fairbairn's country house, brilliantly harmonizes
studies made at different times.

but it may have also developed a certain innate tendency toward shyness and silence and an indisposition toward the exchange of ideas.[26]

A similar situation pertained in the early life of George Nathaniel Curzon, later Viceroy of India, at Kedleston, the great house built by Robert Adam in Derbyshire. Born in 1859, George was supervised for ten years by a Miss Paraman. She appeared on the scene when George was seven years old and set about teaching him and his brothers and sisters (as he later said) "all subjects well." In addition she inculcated in her charges habits of economy and neatness and a dislike of anything vulgar or fast. In her saner moments she was devotedly attached to her pupils;

but there were frequent occasions on which she acted with all the savagery "of a brutal and vindictive tyrant."

From Miss Paraman, George passed to the Reverend Powles's school at Wixenford and another masterly personality in the shape of Mr. Archibald James Campbell Dunbar. As was noted: "This remarkable man left on young Curzon's mind the same uneffacable mark as Miss Paraman had done, and for much the same reason. Like her, he was an admirable teacher; like her, he was often savage and cruel to the boys." Nevertheless, young Curzon's three years at Wixenford brought out something of the quality of his mind. Before leaving he became head of school and during his last term created a record by carrying off five prizes, though one—as with becoming modesty he was careful to point out—was for "the best collection of moths and butterflies," of which, like many boys he was a "passionate pursuer."[27]

By contrast, in *The Scarlet Tree* (1946), the second volume of his captivating autobiography *Left Hand, Right Hand!*, Osbert Sitwell tells how in 1902 he was introduced at an early age to a school in Scarborough that was picked for him by his eccentric father, Sir George, and "mainly supported by superior tradesmen and rich farmers." The playground teemed with "shouting, whistling, roaring schoolboys of different ages and sizes, though all covered with spots, and all wearing caps with the same skull and crossbones." Evidently Osbert had been "expected" and all the larger boys set on him at once with whirling fists and yells of "don't think you're everybody just because your father's a bloody baronet!" As for Osbert's family, they sat primly in the Scarborough "sitting room" and studiously ignored his black eyes, thought he "looked tired," but thought further that in the objectives of all schooling he was destined "to go far." But as his mother saw, after two weeks he was learning nothing and he was returned into the care of his governess, whilst his father was ever preparing him, by subtle hint and visions of a "real fine healthy life," for boarding school at Eton. And there, finally, he saw "a vista of bare corridors, and of classrooms with bare floors, reformatory benches with inkstains, inkstands, and iron clamps," all smelling of rusty iron pipes, ink, and clothes in lockers, which generations of Etonians recall, and it was perhaps ever thus. Eton (plate 22) had been founded in 1440, Winchester in 1382, and between them they schooled many of the peers of the realm and their sons and prepared them for university.

The pride in cool behavior in the face of adversity (the "stiff-upper-lip" ethic) drilled into public school boys partly came from the rough-and-tumble of its games' systems: particularly the game of Rugby football (invented by William Webb Ellis at Rugby School in 1823; the same school that was the locus of childhood cruelty in Thomas Hughes's 1857 novel, *Tom Brown's Schooldays*) and the Eton Wall Game (one of the oldest forms of football, played since 1717).

It is to the range of a school's alumni that its prowess can be traced. The writers Thomas Gray, Henry Fielding, Horace Walpole, Percy Bysshe Shelley, and Robert Swinburne, for example, all attended Eton, as did William Gladstone, Queen Victoria's prime minister. Plenty of other schools were equally capable, as John Milton (an alumnus of St. Paul's) had it, "of giving a virtuous and noble education," with scholarship and rough-and-tumble activities mixed equally into the curriculum.

In the late nineteenth century and the Edwardian years, at the start of the twentieth century, the person most important to a child's development was his, or her, nanny. From the fifteenth century on, such a person had been called a "governess." The use of the word "nanny" came into common use in the early 1900s.

Lady Mersey noted: "Nanny was always in the nursery with the children. She never let them out of her sight and they never seemed to have any time off. Always, always there." Lady Phylliss MacRae, a daughter of the fourth Marquess of Bristol, noted: "My mother did not like nannies. She had had a very middle-class upbringing, and therefore she did not believe in them. She believed in mothers looking after their own children."[28] Nevertheless, with their charges in great black-hooded prams, the nannies were a feature of London and even New York parks on sunny mornings up to the 1930s. Then, like migrating birds, they gradually faded away, each remembered only by those for whom she made frocks and party clothes, let things out, and mended favorite toys. Nanny's birthday card arrived faithfully even when her "little man" was a grown pinstripe-suited diplomat.

For young people all too soon it was necessary to put

18. *"Central Park, New York, in Winter." 1898. Photograph. Museum of the City of New York*

This charming photograph shows a mother and nanny in woolen winter jackets over heavy skirts. The children, also heavily dressed, must have found it difficult to enjoy the snow.

away childish pursuits, at least for a time. It was time to think of further learning in the universities, even if a grumpy tutor had opined, in Francis Bacon's words, that "universities incline wits to sophistry and affectation." [29]

This homily was probably as true of the American gentleman as of his European counterpart. In the late seventeenth century, plantation owners in Virginia helped to consolidate their social positions by establishing the College of William and Mary at Williamsburg. It gave the sons of gentry a Latin grammar and a knowledge of government and of one another. But the status of the American gentleman, who had no right to a title of great antiquity or to a centuries-old family house, was confirmed only by means of personal independence—the freedom from the hard task of achieving wealth and the freedom to seek out the ideas that contained the seeds of the liberal arts. To be a gentleman involved ownership of slaves and large tracts of land—and the role of lawmaker thereby devolved naturally. By 1700 or so the American gentleman had his foot on the first rung of a hard-reared ladder to greater social distinction.

CHAPTER II

Latin, Greek, and the Grand Tour

Travel in the younger sort is a part of education; in the elder, a part of experience. He that travelleth into a country before he hath some entrance into the language, goeth to school, and not to travel.

Francis Bacon, "The Essays: Of Travel" (1625 edition)

Throughout the sixteenth and well into the seventeenth century many writers, from Sir Thomas Elyot in 1541 to Henry Peacham in 1622, were in agreement that the origins of true nobility lay in the pursuit of wisdom and virtue.[1] Education was necessary to create a governing class; instruction, however onerous, was essential to the understanding of grammar, logic, rhetoric, and what Laurence Humphrey, in *The Nobles: or of Nobilities* (1563), called "civility of manners." Though all tutors knew that Aristotle had sketched out gentlemanly characteristics with his twelve public and twelve private virtues in the *Nicomachean Ethics*, the gentleman was really a creation of feudalism.

The private tutor, grammar schools, universities, and Inns of Court catered well for the sons of English noblemen. There had been some disruption in the mid- to late 1530s, when the great religious centers of learning had been dissolved by Henry VIII in his sharp breach with Rome. But new schools were established and others allowed to continue or to be reconstituted under newly enfranchised boroughs. These were mostly for the sons of the squirearchy, the lawyers and merchants, and these "grammar schools" acted as the traditional route for their entry to university.

Aristotle had indicated that the eternal pattern of a good life, which the leading schools aspired to teach, could be realized in different ways. A gentleman had to have a feel for virtue, a capacity to submit passion to reason, and a strong moral code that distinguished between virtue and vice and truth or falsehood.

As for the great schools, such as Eton and Winchester, they had long had affiliations with particular universities: Eton with King's College, Cambridge, and Winchester with New College, Oxford. Many of these schools enjoyed

19. Pompeo Batoni (1705–1787). "Sir Gregory Turner (later Page-Turner)." 1768. Oil on canvas, 53 x 39". City of Manchester Art Galleries

ΑΡΙΣΤΟΤΕΛΗΣ   ΟΜΗΡΟΣ

H.S.E.
JOSEPHUS WARTON S.T.P.
HUJUS ECCLESIÆ
PRÆBENDARIUS
SCHOLÆ WINTONIENSIS
PER ANNOS FERE TRIGINTA
INFORMATOR
POETA FERVIDUS FACILIS EXPOLITUS
CRITICUS ERUDITUS PERSPICAX ELECANS
OBIIT XXIII FEB. MDCCC
ÆTAT LXXVIII.
HOC QUALECUNQUE

20. John Flaxman (1755–1826). Monument to Dr. Joseph
Warton. 1804. Marble. Winchester Cathedral, Hampshire

Warton, headmaster of Winchester school, is shown in wig and
gown holding a book from which he is instructing his scholars.
Busts of Aristotle and Homer keep watch above him.

royal or ecclesiastical patronage, and they were in a unique position to impart the Aristotelian pattern to those already privileged. The ever shifting levels in society were always in subtle-shaded focus. Henry Peacham in *The Compleat Gentleman* (1622) commended strict segregation: "For the companions of your recreation, consort yourself with gentlemen of your own rank and quality. . . . To be over free and familiar with inferiors argues a baseness of spirit and begetteth contempt." When the son of an aristocratic household entered his chosen college as a commoner, "his most important privilege was that of 'commoning' (eating and associating) with the master and fellows rather than the undergraduate body." Parents subscribed to the view

that university education should be imparted to their sons so that it upheld rather than undermined the systems of privilege they held most dear. The proportion of members of Parliament who had attended university has been examined for the years 1563 to 1642, at the four points of 1563, 1584, 1593 and 1642.[2] The percentages were: 1563, 110 of 420, or 26 percent; 1584, 145 of 460 or 32 percent; 1593, 161 of 462 or 35 percent; and by 1642, 276 of 552 or 50 percent. The ruling classes in court and country undoubtedly felt that the universities were offering something worth acquiring, and the colleges, for their part, benefited in gifts of land and endowments from the loyalty created in their graduates.

What did they study, those who bothered to show any considerable application? In 1540 Henry VIII set up five Regius professorships at Oxford and Cambridge in Greek, Hebrew, divinity, civic law, and physic, which added to the endowed readerships and public lectureship. The king obviously hoped this would raise the standard of university education, but his expectations were not realized. The nominated lecturers soon left for more remunerative posts as the fixed stipends took no account of inflation. While the university statutes made provision for fining students for nonattendance at lectures, many were ready to pay the fines. But if persistent and through a regular study of grammar and participation in the thrice-weekly "exercises," a student was expected, eventually, to be familiar with the Latin language. Through the further study of logic he was supposed to be able to think with some precision, and, via rhetoric, to be able to convey these thoughts in a convincing way. But by the time William Harrison wrote his *Description of England* in 1577 he found it necessary to lament that most students "study little other than histories, tables, dice and trifles."[3] The growing tendency for instruction to be provided within individual colleges did something to redress the decline. But Tudor Oxford and Cambridge were far from being in the forefront of new ideas, and arithmetic and the sciences were neglected. John Dee (1527–1608), the mathematician and astrologer, taught at three Continental universities, but refused in 1554 to teach mathematics at Oxford. Instead, the study of Aristotle remained paramount.

Whatever the part played by the universities in a nobleman's development (and there was perhaps little attempt

21. A. C. Pugin (1762–1832). "The High Street, Oxford." 1814. Watercolor, 14 x 24". Trustees of the Victoria & Albert Museum, London

The Oxford High Street, the main thoroughfare of the university town, is one of the world's great streets.
It is on a slight curve, so that its vistas are always changing. It has good and impressive buildings flanking it, colleges,
two churches, trees, modest houses, and at its east termination, Magdalen Tower.

made by such august bodies in the seventeenth and eighteenth centuries to so adapt undergraduate education), their contribution to social mobility can be demonstrated satisfactorily. If there had needed to be long weary hours of concentrating on the ancient classics (or the equal work in so avoiding), they were to be balanced by more enjoyable ones of observing cities and men, councils and governments. It was a process with a long lineage, headed by activity at court and by travel.

The connection between tuition and travel was made by the traveling tutor, or "bear" leader, as he was known affectionately. He was at best "a grave respectable person of mature age," who was retained to watch over the morals and religion of his pupils, vulnerable as they were before the heady complexities of Catholicism "or the fashionable satanism of Venice."

Fathers who had sacrificed to send their sons to university considered travel a necessary final stage in acquiring a quick curiosity, delight in scholarship, and a reverence for classical antiquity. In his essay "Of Travel" (1625), Sir Francis Bacon opined:

The things to be seen and observed are the courts of princes. . . the Courts of justice. . . the churches and monasteries. . . the walls and the fortifications of cities and towns. . . as well as houses, gardens, armories, arsenals, treasuries of jewels, and robes and cabinets of rarities.

As for triumphs, masons, feasts, wedding, funerals, capital executions, and such shows men need not to be put in mind of them, yet they are not to be neglected?

He urged having a servant or tutor who knew the country well and a guidebook, and he advocated keeping a diary. It was advice too many ignored.

At St. Paul's School in London the classical learning necessary for such travelers was first in the charge of William Lily (1468–1522), who had entered Magdalen College, Oxford, in 1486. Lily had studied Greek and Latin and classical antiquities in Italy, becoming High Master of

St. Paul's in 1512. One of his pupils was John Leland (1506–1552), who went on to Christ's College, Cambridge, then to All Souls, Oxford, before embarking in the mid-1520s for Paris, then the home of humanist studies, under the aegis of Guillaume Budé, the philologist and lawyer. When he returned to England in about 1528, the Duke of Norfolk engaged him as a tutor for his younger son, Lord Thomas Howard. He was able to use this service to obtain royal patronage and was soon putting in order the royal family's library at Whitehall and establishing his career as a "royal antiquary."

The perfect courtier, the ideal of the *uomo universale* in a Renaissance sense, may be first applied to Henry

22. *William Evans (d. 1877). "The Eton Wall Game." 1839. Watercolor, 27 x 37". The Provost and Fellows of Eton College*

Evans, who was drawing master at Eton, must often have witnessed the famous athletic tussle played out on a narrow strip of land—the mud, sweat, and heaving incomprehensibility of it all. Windsor Castle is silhouetted in the distance.

23. William Blaikie. *"System of Gymnastics at the 5th Avenue School, New York." c. 1880–1890.*
Photograph. Museum of the City of New York

Mr. Blaikie's system, muscular coordination personified, was practiced at his school for young gentlemen on West 59th Street.

Howard, Earl of Surrey (plate 30), the "Poet Earl." As a young boy his mornings were spent studying classics and the sciences under the eye of his tutor, John Clerk, Fellow of Magdalen College, Oxford, who had traveled in France and Italy and spoke those countries' languages and Latin. Clerk introduced Surrey to Latin, French, Spanish, and Italian. In his *Treatise of Nobility* (1531), dedicated to the earl's father, the third Duke of Norfolk, Clerk praised the young boy's translations from those languages. By the spring of 1530 Surrey was serving at court and was part of the entourage that accompanied Henry VIII to meet Francis I at Calais. The earl stayed on to spend a year at the French court.[4]

Sir Philip Sidney (1554–1586), soldier, statesman, and poet, was educated at Shrewsbury School and Christ Church, Oxford. After a few months spent at Queen Elizabeth's court he left England in 1572 for Paris, accompanied by three servants, a half-Italian tutor, and four horses for his carriages. He traveled to the French court but left it after the troublous time of the St. Bartholomew's Massacre for Lorraine, Germany, and Italy. In Venice he met the painters Tintoretto and Paolo Veronese, then visited Poland, and resided for a time in 1575 in Austria, before returning the following year to England. At the battle at Zutphen in 1586 Sidney was wounded in the thigh and died, after twenty-six agonizing days, at Arnhem. His widow, Frances, daughter of the statesman Sir Francis Walsingham, remarried in 1590 to Robert Devereux, second Earl of Essex (1566–1601; plate 29), who had survived the battle at Zutphen. He had been educated at Trinity College, Cambridge, in the late 1570s and became a favorite of the queen's before displeasing her with his marriage to Lady Sidney. Perhaps the insistent point to make is that, accomplished soldier that he was, Devereux was fitted to be "the perfect courtier" in that he wrote numerous sonnets and was credited by the diplomat Sir Henry

24. Giulio Pignatta (1684–1751). "Sir Andrew Fountaine and Friends in the Tribuna." 1715. Oil on canvas, 58 x 47".
Commander Andrew Fountaine, Narford

This canvas is the earliest depiction of the Tribune Gallery in the Uffizi Palace, Florence.
Sir Andrew Fountaine leans against the base of the "Venus Victrix," holding a medallion in his hand.
The other gentlemen, Captain William Price (with tray of coins), the Hon. Anthony Lowther (behind him), the Hon. Richard Arundel
(seated), and a Frenchman, the Marquis de Senville (at right), were typical of those well received on the Grand Tour.

Wotton (1568–1639) with special skill in masques. Both Devereux and Wotton—who, after his early years at Winchester and New College and Queen's College, Oxford, traveled on the Continent and then entered one of the Inns of Court, before settling in Venice—are typical of those whose wide knowledge was fused with deep experience. As George Savile, Marquis of Halifax (1633–1695), wrote: "Great Reading, without applying it, is like corn heaped, that is not stored, it groweth musty."[5]

Such opportunity was denied to most young ladies. They had time enough for reading but rarely as part of a defined course of study. The responsibility of educating young ladies was entrusted from the seventeenth century on to many boarding and finishing schools. Some, like that of Bathusa Makin (who had been a governess to Princess Elizabeth, daughter of Charles I), made much of intro-

25. *Nicholas de Largilliere (1656–1746). "Sir Robert Throckmorton, 4th Baronet." 1729. Oil on canvas, 53 x 47".*
The National Trust (Coughton Court)

This portrait of Sir Robert Throckmorton (1702–1791), painted in Paris, where three of his sisters were
Augustinian nuns, is one of the last portraits painted of a man in armor.

ducing pupils to a wide range of study, including languages, both classical and modern, the sciences, and mathematics. There was a greater need, however, that the gentlewoman should recognize and understand the niceties of a household's economy and the properties of medicinal plants for tending the sick, for both lay to her eventual duty, unremittedly. As it was the lady of the household who educated her children in the first few years of their lives, such prominent thinkers as John Locke advocated that women should receive more complete education, and

Jonathan Swift and Daniel Defoe believed that this would make them better companions and not simply ornaments for their husbands.[6] But for the most part even a well-educated woman was restricted to the domestic vocation of service to her husband and children.

The excursions were still not without danger. The traveler Fynes Moryson (1566–1630), after leaving Peterhouse, Cambridge, in 1587, obtained a license to travel. From 1591 to 1595 he visited Germany, the Low Countries, Denmark, Poland, Italy, Switzerland, and France. He had

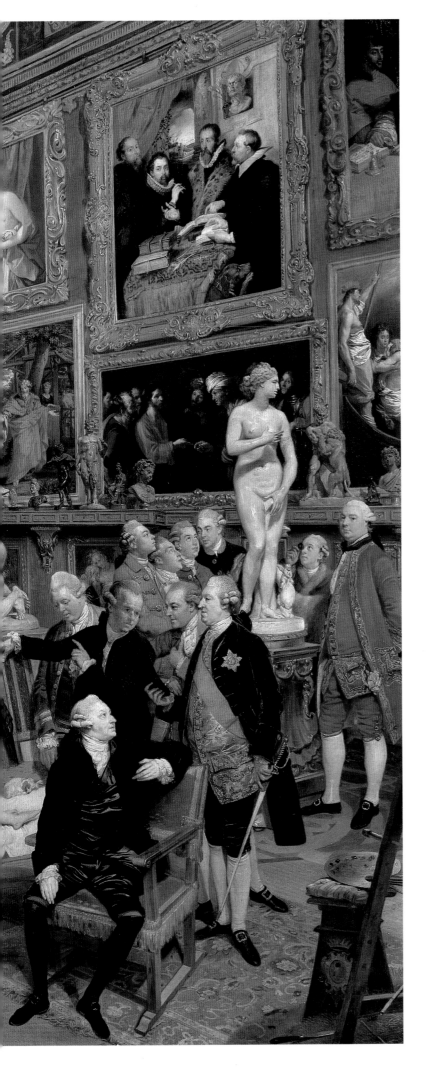

sailed from Leigh-on-Thames on May 1, 1591, and then spent a great deal of time nervously avoiding Spanish freebooters, thieves in France and Italy, and Turkish pirates. As a Protestant visitor to Rome, he was robbed in France by a gang of disbanded soldiers, who took all his money, his sword, cloak, shirt, and even his hat. He was also in some additional danger from the long arm of the ubiquitous Inquisition, which kept a watch on all inns to discover visitors failing to take the sacrament. While Thomas Coryate, an inveterate traveler (mainly on foot), believed that "of all the pleasures in the world" travel was "the sweetest and most delightful" (some part of which he set out in *Coryat's Crudities. Hastily gobbled up in five Moneths travells in France, Savoy, Italie* [1611; republished 1905], his troubles were little compared with Fyne Moryson's). The latter, almost wearily, set out his thoughts in his own book *An Itinerary Containing His Ten Yeeres Travell* (1617; reprinted 1907). However, following the marriage of Charles I to the Catholic Henrietta Maria, in 1625, the English traveler was less at risk from the attention of the Catholic authorities, and John Milton toured Italy in 1638–1639 without needing to hide his Protestant allegiance.

One of the considerable hazards of foreign travel was the risk of incurring a serious illness. Many travelers became so ill when abroad that they never returned to England, or, like the young Robert Corbet, died a little time after returning. Having come back from Italy about 1576 in a weakened state, Corbet died before he could accomplish his plans for implementing his newfound knowledge of building.

The historian William Camden wrote in the 1610 edition of his *Britannia*:

> . . . within our remembrance Robert Corbet carried away with the affectionate delights of Architecture,

26. Johan Zoffany, RA (1734–1810). "The Tribuna of the Uffizi." 1772–1778. Oil on canvas, 48 x 61".
By gracious permission of Her Majesty, Queen Elizabeth II

Zoffany's depiction of the Tribune, more elaborate than Pignatta's (plate 24), was commissioned by Queen Charlotte. The Grand Duke of Tuscany's collection housed there was considered among the finest in Europe. The room was built in 1585–1589 for Francesco de' Medici. The English Grand Tourists gathered in various groups are all identifiable (Sir Horace Mann is at the right with the Garter Star on his left breast), as are the paintings and sculptures.

began to build in a barraine place, a most gorgeous and stately house after the Italian modell.

Corbet wanted to build an addition to Moreton Corbet Castle in north Shropshire. He covered the south Elizabethan stone façade with cyphers and strange signs, exemplifying, even in its incomplete state, the results of mannerist studies on the Grand Tour. Flemish influence, ever pervasive, had been ushered away, here and elsewhere, before the seduction of the crisp engravings of the Renaissance architect Sebastiano Serlio and other Italian theorists.

During the seventeenth century the term "Grand Tour" was coined. In 1670, Richard Lassels noted in his *Voyage in Italy* that no one could understand Livy and Caesar "without having made the Grand Tour of France and Giro of Italy." The tour established itself as a means of giving taste and knowledge to a young gentleman in addition to his learning at university. It supplanted the desire for military service as the only adventurous course of action, and it was essential preparation if fluency, or even passing competency, in foreign languages was needed.

During his travels in 1641, the diarist John Evelyn caught smallpox in Geneva, and although he fully recovered in time to go to the Continent again in 1643 (mainly to avoid the growing political dispute and the onset of civil war at home), it was a sharp reminder to him of the continual danger of contracting a mortal disease. In such arduous political times, and for other reasons, mainly religious ones, an increasing number of young nobleman were sent to Europe to continue their education. The world of many parents had been ruined by the execution of Charles I and the defeat of his son at the Battle of Worcester. The young Charles fled to the Continent, not to return until 1660. The need to ensure some kind of a prospect for a generation deeply committed to the past caused many noble sons to travel and to learn abroad in the 1650s. Some needed to join seminaries to avoid persecution for being Catholic, while Protestants went to study in places like the university town of Leiden. Indeed, Protestant travelers may well have carried with them James Howell's *Instructions for forreine travel*, issued in London in 1642. His first stipulation for the ideal traveler was that he should be a firm Protestant and have some understanding of Latin

as a basis for his study of Italian, French, and Spanish. An experienced diplomat, Howell knew the dangers of endlessly prolonging a journey and thus advocated travels lasting "three years and four months."[7]

By the beginning of the eighteenth century the Grand Tour had become the most convenient means of training for "diplomats, public servants, and soldiers" and "an ideal finishing school for a young gentleman of fortune after he had been whipped through a public school and acquired the doubtful benefits of its narrow curriculum."[8]

Some intrepid women traveled too, although for reasons other than finishing their polite education. Aletheia Talbot (d.1654), daughter and eventually heir of Gilbert, seventh Earl of Shrewsbury, in 1606 had married Thomas Howard, the second Earl of Arundel. When the earl set out in 1613 on his second journey to Italy, the countess accompanied him. After a time in Venice, where they were received in great splendor and given a banquet in the Arsenal by the Doge, Lady Arundel stayed at a villa in Padua while the earl and the architect Inigo Jones journeyed to Vicenza to look at Palladio's villas. (Jones returned to England with an appreciation of Palladio's achievements, which was a springboard to his introduction of classical building into England.) She rejoined her husband at Siena, and they then spent six months in 1614 in Rome acquiring books, antiques, and copies of ancient statues and visiting assiduously, with the earl even doing some excavation in the Forum and discovering marble statues, perhaps "planted" previously. When the earl and his countess arrived in England in 1615, after journeying from Genoa to Paris, the philosopher Sir Francis Bacon, on seeing all the statues, exclaimed, "My Lord, I see the Resurrection is upon us."[9] Busy as they all might have been with their Italian grammars to stay ahead of the sightseeing demand, it was the Earl of Arundel's sure perception that "arts and learning added to the honour and dignity of great men" that gave his Italian journey "a special place in the history of English culture." The journey made him, in Horace Walpole's words, the father of *vertu* in England, for he now recognized the connection between "life and art, manners and actions, collecting and ethics."

The best and most expensive way to travel from England was with coach and servants. The Earl of

Castlemaine set out in 1686 with coaches so lavish with gilt brasswork that the window frames on one coach alone cost 100 pounds. But less illustrious travelers journeyed more simply, and more uncomfortably, by *carosse* or *diligence*, which carried sixteen or thirty passsengers, respectively. Italy was reached by small vessel (*felucca*) from southern France or via the cold passes of the Alps.

For over a century English Reformation travelers wanted to study firsthand the remains of classical antiquity and the new art and architecture in Italy. The diplomat, courtier, or artist could perfect his professional skills on such a journey, and the sons of the rich could practice social graces previously acquired only from narratives and treatises aimed at the humanist dilettante.

The cost of a Grand Tour, often prolonged several years, allowed only the rich to participate. Some 2,733 pounds were paid out for the second Viscount Townshend's travels and purchases in Italy in 1695–1696 and some 2,917 pounds for purchases of pictures and statues on behalf of Thomas Coke.

In 1776 Dr. Samuel Johnson told James Boswell (who recorded it in his *Life of Johnson*):

Sir, a man who has not been in Italy is always conscious of an inferiority, from his not having seen what it is expected a man should see. The grand object of travelling is to see the shores of the Mediterranean.

It was advice many had already anticipated. When the essayist Joseph Addison (1672–1719) traveled in Italy in the early years of the eighteenth century, he compared what he saw with descriptions of the same places by classical authors. In his *Remarks on Several Parts of Italy, 1701–1703* (1705), Addison set out, smugly enough, for forgetful readers a transcription of the appropriate quotations. The later literary traveler Laurence Sterne waspishly said that Addison journeyed "with his satchel of school books hanging by his a. . . . "

A study of the effects of the Grand Tour on the specific English region of Norfolk[10] draws attention to the important journeys made by Sir Andrew Fountaine (1676–1753) and Thomas Coke, first Earl of Leicester (1697–1759). So accomplished was Fountaine in his Latin (after being educated at Eton and Christ Church, Oxford)

that he had been chosen in 1698 by his tutor, Dr. Henry Adrich, to make the oration in Latin to William of Orange upon the king's entry into Oxford. The king knighted Fountaine the same year at Hampton Court, and the nobleman's foreign travels began in 1701 when he was chosen to accompany Lord Macclesfield to carry the Act of Succession to the Elector of Hanover—the invitation to become king of England. From the elector and Electress Sophia he was given valued introductions to the courts of Europe. Sir Andrew was noteworthy for his percipient collecting, and he made a second tour of France and Italy in 1714–1715. "It appears likely that he was accompanied for considerable periods of time, by those friends with whom he was depicted in the Tribune Gallery of the Uffizi, Florence, by Giulio Pignatta in 1715" (plate 24).[11] He became a good friend of Duke Cosimo III: they wrote to one another; the duke sent gifts of wine and his portrait by Domenico Tempesti, which is still at Sir Andrew's family home, Narford Hall, Norfolk. Fountaine's journeying led him to commission murals for Narford from Giovanni Antonio Pellegrini, the accomplished Venetian painter who had been brought into England in 1708 by Charles Montagu, fourth Earl of Manchester, to work at Kimbolton, and also enabled him to gather extensive collections of majolica, paintings, and sculpture.

Thomas Coke's grandfather, Sir John Newton, was told by his cousin and guardian, Sir Edward Coke, that the young man spent too much time "on hunting with the gentlemen about us, which I find makes him grow cool to his studyes." He recommended "that his education would be better answered to have him forthwith sent abroad," in the care of a tutor, Dr. Thomas Hobart, a Fellow of Christ's College, Cambridge. The two left in August 1712 with a coach and four horses, two grooms, two valets, and one Edward Jarrett, who was to pay all the bills. They did not return until May 1718, having made a long, eighteen-month journey through France to Rome, a major, two-year excursion from Rome into eastern France, Germany, Italy, Sicily, and Malta, and then almost two years on the homeward route, via Vienna, Prague, Berlin, Amsterdam, and Paris. Coke (plate 28) constantly collected drawings, paintings, manuscripts, books, and sculpture. He studied all of them, carefully, and what still delights at Coke's great Norfolk house of Holkham, erected in the 1750s partly to

his own designs, are the abundant trappings of the active journeyings made years earlier under hot Italian skies.

The Grand Tour was a costly enterprise. In February 1728 the young George Lyttelton, a tall, ungainly young man of nineteen, was waiting in London for his father, Sir Thomas Lyttelton, to obtain a servant for him in order that he might embark for Calais on the first step of his Grand Tour. He wrote many subsequent letters to his father from the Continent, two of which indicate the social side of such travels. At Luneville in 1728 George had bought five suits: a blue hunting suit, a handsome summer suit, a lighter suit for everyday wear "of a light silver stuff, the westcoat lined Blue Silk, laced with silver, a fine cloth suit 'for the duke's birthday'"—seemingly any duke—and a black suit for mourning "for the Queen of Sardinia, who was a Sister of the Duchess." With his footman's livery, his purchases cost more than one hundred pounds. He had taken up a second hundred and broken into a third. The thought gave him so much concern that

he almost entreated his father to recall him to England to save such charges. But "No," he continued, fearful lest he be taken at his word: "The world would Judge perversely and blame you for it. I must go on, and you must support me like your son. . . . I can only assure that if I live and return to England I will marry the first advantageous match you offer to me." There would be dalliance along the long way back, by the most circuitous route, charted merely by further withdrawals of money.

Sir Thomas Lyttelton began to complain that his son was spending a great deal, considering that his business was "improvement and not show." George argued back in sanded, red-sealed letters, which took a long time to arrive in rain-swept England, that "without shew abroad, there is no improvement." He needed a second suit, a nightgown, "my old one being so dirty that it is not fit to wear." Coach hire, fencing, and dancing were also costing him a good deal more, but he believed it was cheaper in the long run to pay the price than to learn from bad masters. Were Eton and Oxford capable of teaching him all that? As his father (as perhaps all fathers have to do on occasion) wrote in November, 1729:[12]

My dearest George, you have many rare and excellent qualities for which I love you from my soul, and have no pleasure equal to that of making you happy . . . but I have not wherewithal to support you at this rate.

Many travelers less knowledgeable than Coke and keener than Lyttelton often used the services of a resident English artist, or long-time dweller in a city, to help in selecting suitable works of art and arrange for their being sent home from Italy. Two such intermediaries were Thomas Jenkins (1722–1798) and James Byres (1734–1817).[13] Jenkins had been born in Rome and became the "richest and most influential figure in the English Colony in Rome during the second half of the eighteenth century." He helped to form some of the greatest collections of ancient marbles in England, including works in the collections of Charles Towneley and William Weddell. He was on close terms with the painters Anton Raphael Mengs and Pompeo Batoni, who specialized in painting Englishmen visiting Rome (plate 28) and acted as banker,

28. Pompeo Batoni (1705–1787). "Thomas William Coke (later 1st Earl of Leicester)." 1774.
Oil on canvas, 96 x 67". The Viscount Coke, Holkham

On leaving Eton in 1771 Coke traveled in Italy until 1774. Here he was painted by Batoni in a "Van Dyck style" costume,
possibly worn to a masquerade ball given in 1773 by Louise Stolberg, Countess of Albany.

dealer, and friend to many, including the Royal Academician Angelica Kauffman. He put up money for excavations and sold the discovered fragments, which had, in the meantime, been transformed by expert restorers.

Byres, the son of a Scotch Jacobite, arrived in Rome about 1756 and set himself to work under the painter Mengs and his pupil Anton Maron. However, by 1762 he had become a student of architecture and within a year or two an antiquarian, a much more lucrative calling in the fevered atmosphere created by those building up collections. Nevertheless there are many architectural designs and projects that Byres involved himself with. He obtained

29. *Sir William Segar (working before 1585; d. 1633). "Robert Devereux, 2nd Earl of Essex." 1590.*
Oil on panel, 44 x 34". The National Gallery of Ireland

Essex was the last but not the least brilliant favorite of Queen Elizabeth I. He was beheaded after the failure
of his plot to seize power in London in 1601. Essex was ever a soldier, traveler, and adventurer, proceeding against the Spaniards
and the Irish and commanding the Ordnance. He was but thirty-four years old at his death.

works of art for many and even conducted Edward Gibbon to see the sights of Rome—the usual time allocated for this was six weeks, but they took twelve. Byres's most important purchase, made in 1780, was the cameo glass "Portland Vase" (now in The British Museum) from the Princess Barberini, which he sold for 1,000 pounds to Sir William Hamilton. He was not above descending to trickery (nor was Thomas Jenkins) to get what he wanted, and he remained in Rome, exporting works of art, until 1790. He then retired to his native Scotland, thriving for another twenty-seven years in what his friends felt to be a terrible climate for one used to the orange heat-hazes of Italy.

What Coke, Lyttelton, and others realized was that they and their contemporaries should be more widely cultivated than their predecessors. The Grand Tour, whatever it did for their morals or for the family bank balance (and Jenkins, Byres, and others sharpened these considerations), it "polished manners, enlarged their interests and educated their taste." The old Castle of Henderskelfe was replaced by the heavily rusticated wonders of the "great fine house" of Castle Howard, built from 1699 onward for the third Earl of Carlisle, fresh from his Grand Tour. The half-timbered family home of the Lytteltons, Hagley Hall, was pulled down for a new Palladian box (1754–1760) by Sanderson Miller, the design of which Horace Walpole said had been copied from his family house of Houghton. He was horrified that "both their eating room and salon are to be stucco with pictures."

The architect Robert Adam (1728–1792), who had spent four years (1754–1758) in Italy training to be a better architect, was ready to put "all of Rome" into ideas and plans and to be at the service of many patrons, including the newly created (1761) Lord Scarsdale at Kedleston. In England, Francis Hayman, Sir Joshua Reynolds, and Thomas Gainsborough painted the portraits of traveling gentlemen and those of their wives and children, when accompanying them. As their libraries suggested, from the vellum-bound books in the early traveling cases (plate 32) to the shelves of the latest leather-bound and gold-tooled "modern" treatises, they esteemed learning and literature. In a gentlemanly sort of way, perhaps even indolently, they fished, shot at everything, gathered in grand salons, ostensibly to talk (plates

30. *Anonymous, 17th century. "Henry Howard, Earl of Surrey (1517–1547)." Oil on panel, 62 x 43".*
National Portrait Gallery, London

By the age of thirty, the "Poet Earl," as he was titled, had distinguished himself as poet, scholar, and soldier. But he was then unjustly charged with treason and executed in 1547. The architectural framework, inspired by Italian examples seen on the Grand Tour, may have been designed by Inigo Jones as part of the decoration of Arundel House in the Strand.

24 and 26)—but perhaps never talking at all, at least to their nearest and dearest—to take tea and play cards, ever wriggling hard in starched new clothes. But what they were was a politically and socially effective *élite* who took their responsibilities keenly, tended their widespreading estates, and reared their children, hopefully, in the pursuit of happiness.

Travel abroad was not of course the prerogative of the British aristocracy. From the middle of the seventeenth century many affluent New Englanders visited London. When Increase Mather was abroad in 1689 he passed time with Harvard alumni at the New England Coffeehouse. In the eighteenth century they came to London and elsewhere to study law or medicine. William Shippen, Jr., who was in London to study medicine, noted in his diary that in July 1759 he supped with Governor Hamilton of Pennsylvania, William Smith, provost of the College of Philadelphia, and Josiah Martin of Long Island, a student at the Inner Temple. Benjamin Franklin spent some fifteen

31. Sir Anthony Van Dyck (1599–1641). "Lord John Stuart with His Brother, Lord Bernard Stuart." c. 1639.
Oil on canvas, 93 x 57". The Trustees, National Gallery, London

This fine double portrait was painted before the young men set off in 1639 for a three-year tour of the Continent.
Within five years, both had died in the battles of the Civil War. Van Dyck is at his most fluent with the wonderful depiction
of the silvery cloak. Gainsborough painted a copy of the picture (St. Louis Art Museum).

years in England as a colonial representative, and in the 1770s he was active in helping his itinerant countrymen.

Leading American painters, including Benjamin West (1738–1820) and John Singleton Copley (1738–1815), found it essential to travel and work in Europe. West, of Pennsylvania Quaker stock, spent his mid-twenties (1760–1763) in Italy, where he visited Rome, Florence, Bologna, and Venice. In Rome he was in close contact with the circle of Mengs and the Scottish history painter Gavin Hamilton (1723–1798). He improved his skills in a milieu well versed in the ways of painters and then set up in London in 1763. He entered paintings in Society of Arts exhibitions, enjoyed the patronage of George III, and became a founding member of the Royal Academy of Arts. He was also very generous to art students from the colonies who called on him.

It was left to Copley "to exploit the popular subjects from contemporary history, for which West had led the way."[14] In 1774 he left America, traveling first to Italy. At the end of 1775 he settled in London. Copley noted that he found help there from fellow Americans. Once Governor Hutchinson of Massachusetts was in England in 1774 New Englanders of Loyalist persuasion visited him. Copley described a dinner at Hutchinson's table where "there was 12 of us altogether, and all Bostonians, and we had Salt Fish for Dinner."[15] He competed for commissions with his fellow Academicians Sir Joshua Reynolds and Benjamin West, who were also active in painting portraits and historical subjects. Three of Copley's major paintings (*Brook Watson and the Shark*, 1778; *The Death of Chatham*, 1780; and *The Death of Major Pierson*, 1783) made a significant contribution to the development of history painting in England.

The architectural impact of Europe on the eighteenth-century American gentleman is best illustrated in the achievements made by Thomas Jefferson. The years of

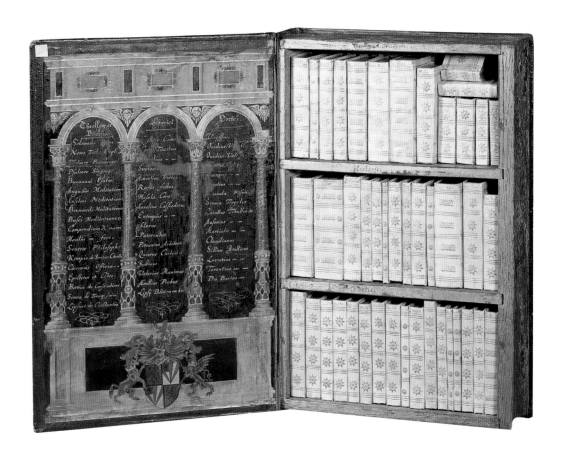

32. *Traveling library of Sir Thomas Egerton (later Lord Ellesmere). c. 1615. Gilded box containing 44 volumes.*
The Henry Huntington Library, San Marino, California

The volumes, bound in vellum, are divided into religion and philosophy, history, and poetry. Sir Thomas was a prominent lawyer and judge under Elizabeth, and Lord High Chancellor under James I.

experimentation (1796–1809) with Palladian motifs in his own house, Monticello, in Virginia, was added to the inspirations from his years of residence (1784–1789) in France (with a developed admiration for the brilliance of French planning). His carrying forward of classical ideas into the façades of the Virginia State Capitol (1789) and the University of Virginia is adequate testimony to a passionate devotion to realizing his informed dreams.

Notwithstanding his passionate interest in architecture, Jefferson had a somewhat jaded view of sending an American east to Europe for education. On October 15, 1785, he wrote from Paris to a young man, J. Banister, Jr., who, having been sent abroad because of ill health, was being educated in France, where he was recommended to Jefferson's care. He suggested to Banister that there were advantages in being in Geneva to learn French and in Rome of acquiring "a true pronunciation of the Latin language; a just taste in the fine arts. . . and lastly, the advantage of a fine climate for health." He accepted that "the habit of speaking the modern languages cannot be so well acquired in America," but every other article of education "can as well be acquired at William and Mary College [in Williamsburg] as at any place in Europe."[16]

In the nineteenth century many prosperous politicians, merchants, architects, and painters traveled in Europe, Americans among them. Significant were J. M. W. Turner (1775–1851), who painted his mighty canvases of Venice, including the famous *Fighting Temeraire* (1839) in the 1830s, and the American painters Thomas Cole and Frederic E. Church. As America's leading landscape painter, Cole felt it necessary to visit Europe. He called in 1831 at London and Paris on his way to Italy, where he "filled his imagination with high-minded themes and ideas." A second trip to Europe in 1841–1842 advanced his use of color and representation of atmosphere. He became well acquainted with the paintings of Claude Lorrain, of whose work he approved without reservation, regarding him as the greatest of all landscape painters. He occupied Claude's studio whilst in Rome and daily immersed himself in studying the rich remnants of classical and medieval antiquity. He returned to America in late 1832, intellectually and technically equipped for greater things.[17]

Cole encouraged the career of Frederic E. Church, and in 1868 Church with his wife, mother-in-law, and young son traveled to Egypt and journeyed extensively in the Middle East, then by steamer up the Danube to Vienna, through Austria and Switzerland, and arrived in November 1868 in Rome at Hotel Russie on the Pincian. This last venue inspired him to start in 1869 the great canvas *The Arch of Titus* (Newark Museum), which he did not finish until 1871. After leaving Rome in April 1869, Church and his family traveled to Corinth and Corfu, saw Paestum, and then returned to Paris and London before sailing for New York in June. He was now ready to start the building of his great Hudson River hilltop house, Olana (1870–1874), and Mrs. Church was almost ready for the birth of their fifth child.[18]

The travels of the nineteenth-century English gentleman may be demonstrated best from countless choices by the wanderings of the critic, writer, painter, and social reformer John Ruskin (1819–1900). Ruskin's family had taken him on almost annual visits to Italy during his early years, but his mother and father were pursuing the picturesque rather than pictures, Byron's *Childe Harold* rather than Raphael or Michaelangelo. The young Ruskin already drew to near-perfection, and he wrote with a rare ability. Ruskin made his first visit to Venice in 1841, but in 1845 he set off again for Italy and for the first time without his parents. His "peregrination through Europe became an annual event for so long as he had strength to make it," informing his eye and mind, fitting to the business of an intending art critic.

In 1849 Ruskin published *The Seven Lamps of Architecture*—setting aside for a time his long work, *Modern Painters*. His famed essay "The Seven Lamps" was an introduction to *The Stones of Venice*, which appeared in three volumes to 1852. He evoked Venice with all its splendor, grace, "noise, narrowness and confusion," seeing the structure of its marbled, well-crafted buildings through the eyes of an ardent disciple, and with all the passion he later brought to championing the causes of the Pre-Raphaelite Brotherhood. Three of his friends, the artists Millais, Rossetti, and Burne-Jones, were members, although the friendship with Millais ended disastrously when the latter, in 1854, fell in love with Mrs. Ruskin and finally married her.[19] As for Ruskin, in old age he came to loathe *The Seven Lamps of Architecture*, which was poorly published, and much of *The Stones of Venice*, too, but the range of his comments and the degree of observation informing his drawings made him a traveler apart from the similarly black-suited, watch-chained but pompous cotton merchants of Manchester, or the rubicund wool barons of Bradford. Significantly, it was but trade that allowed them, as Mr. Butterfield of Keighley (plate 142) or Mr. Frick of New York, to travel, and, like their eighteenth-century forebears, to acquire what the novelist James Fenimore Cooper (1789–1851) had observed as early as 1828.[20] Homes in New York, and I'm sure elsewhere, had, as he put it:

> French clocks, English and Brussels carpets, curtains from Lyons, and the Indies, alabaster from France and Italy, marble of their own, and from Italy, and, in short, every ornament below the rarest that is known in every other country in Christendom and frequently out of it, is put within the reach of the American of moderate means, by the facilities of their trade. The more elusive gain of knowledge and perception, even wisdom, from carefully arranged travels remained the perquisite of the rarer souls such as Jefferson and Ruskin.

During the nineteenth century the means of travel for gentlemen and their families leaving the city or the country was improved by the growth of the railway system. They could move themselves, servants, and plate with ease. There was now also the convenience of "the special treatment which stationmasters reserved for the great, or the special halts, at private stations, which companies sometimes undertook to make."[21] There was also little need for servants to be in elaborate livery to accompany their masters. Whilst the stationmaster might not be visible in W. P. Frith's painting of Paddington Station (plate 112), the soaring expanses of the train shed, a "lofty pagan temple consecrated to the god of steam," are. And once Queen Victoria and Prince Albert started to travel by train, from 1842, giving the means of locomotion the seal of royal approval, the gentleman's prejudice against railways slowly declined. By the end of November 1845, 623 new railway construction bills were before Parliament, representing a vast capital outlay of some 563 million pounds.[22]

Still, the youngblood intent on roaring down to pater's seat by car had difficulties until after 1896. The Red Flag Act (repealed in 1896) had prohibited the use of self-propelled vehicles on British roads. The Frenchman Etienne Lenoir had produced a gas engine for power transmission in 1860, but British inertia long delayed the first practical motor car. In America there was greater eagerness to seize the advantages of traveling at more than a walking pace. At Mr. Edsel Ford's house in Detroit, it was considered normal by 1920 for there to be an eight-car garage—with a turntable for moving the cars and thereby eliminating the annoyances of "backing the car out." In the meantime there was always the bicycle, unaffected by highway legislation and safe enough for even a stiff-corseted, long-skirted, younger daughter. The wire-spoked tension wheel (1868) and the Dunlop pneumatic tire (1888) may never have been touched by their delicate fingers, accustomed hitherto to the intricacies of Berlin wool-work. But the bicycle enabled them to pedal to the top of the nearest hill from which, with an appropriate cacophony of sound, the Lanchester, with its epicyclic "early change" gearbox, hove into sight, bearing the love of their life, or, at least, of their dreams. Thoughts of marriage could survive the young man's obsessions with "splined shafts," "worm-drive," and "live" rear axles in a girl of some breeding and determination. And the young man, when his oily fingers were clean again, knew that marriage, the alliance of great names and greater estates, was a destiny. It was laid out as straight and inexorably before him as the shining steel struts supporting the gray canvas roof of the "lovable" machine on the graveled forecourt below.

CHAPTER III

Married, for Love and for Land

> *He that hath wife and children hath given hostages to fortune,*
> *for they are impediments to great enterprises, either of virtue*
> *or mischief. Certainly the best works, and of greatest merit for the*
> *public, have proceeded from the unmarried or childless men, which*
> *both in affection and means have married and endowed the public.*
>
> Francis Bacon, "The Essays:
> Of Marriage and Single Life," 1612

Despite Francis Bacon's strictures on wives and children being "impediments to great enterprises," the pursuit of marriage, for many reasons, was a generally held intention. Some may have been amused at the seventeenth-century diarist John Evelyn's views on the diverse problems associated with love, if that is what marriage was meant to signify: "Too much frequency of embraces dulls the sight, decays the memory, induces gout, palsies, enervates and renders effeminate the whole body, and shortens life."

The possession of a large estate encouraged proper arrangements for marriage and inheritance. Love was available to all; but for the rich, marriage was the establishment of an indissoluble union, broken only at death. In consequence, care was needed in selecting a suitable spouse.

In that most significant of manuals of advice, addressed in the late sixteenth century[1] to his son Robert, William Cecil, first Lord Burghley, advised on the choice of a wife:

Enquire diligently of her disposition and how her parents have been inclined in their youth. Let her not be poor, how generous so ever, for a man can buy nothing in the market with gentility. Nor choose a base and uncomely creature altogether for wealth, for it will cause contempt in others and loathing in thee. Neither make choice of dwarf or fool, for by the one thou shalt beget a race of pigmies, the other will be thy continual disgrace and it will irk thee to hear her talk. For thou shalt find it,

33. *William Hogarth (1697–1764). "The Wedding of Stephen Beckingham and Mary Cox." 1729.*
Oil on canvas, 50 x 40". The Metropolitan Museum of Art, New York, Marquand Fund, 1936

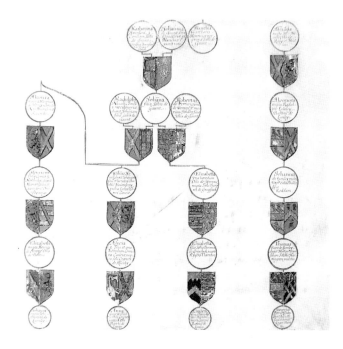

*34. Page from the "Lumley Inventory" of 1590. 16 x 11".
Prepared by John Lampton, Steward to John, Lord Lumley
(1534?–1609). Trustees of the Earl of Scarbrough's Settlement*

*Lord Lumley, one of the great collectors of his age, was much
occupied with the commemoration of his family. This immense family
tree improbably traces his ancestry back through Charlemagne to
Adam and (in gilded letters) to "DEUS."*

*35. "The Descent of the Grenville and Temple Families." c. 1780.
Engraving. Colonial Williamsburg Foundation*

*The Stowe estate had been acquired before 1590 by the Temple
family, who became Lords Cobham and married into the Grenvilles
of neighboring Wotton. As the coat-of-arms show,
that is but the start of an involved story.*

to thy great grief, that there is nothing more fulsome
than a she-fool.

The problem Cecil touched on, of a shrewlike woman
given to much scolding, was one often recognized in the
books of advice.[2] Thomas Bentley, in the third volume of
his *The Monument of Matrons* (1582), counseled that a wife
should hold these principles dear:

In my conversation modest, and honest; make me in
visage shamefast, in words temperate . . . take from me
all crabedness, curtness, stubborness and shrewdness.

The books of advice and printed strictures of many a
Puritan divine were issued freely from the London presses. A selection of titles explains their message clearly
enough. Across the years the purpose was largely religious
instruction leading to the betterment of life. John Dow-
name's *Guide to Godliness* (1622), Jeremiah Dyke's *Good
Conscience* (1624), and Richard Bernard's *The Ready Way
to Good Works* (1635) were paralleled by Isaac Watt's
A Caveat against Infidelity (1729) and in the nineteenth
century by Susan Moodie's *Homilies on Marriage* (1857);
being "seen but not heard," alas, applied to more than
children.

Women were expected to suffer their husband's anger
in silence, but this was not the case with those well versed
in forwardness and shrewishness. The outstanding example was Elizabeth, Countess of Shrewsbury ("Bess of
Hardwick"). The earl claimed that his wife called him
"knave, foole and beast" and "scolded like one that came
from the Bank."[3] But as William Overton, the Bishop of
Coventry and Lichfield, wrote to Lord Shrewsbury in
October 1590 (when asking him to put aside complaints
against his wife): "If shrewdness and sharpness may be
just cause for separation I think that few men in England
would keep their wives for long, for it is common jest . . .
that there is one shrew in all the world and every man
hath her."[4] A final quotation of such intractability
(although so alien from our own age of welcome emancipation for women) is evidenced in Henry Smith's
Preparative to Marriage (1591). In his view women were
"stubborn, sullen, taunting, gainsaying, with such a bit-
ter humour that one would think they were molten out

36. *Attributed to Rowland Lockey (active c. 1592–1616). "Elizabeth, Countess of Shrewsbury,*
'Bess of Hardwick.' " c. 1590. Oil on canvas, 40 x 30". The National Trust (Hardwick)

This imposing portrait shows Bess in black, mourning the death of her fourth and last husband,
the 6th Earl of Shrewsbury (d. 1590). However, she added his fortune to her building fund and urged Robert Smythson
to design the "New" Hardwick Hall, 1592–1597.

of the salt pillar into which Lot's wife was transformed."[5]

But for most noble husbands at least marriage meant an alliance of great names that enabled enhancement of their position and extension of their estates. The bargaining that predated the match was often extended over months, with the amount of the dowry and the jointure (the portion granted to a widow) being of great relevance. Every enter-

prising lawyer played at his own skilled game of interpretation, particularly for the husband, few of whom had heeded the wise words of Sir Walter Mildmay, who advised his son in 1570 "choose thy wife for virtue only."[6]

Fathers such as Sir William had to contend with the fear that if they died before their heir was twenty-one, their land would be taken by the Crown and be administered

37. *Sir Anthony Van Dyck (1599–1641).* "*Thomas Howard, 2nd Earl of Arundel, with Aletheia, Countess of Arundel.*" *c. 1639.*
Oil on canvas, 55 x 83". His Grace, the Duke of Norfolk

This painting recalls the revival of a scheme to colonize the Island of Madagascar to which the earl, wearing Parliamentary robes,
is pointing on the globe. The project was finally abandoned, perhaps because of his illness and his discovery that the island was infested
with fleas. Nevertheless, this is a significant portrait of a husband and wife reviewing an acquisition.

Opposite: 38. George Gower (working before 1573, d. 1596). "*Elizabeth Littleton, Lady Willoughby.*" *1573.*
Oil on canvas, 29 x 25". The Lord Middleton

Seen here when she was twenty-seven, Lady Willoughby lived in great style at Wollaton Hall, one of the most grandiose
of the late sixteenth-century houses. Her husband's wealth from his landed possessions gave her a steady and significant allowance.

An° dñi 1573.
ætatis suæ 27.

39. Attributed to Jan Van Belcamp (?–1653). "Lady Ann Clifford and her Family." 1646.
Tryptych, oil on canvas, 100 x 100″, center panel. Kendal, Abbot Hall Gallery

Lady Clifford is with her parents and immediate family in this extraordinary series of portraits within portraits.

by the Office of Wards until the heir was of age. It was a system based on the medieval requirement of raising an army quickly. The Crown would award lands in return for the provision of a mounted knight when one was needed— knight service. While knights in heavy armor became almost useless in war, the Crown's long memory saw that the claim to service was not forgotten. Henry VII revived the office's powers (soon known as the Court of Wards), and Henry VIII, ever in great need of revenue, strength-

ened its hold on the estates of minors and the right for it to sell the marriage of a ward. The age of consent in marriage for women was held to be twelve, and that of men, fourteen. Wards under these ages could be married off at the desire of their guardians, who were always anxious to escape the prying attention of the Master of Wards.[7] The usual aim was to achieve a marriage for money, however disapproving one's friends and neighbors might be, on the surface at least. It has been shown[8] that in the pursuit of

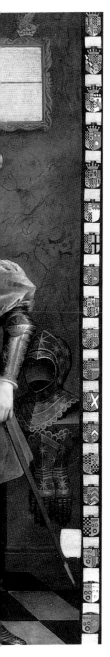

age dependent on the consent of their parents or guardians.

An unmarried woman was seen by her family as a considerable burden. The head of the family had to provide for her maintenance, usually by an annuity of no investment potential to the grantee. But in contrast a bride was maintained by her husband in return for the one-time provision of a marriage portion. In the event of his death she was awarded a jointure.

There was a contract between the fathers of the groom and the bride and another in which the groom's father settled his estate to trustees. Frequently they were one and the same complex piece of written parchment. The father of the bride provided a cash sum (the portion) payable in several installments, "the bride's" trousseau and jewels, and the marriage feast as well. The groom's father was put to more trouble and expense. The most important claim on his estate was the provision of an annual allowance (the jointure) to support the bride, if and when she became a widow. The jointure usually involved both a cash sum (on the size of which there could be substantial disagreement) and the ownership of land and a house, or rooms, in which to live.

All grooms today might wish that the practice of an allowance made to them in their father's lifetime still continued. This was often in the form of an annuity, popular since the early seventeenth century, or, as with the jointure, a transfer of land and a house. After about 1620 a sum of "pin-money" was made available to the bride to be spent at her discretion. The groom's father also needed to make clear what proportion of his estate he proposed to settle at his death on his eldest son.[10]

Throughout the sixteenth and seventeenth centuries there were many devices introduced by clever lawyers to prevent marriages breaking up estates and redistributing land. The large sums of money necessary to marriage had led to selling land to raise portions for daughters. Families had an urgent desire to establish a dynasty, and by the middle of the seventeenth century (hastened by the bloody progress of the Civil War), protection of property was essential. With the abolition of the iniquitous Court of Wards in 1660, the legal device of the strict family settlement emerged to protect the inheritance. This provided that estates would pass to the eldest surviving male heir from generation to generation, that estates could be set-

heiresses the Howards, Earls of Arundel, married four between 1555 and 1606; the Howards, Earls of Suffolk and the Norths, each three in a row; and the Russells, Earls of Bedford, four. In the early seventeenth century one marriage in every three by a peer was to an heiress, probably in an "arranged" context. Henry Hastings, the fifth Earl of Huntingdon, had reminded his son in 1613 that "without means honour will look as naked as trees that are cropped."[9] He had himself married when a child, happily as it happened, but forced marriages were usual, with no right of veto to the son or daughter under the age of eighteen until the early seventeenth century. In any case the canons of 1603, issued in the year of Elizabeth I's death, had made marriage of children under twenty-one years of tled on unborn children, and that, beyond the wife's join-ture, like provision was made for younger sons and daughters. The stability of landed society was a view that the courts inevitably endorsed as disputed cases came before them in the Chancery Court. By 1764 it was estimated by Sir John Dalrymple that nearly half of all English land was still settled, and even as late as 1901 most of the greater estates remained that way.

In all the complexities of ensuring succession few parallels might seem relevant between the strict Puritan world of the seventeenth century and the position of a family in the nineteenth. Yet few Victorian misses would deign to defy their glowering top-hatted fathers with an unsuitable match. Morals were strict (if more easily evaded), and there was an overriding concern, with war clouds over Europe still distant, to preserve the value and extent of family life.

For the system to work (with lawyers thereby enriched), a new settlement was agreed in each generation between the tenant for life and his son (known as the *tenant-in-tail*). This usually took place at the marriage of the heir, and the process of discussion is illustrated graphically by William Hogarth in his painting *The Marriage Settlement* (plate 40), from his Marriage à la Mode series. There was an incentive to acquire more land to add to the strength of an estate. The events in revolutionary France at the end of the eighteenth century reinforced the stability of landed society as a firm argument by Edmund Burke and others for ensuring stability in the country.[11]

When marriage had been entered into, it was but the beginning of an association in which the principal players might still be almost strangers. Nevertheless, it was in the interest of parents, anxious to avoid the Court of Wards seizing on heiresses, that they be married as soon as of legal age and that the union be quickly consummated. The young man might be about to leave on his Grand Tour, for it was a usual practice—at least in the early seventeenth century—for the marriage to take place a day or two before the prolonged journey was undertaken. The wife did not accompany her husband, and her presence in England was meant to discourage any contemplation of unsuitable liaisons when abroad.

In the world of the Puritan gentry, it was believed that compatibility in marriage was only achieved through the working of God's will. Sir William Waller noted that following the death of his first wife in 1633 he prayed that he might be granted a second marriage to a religious woman. As a result, he believed, of divine intervention, he was directed to Lady Anne Finch, the daughter of Thomas Finch, Earl of Winchelsea. After the settlement of the essential financial arrangements, Sir William and his intended wife agreed to set a day apart to seek God's blessing on the marriage—they became "one soul in two bodies." The second wife soon dying, his prayers were answered yet again; Lady Anne Harcourt was sent as the intended third wife. She recorded that Sir William was a "religious, wise and faythfull loving husband."[12]

Puritans believed that the Bible gave all things necessary to salvation, that preaching the gospel could always forward the cause of a goodly life, and that days of fasting and confessing of sins were necessary adjuncts to a religious household. These benefits were strengthened by the conviction that God took care of the elect while they were on earth. There were some gentlemen who modified these strictures, which were fed by a vast pious literature, to suit their own position. The outstanding Puritan gentleman and antiquarian writer Sir Simond D'Ewes (1602–1650) observed in his autobiography that when he was seeking a wife he put considerable emphasis on religion, though he also wished to "ensure his posterity with good blood." He lighted, in April 1626, on the fourteen-year-old Lady Anne Clopton, who had been "verie religiouslie educated" by her grandmother. The wedding took place in May, and D'Ewes was soon boasting to a friend that he was "linked either nearelie or moore remotelie to all or the most parte . . . of all the ancient nobilitie of England."[13] D'Ewes, as with others of his generation, had little difficulty in reconciling spiritual and worldly matters. A year after his wife's death in 1642 he was married again, to the daughter (and heiress with 1,000 pounds a year) of a Derbyshire baronet. Sir William Waller chose in succession three wives from a similar and faultless background. They were all concerned, nevertheless, with their financial interests. Sir Christopher Yelverton waged a long battle over the terms on which his only daughter would be allowed to marry Lord Mandeville, notwithstanding the young man's piety and owning of the ways of God. There were also long negotiations over the portion, maintenance,

40. *William Hogarth (1697–1764). "Marriage à la Mode; The Marriage Settlement." 1745.*
Oil on canvas, 27 x 35". The Trustees, National Gallery, London

Hogarth's painting (one of six) shows that the earl and the merchant will decide on the marriage of their children, advised by the usurer.
The lawyer, Silvertongue, whispers to the intended bride, and the foppish groom has taken to snuff.

and jointure in the projected marriage of John Dryden and Elizabeth Isham, both of prominent Puritan families in Northamptonshire. Sir Erasmus Dryden refused to take a generous stance, and in December 1631 his son died unmarried; one intermarriage between Puritan families was therefore thwarted.[14]

The protection afforded by marrying into chosen families, with a likelihood of good, sober living and pious children, was a dream often broken. First, the House of Commons had refused, after the Restoration of Charles II to the throne in 1660, to join the Lords in tightening the marriage laws. In 1677 the Lords had prepared a bill that noted the danger to young children when "their fathers, having no means to avoid such marriages, are often reconciled thereto rather than wholly desert their children." The House of Commons ignored the premise, as it did again in 1685, 1689, and 1691. The matter was taken up again in 1697, in 1711, and in 1735, always unsuccessfully. It was not until 1753 that Lord Hardwicke's Marriage Act, which strengthened parental authority, became law, although Horace Walpole thought it one that "breathed the very spirit of aristocracy and insolent nobility," and there was much oratorical opposition to it from such prominent politicians as Charles Townshend, Henry Fox, and others.[15]

One of the relationships the House of Lords tried to legislate was marriage without parental consent. The matter may be illustrated by the case of Lord Ossulston (he later became third Earl of Tankerville), who in about 1714 started courtship of Camilla Colville, daughter of a Durham butcher and grazier. He had met her at an assize ball in Newcastle and pursued her to Rotterdam, where she had been sent by a prudent father. It is said that the linden walks there lent their shade to meetings of the lovers "and. . . his lordship made signals from the street, which Camilla could furtively read in the friendly mirror projecting from the parlour window"; Camilla was therefore sent back to England, but Lord Ossulston secreted himself on board ship in a cask. They landed together at South Shields at some point in 1715 and soon afterward were married at Jarrow Church, which had long been a resort of young couples "seeking to enter the bonds of wedlock without the consent of parents."[16] Edward Colville, Camilla's father, had been aware of Lord Ossulston's father having been suitor to two wealthy ladies and paying court to many less desirable, and perhaps feared his daughter was being courted with no firm intention of marriage. The two young people proved him wrong. His daughter, now a countess, was able to become the Lady of the Bedchamber, or personal attendant, both to Queen Caroline and to the Princess Augusta, a striking example of upward mobility in status.

In his *The Complete English Gentleman* Daniel Defoe set out a list of "inferior ladies . . . married to persons of rank and dignity."[17] While doubt has been cast on most of his names, Defoe did touch on an important issue that agitated parents did their best to control. One of the most celebrated cases of the early eighteenth century in the withholding of parental approval to marriage was that of Edward Wortley and Lady Mary Pierrepont. In 1710 Wortley, eligible and an ardent suitor, sought to marry Lady Mary. Her father, Evelyn Pierrepont Kingston,

Marquess of Dorchester (and later first Duke of Kingston), insisted, firmly, that the Wortley estate be entailed on the first son born to the marriage. When Wortley refused to agree to this Lord Dorchester refused his permission to the marriage.

In *The Tatler* of July 18, 1710, Wortley's friend Sir Richard Steele set out an eloquent argument against mercenary marriages. One of the abuses was the bridegroom assigning his estate without knowing whether he would be succeeded by anyone of merit. The woman was set up as though at auction: "Her first lover has ten to one against him. The very hour after he has opened his heart and his rent rolls he is made no other use of but to raise her price." The arguments went unheeded by Lord Dorchester, but Steele continued the attack. To prove the absurdity of entailing estates he continued, ironically, in his essay of September 12, 1710, on the usual marriage settlement:

The suitor declares that: "in full and perfect health of body, and a sound mind, not knowing which of my children will prove better or worse, I give to my first-born be he perverse, ungrateful, impious, or cruel, the lump and bulk of my estate. . . hereby further confessing and covenanting that I am from henceforth married, and dead in law."

Lady Mary's father remained unpersuaded and advanced other suitors to his daughter. She still bore the irrevocable gift of her title and wed plain "Mr. Wortley" on August 20, 1712.[18] He had to contend with the loss of her 20,000-pound dowry as well as incurring his father's anger. She would lose the attractive terms offered by her Irish suitor, the Hon. Clotworthy Skeffington—500 pounds a year as "pin-money" and 1,200 pounds a year if he died, together with 8,000 pounds raised by her father on her brother's marriage and 6,000 pounds from her grandmother's will. She told Wortley in August 1712 that she was ready to abandon all for him—fame, family, and settlement. Instead she would substitute Love, Solitude, and Economy as the articles of their private settlement. When Lady Mary met Joseph Spence in Rome, some thirty years later, she confessed that for a month prior to her marriage she was kept awake by the vast number of offers of marriage and "who to fix upon." She elected that she would be married to somebody and not to the man her father advised her to. In later years, when she read Samuel

41. *John Michael Wright (1617–1695). "The Family of Sir Robert Vyner." 1673. Oil on canvas, 57 x 77".*
The National Portrait Gallery, London

This is one of the great family portraits of seventeenth-century British painting. Sir Robert Vyner (1636–1688), who,
as a city goldsmith, made the regalia used at Charles II's coronation in 1661, is shown with his second wife and the children from
both his marriages. The garden is almost certainly that at Swakeleys, their Middlesex house.

42. *Arthur Devis (1712–1787). "Thomas Lister and His family." c. 1740–1741. Oil on canvas, 44 x 39".*
The Art Institute of Chicago, gift of Emily Crane Chadbourne

The Lister family, painted here at Gisburne Park in Yorkshire, were among Devis's most important patrons.
Thomas Lister had rebuilt the house at Gisburne in 1724; prominent also, in the middle distance, are its famous breed of white cattle.
Lister is shown with his land agent and four of his children: Mrs. Lister had died in 1728.

Richardson's novel *Clarissa Harlowe*, she saw Clarissa as herself, with her father insisting on the rich ugly Solmes and the libertine Lovelace as Wortley, although Edward lacked both Lovelace's charm and his vices. The novel, issued in 1747–1748, is about Clarissa Harlowe, a young lady of excellent family, who is wooed by Lovelace, an attractive but unscrupulous man of fashion. Secretly fascinated, and against her family's wishes, Clarissa succumbed to Lovelace and then died of shame; Lovelace was killed in a duel by her cousin, Colonel Morden. Richardson's title page carried the legend that the novel was a warning of "the Distresses that may attend Misconduct both of Parents and Children in relation to Marriage."

All young couples, intent on listening to each other rather than to the dull advice of their fathers and the lawyers, might have aspired to George Grenville's situation. It was, observed a friend, his unvaried practice "in all situations to live on his own private fortune, and save the emoluments of whatever office he possessed." Back from a Grand Tour, intent on a grand Palladian house to which his friends' coaches could come and go, a young man's life might seem good and eventful. But to marry, to have a bevy of healthy but not particularly good-looking daughters, too much had to be raised in extra dowry to render them eligible to someone.

A rarer practice, of marrying into business as well as into the aristocratic landed circles, had grown spasmodically from the seventeenth century. The most noted example was the marriage in 1677 of Sir Thomas Grosvenor to Mary Davis. She was heiress to the manor of Ebury, which became in due course a valuable part of the West End of London, ensuring by its development the largest of private fortunes to subsequent Grosvenors, Dukes of Westminster.[19] The second Earl of Warrington, anxious for money to ease his financial plight, used two agents at a cost of 1,000 guineas to find him a wealthy wife. They found him Mary Oldbury, daughter of a rich London merchant with a portion of 40,000 pounds.[20] However, the stuffy prejudice against such marriages had reached an overwhelming level by the nineteenth century, when a few marriages to bankers' daughters—and to Americans—set the pace. Nevertheless the pursuit went on at house parties and in the encouraging conversation of the older members of a family.

William, the sixth Baron Monson, who had in 1841 succeeded his cousin Frederick to the title, was always urging his son William to marry a girl with a fortune, to rescue his household from its varied predicaments. Some of these had been caused by the prolonged jointure payments to two dowagers (one survived to 1891). Lord Monson told his son about his aunt:

[She would] like to see you married to a nice girl with a good fortune—Miss Clara Thornhill who is just coming out promised to be a very nice girl and has nine thousand a year (that would do, eh!). . . there are two younger daughters of £40,000 each, not bad, but the first is the largest prize, I should be very sorry for you to marry for money but a nice wife with it would not be bad.

Three days later, the inquisitive Lord Monson revised his knowledge of Miss Thornhill's annual income upwards, to 15,000 pounds. But, alas, young William Monson let all these financially endowed young ladies slide through his fingers. He waited until 1869, seven years after his father's death, for the hand of Maria Adelaide, widow of the Earl of Yarborough. Fathers must have often experienced some shimmering mirage in which they, who had failed to find any such affluent, nay, pretty foreign creature, imagined that their son would certainly succeed in doing so. She would, moreover, only need a modest jointure, as an heiress, set at but 1 percent of the capital value of her inheritance. The imaginings of any father such as this might be dismissed as mere dreams or the vaporous meanderings of one too affected by imbibing crusted port laid down in the reign of George III.

The Baring firm had been established in 1763 by the first baronet, Sir Francis Baring. At first they were merchants with an extensive mercantile trade, but in the early nineteenth century greatly expanded banking and finance became more important, which continues to the present. In 1830 Harriet Baring married Lord Henry Thynne, one of the Marquess of Bath's younger sons. Into the marriage chest Lord Henry put 10,000 pounds: his intended wife complied with 50,000 pounds. Harriet's jointure was fixed at 2,500 pounds, or 5 percent of her fortune. Stepping this up could be done by bequests in a will, but there was always need for a nicely judged smoking-room conversation between the male in-laws on the exact relationship between marriage portion and jointure.

More immediate money, spent on the London season, on levees, soirées, balls, operas, visiting galleries, having one's portrait painted, parading to be seen, all this was worthwhile expenditure if it led successfully to finding a husband. It was money parents provided, ever protesting, but secretly rejoicing—the more so if the prospective young man had a title, a coronet, an ermine-decked robe, and even a moderate house in the country. But peers were not above considering personal pleasure rather than financial advantage in seeking out actresses to marry. There were nineteen such marriages in the twenty years before the First World War. The new merchants, Sir Ernest Cassel and Sir Thomas Lipton for example, were ever in Edward VII's company, and, in such an atmosphere (as

43. *Arthur Devis (1712–1787). "Robert Gwillym of Atherton and His family." c. 1745–1747.*
Oil on canvas, 39 x 50". Yale Center for British Art, Paul Mellon Collection

While there is some confusion as to whether Devis has represented Atherton Hall or another Gwillym house,
there is ample evidence of a burgeoning family: Robert, with his father, points to Elizabeth, their four children, and one of his brothers.

Opposite: 44. Thomas Hudson (1701–1779). "Sir John Pole, 5th Baronet, and His Wife, Elizabeth."
1755. Oil on canvas, 94 x 71". The Trustees of Sir Richard Carew Pole

Hudson painted this delightful work after some observation of Van Dyck and Lely.
There is a rococo gaiety in the color and a daring display of ankle for the lady.

45. Sydney Prior Hall (1842–1922). "The Marriage of Princess Louise to the Marquess of Lorne." 1871.
Oil on canvas, 50 x 40". The Trustees of the 10th Duke of Argyll

Princess Louise was the fourth daughter of Queen Victoria. Married to her in St. George's Chapel, Windsor, in 1871,
her husband, who became the 9th Duke of Argyll in 1900, was Governor-General of Canada.

F. M. L. Thompson has noted in his *English Landed Society in the Nineteenth Century*, 1963), "the adulation of gold and diamond millionaires, financiers, and rough self-made men became fashionable and respectable," and their eligible daughters equally so.

In America, as in England, marriage concerned the establishment of dynasties. Before the Revolution, Benjamin Franklin had opined that marriages in America were "more general, and more generally early than in Europe." This he thought was due to the abundance of land and the relative ease of subsistence, which "banished forebodings and led to readiness for early marriage." Early marriages were common and even, on occasion, those that seemed destined to fail. James Fenimore Cooper wrote in 1828:[21]

> From all that I can learn, nothing is more common, however, than for young men of great expectations to connect themselves with females, commonly of their own condition in life, who are penniless; or, on the other hand, for ladies to give their persons with one or two hundred thousand dollars to men who have nothing better to recommend them than education and morals.

46. *John Singer Sargent, RA (1856–1925). "Lord Ribblesdale." 1902.*
Oil on canvas, 101 x 56". The Trustees, National Gallery, London

Lord Ribblesdale, a liberal-minded aristocrat, was married twice, first to one of the Tennants and then to the widow
of John Jacob Astor. He kept company with the leading literary figures of the day, but his dandified hunting outfit
almost renders him an elegant caricature of the stylish gentleman.

47. James Tissot (1836–1902). "The Bridesmaid." 1883–1885. Oil on canvas, 88 x 57".
Temple Newsam House (Leeds City Art Galleries)

Tissot, an immigrant French artist working in England, specialized in the depiction of everyday scenes,
investing them with rich color and sometimes mischievous observation.

In 1867 Auguste Carlier[22] asserted that the greatest ambition of a young American girl was to wed a title—a European of whatever title could be sure of a rich wife:

Place before her two men, one of whom has but his noble title; and the other a man distinguished in science, in letters or in business—there will be no doubt of the young American's choice.

This view was confirmed by the Frenchman Duvergier De Hauranne. Writing in 1866 he noted, "A European title, tho old and ruined, still has a chance to find a wife in America."[23] A few years before, in 1862, Charles Woodruff wrote in his cynically titled *Legalised Prostitution* that when two young people contemplated marriage society warned that they must be of equal rank "or else public opinion will frown upon them so terribly that one or the other shall lose caste and be banished from all intercourse in certain cliques or grades of life." Nevertheless, they needed, perhaps, to make their own way, if the German Joseph Kleiber is to be believed. Writing in 1877 in his *Amerika wie es ist*, Kleiber noted that "the Yankee as a rule gives his children no dowry, and if he is approached in that regard asks whether the man wants to marry his daughter or his property?" While Samuel Day stated[24] categorically that "American damsels . . .will not marry you, save upon the cold, careful consideration of how you stand with your banker . . . she takes quite a business view of the marital relationship."

From the English side of the Atlantic there had certainly been interest shown by some aristocrats in marrying an American wife. The fact that American fortunes could pass to daughters, as well as to sons may have been a contributory factor. With declining rents and a fall in the value of property, many English peers needed their capital regenerated. What they could offer to those who had most material possessions was a social position based on the certainty that primogeniture was unfailing. As one writer has put it:[25] "If one's daughter were a duchess, one's grandson would without question be a duke." The lure was irresistible.

Lord Randolph Churchill, attending the Royal Yacht Squadron Cowes Week grand events in August 1873, met Jennie Jerome, one of the three charismatic daughters of the Wall Street banker and racehorse owner Leonard Jerome. Lord Randolph was captivated by Jennie, and it probably did not escape her notice that he was a younger son of the seventh Duke of Marlborough. He was an active member of the Prince of Wales' circle, known as the "Marlborough House set." Despite his family's predilection for marrying within their own social class there was the attractive question of Jennie having access to her father's money. Leonard Jerome's lawyers fought a hard fight, and when sums had been agreed, the marriage took place. Soon the Churchills were at every social event but there was eventually much talk of the prince's obvious interest in her, to the point where Randolph was sent to Ireland as private secretary to the seventh Duke of Marlborough, who had been appointed Viceroy of Ireland. On return to England Randolph's parliamentary career flourished and Jennie, as his ardent advocate at the elections, had conferred on her by Queen Victoria the Insignia of the Imperial Order of the Crown of India. It is not to our purpose to chronicle Jennie's further indiscretions with the prince, the failing of Randolph's mind and his death in 1895, or Jennie's metamorphosis as a hostess of the naughty nineties. The task has been done by her biographers.[26] Suffice it for us to look at further American marriages by the Marlboroughs.

Jennie's niece by marriage was Consuelo Vanderbilt, who was introduced to London society through the eager efforts of two more American wives of peers, Minnie, Lady Paget, and Consuelo, Duchess of Manchester. At Lady Paget's London house in Belgrave Square, Consuelo met her future husband, the ninth Duke of Marlborough. He fell in love with her, followed her back to New York, and they were soon married, on November 6, 1896, at St. Thomas's on Fifth Avenue. Consuelo's father, the enormously wealthy William Kissam Vanderbilt, had by then died, but her mother had strong social ambitions for her daughter. Whether the duke had in mind that his own father had married an American (Lilian Warren, the daughter of Cicero Price, a commodore in the U.S. Navy) was not precisely relevant to his own situation, but an interesting gloss on it, nevertheless. Consuelo found the duke intended to school his wife rigidly in aristocratic niceties and in the lineage and intricacies of family connections and to conduct prayers each morning in chapel. He even

48. John Singer Sargent, RA (1856–1925). "The Marlborough Family." 1905. Oil on canvas, 131 x 94".
His Grace, the Duke of Marlborough

This grandly posed portrait shows the 9th duke and his American wife, Consuelo Vanderbilt, whom he married in 1896.
"Sargent," the duchess recalled, "chose a black dress whose sleeves were lined with deep rose satin,"
basing it on a costume worn for Van Dyck's portrait of Lady Morton and Mrs. Killigrew, also at Blenheim Palace.
The future 10th duke is shown as a boy of eight; his younger brother is at the right.

equipped her with a page in oriental costume.[27]

One of Consuelo's friends was Mary Victoria Leiter, the daughter of business magnate Marshall Field's partner in Chicago, Levi Leiter. She and her two sisters were, as with Jennie Jerome and her sisters, all to marry Englishmen. After a five-year courtship, the last two as an engaged couple, Mary married George Curzon of Kedleston, at St. John's Church in Washington, D.C., on April 22, 1895.

George, was eventually elevated in the Irish peerage as the Baron Curzon of Kedleston, so enabling him to continue as a member of the House of Commons. But more important, in the summer of 1898, he was offered and accepted the Viceroyalty of India. Mary as his Vicereine reveled in the new and important social role, the state dinners, balls, receptions, all of it partly paid for from her own fortune. But the teeming life and strains of the Asian subcontinent

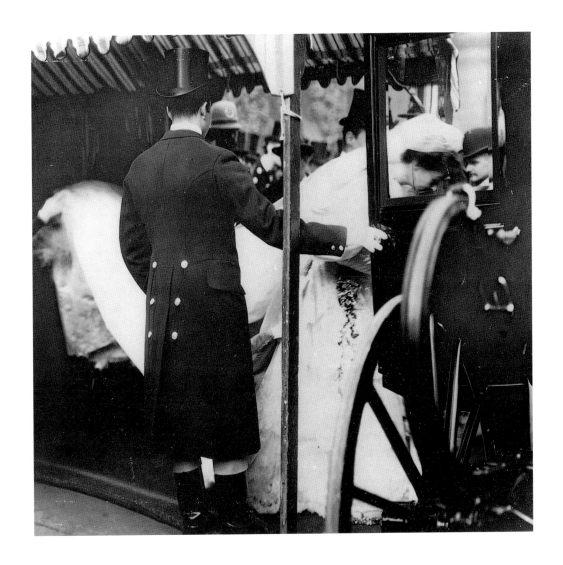

49. "The Marriage of the 9th Duke of Marlborough to Consuelo Vanderbilt," New York. 1896.
Photograph. Byron Collection, Museum of the City of New York

The 9th duke's father, who died in 1892, had also married, as his second wife, an American, Lilian Warren.
This ceremony took place at City Hall. On November 6, 1896, his son was married at St. Thomas's on Fifth Avenue.
It was a social occasion that brought New York to a halt. (See also plate 48).

took their toll on Mary's health. She returned home in 1903, alone, to Kedleston and the London house, 1 Carlton House Terrace, which had been bought for George and herself by her father. She died there in July 1906, at the early age of thirty-six.[28]

Whatever marriage did for the stability of a household, of its nature it was always fragile. Consuelo eventually divorced the duke and became an active figure for women's rights. There were also the looming storm-clouds of the First World War with all that did in the annihilation of the eldest sons. Large quantities of land were on sale even before the war, with perhaps a million acres having

changed hands by its end and five times as much by 1921.[29] The stable conditions of the mid-nineteenth century had gone, and the aristocracy was irreparably weakened, but not dissolved, after the war. It had a long historical tradition, which even those opposed to the position of the aristocracy, and even of the monarchy, have not abandoned either. Great estates may have been broken up and the constitutional position of the House of Lords eroded, but "all the world loves a lord," men (and women too) of consequence, with no worry about "always knowing quite why."

CHAPTER IV

The Noble Seat and the Goddess of Taste

If you are not able to handsomely contrive it yourself,
get some ingenious gentleman who has seen much of that
kind abroad. . .to do it for you.

"Notebooks of Sir Roger Pratt," 1660, cited by R.T.
Gunther, "The Architecture of Sir Roger Pratt"
(1928)

From the Tudor period on, there had always been those gentlemen who earned money by their abilities, or by guile, and were then forward in architecture and building. Henry Percy, the ninth Earl of Northumberland in the late sixteenth century, was assiduous about his buildings at Syon House on the Thames near to London, and he possessed many foreign architectural books. Sir John Thynne at Longleat and William Cecil, first Baron Burghley (plates 4 and 74), were equally active in the late years of Elizabeth's reign in building grand houses.[1] The demands of such building needed the provision of money in more than ordinary quantity. In the early seventeenth century, for example, Sir Arthur Ingram gathered a large fortune by the granting to him of monopolies by James I, and he became one of the ablest and most unscrupulous financiers

of the period; he founded the fortunes used by his ancestors who lived at Temple Newsam House, Leeds, for the two and a half centuries after he had acquired the land in 1622 for 12,000 pounds.[2] Lord Conway wrote to his cousin Sir Edward Harley in 1677 of his Warwickshire home, Ragley Hall: "Here you find me playing the foole in laying out money upon building, having cheefely undertaken it because I find my grandfather designed to build here."[3]

One of the main concerns of the earlier medieval builder had been the defense of his home, and comfort was secondary to this aim. Across the deep reedy moats of fortified houses, owners could feel secure, dining in their great halls, which were set away on the side of the inner courtyard farthest from their castellated gatehouses. But by the early sixteenth century the concerns of the Tudor builder

50. Jan Siberechts (1627–c. 1700). "Wollaton Hall and Park, Nottinghamshire." 1697.
Oil on canvas, 75 x 54". Yale Center for British Art, Paul Mellon Collection

51. *Wollaton Hall, Nottinghamshire, South front. 1588.*

Many of the architectural details on Wollaton's façades are based on books of designs by Jan Vredeman de Vries,
published in Antwerp and Paris, 1563–1565. The building, which epitomizes the early country house,
was built for Sir Francis Willoughby by Robert Smythson.

related more to the overall symmetry of his expensively contrived façades and less to defensive towers. The hall window bays could thus be spaced out equally on the high main front, with side-wings balancing each other as they swept forward to enfold the amazed onlooker. Visual impact was equally a concern of any patron intent on lavish building. He wished to demonstrate that he could outdo all his rivals and that his status was announced prominently not only by the elaborate façades of his house, decked in expensive materials, but by the swirling acres of its encircling park, which stretched as far as envious eyes could encompass. And if such a building could be grand enough for King Henry VIII to visit, or for Queen Elizabeth I to journey to on one of her lavish summer progresses, it was worth the beggaring expenditure. The

queen was not above complaining if all was not well. In 1572 she told her Lord-Keeper of the Great Seal, Sir Nicholas Bacon, that his brick courtyard house at Gorhambury was too small, and at once he set to enlarging it.[4] In 1579 Lord Burghley referred to the expense of his own great house of Theobalds in Hertfordshire, which he had acquired in 1564, and to that of his friend Sir Christopher Hatton's Holdenby Hall, Northamptonshire, which was copied (as Sir Christopher owned) from Theobalds. Cecil noted that both were built to honor the queen, "for whom we both meant to exceed our purses." Hatton further described Holdenby as his "other shrine" and hoped, blasphemously, "that holy saint" Queen Elizabeth "might sit in it."[5] Both houses were destroyed during the Commonwealth (1648–1660), with but fragments remaining. The Commonwealth, the period between the execution of Charles I and the Restoration of Charles II in 1660, had seen a republican government established, led by the Protector, Oliver Cromwell (1599–1658).

By the end of the sixteenth century the concerns with architectural practice seem to have adjusted to changes brought about by the importation and acceptance of Renaissance ideas. A wise builder now followed a set process of obtaining a careful estimate of the cost of his proposed works from a "surveyor," who submitted drawings and a model in wood. It was obviously desirable, as Bardolph quoted in Shakespeare's *Henry IV, Part II*, to keep a careful check on building expenditure: to "rate the cost of the erection," "question surveyors," and "know our own estate." And yet the employer of all these could become too obsessed with detail, and Gerbier in 1662 found it necessary to emphasize (even if he was doing some special pleading) the undesirability of such interference during building operations:

The builder having made choice of his surveyor and committed to him all the care and guidance of the work, never changes on the various opinions of other men. . . .They know that a well-experienced surveyor must not be disturbed in his task and undertaking.

Presumably Bess of Hardwick argued with her "well-experienced" surveyor, Robert Smythson, over the details of building Hardwick Hall for her in the late 1580s. For example, there is the innovation that the axis of the hall is aligned with the main entrance, rather than cutting across it, with entry to a screens-passage. This was a scheme betokening some knowledge of villa plans, as set out by Andrea Palladio in 1570 in his *Quattro Libri* and perhaps derived from the Valmarana Villa.[6] While Smythson would have known that, his patroness still needed to approve. Andrea Palladio (1508–1580), one of the greatest Italian architects, evolved a calm simple style for his Veneto villas that attracted English builders as sophisticated as Smythson by the strict attention to rules of proportion. An essential characteristic was the correct rela-

52. Peter Robinson (1776–1858). "Hardwick Hall, Derbyshire, The High Great Chamber." 1835.
Engraving in "New Vitruvius Britannicus." The National Trust, London

This view shows Hardwick's finest room, where Bess received her visitors. The frieze alludes to Diana and her court.

tionship of the proportions of the component parts of a building one to another. That Bess wished her great house to express her status is exemplified in the initials "E.S" (Elizabeth, Countess of Shrewsbury) displayed at large in the stone parapets to all its six towers. As with Wollaton Hall, completed by Smythson in 1588 for Sir Francis Willoughby, Hardwick is on a hilltop, visible for miles and with great windows from which to gaze at the "prospect" of the estate. Bess's master mason, Thomas Accres, had embellishied Wollaton's stone façades (plate 51) with rich carved decorations based on engravings by Jan Vredeman de Vries. Bess also visited Holdenby and Wollaton in 1592, on her way back from an eight-month stay at her London home, Shrewsbury House, in Chelsea, and attendance on the queen at court. Holdenby was then empty, except for a small retaining staff. This visit was largely for Bess to inform herself of their comparative scale and plan—as she moved between Chatsworth and the old Hardwick Hall,

53. *William Henry Hunt (1790–1864). "Hardwick Hall, Derbyshire, The Long Gallery." 1828.*
Watercolor, 15 x 22". Devonshire Collection, The Chatsworth Settlement Trustees

Hardwick's Long Gallery, 162 feet long, amazes by the profusion of portraits laid over the thirteen tapestries
acquired by Bess of Hardwick in London in 1592.

Opposite: 54. Knole, Kent. The staircase. 1605–1608. The National Trust

This staircase was remodeled for Thomas Sackville, 1st Earl of Dorset. The leopards from his coat-of-arms are carved above
the newel posts. The paintings, after designs by Marten de Vos, were carried out by Paul Isaacson, who had worked previously
for Queen Elizabeth I and for King James I.

all the time watching the rearing progress of her new house. She moved into the new Hardwick Hall in October 1597, but the bustle, banging, painting, and furnishing went on apace until 1601 and absorbed nearly half of her gross annual income.[7]

Hardwick's façades are pierced by great areas of glass windows, a magnificent statement of Elizabethan opulence. Its gallery, 162 feet long, was a useful space in which important visitors could be received, or exercise taken on inclement days. A gallery was also a place to hang paintings, and to have "entertainments." It was entered at Hardwick from the High Great Chamber, arguably one of the most beautiful rooms in Europe. It is approached, winding up through the light and dark areas of the house, by a stone staircase that never reveals where it is going until the last sharp turn to a bright, tapestry-bedecked landing. Bess's coat of arms is set in plaster over the elaborately paneled door and below the deep, robust frieze symbolizing "Diana and her court." The sheer scale of the space was intended to impress and, with an assurance born of her position as the wealthiest widow in England, even to aggrandize the owner. The "DIEU ET MON DROIT" has

the "ET" changed to "EST," another deliberate incorporation of the owner's initials. Bess of Hardwick's land, great house, coal mines, glassworks, and burgeoning fortune placed her ahead of most men.

The first English architect to understand the classical orders that Bess of Hardwick had toyed with was Inigo Jones. He was born in 1573 and might be classed as belonging to the Elizabethan period, except that his work differs so fundamentally from that of his contemporaries. The first of the Palladians, he brought the classical style into England, having formed a keen appreciation of both Roman monuments and Palladio's buildings during his eighteen months in Italy in 1613 in the entourage of the "Collector" Earl of Arundel (plate 37). He set a fashion to think of building according to rules that looked back, via Palladio, to the Roman architect Vitruvius.

In 1624 Sir Henry Wotton, ambassador at the court of Venice in the early seventeenth century, wrote in his *Elements of Architecture:*

Everymans proper *Mansion* House and *Home*, being the *Theatre* of his hospitality, the seate of *self-fruition*,

55. *"Belton House, Lincolnshire." c. 1690. Oil on canvas, 30 x 44". The National Trust (Belton House)*

This painting, showing the house two or three years after its completion, is attributed to the house-porter Henry Bugg.
He painted himself as the outsize figure holding his mace of office and looking after his master's domain.

the Comfortablest of his owne *life*; the *noblest* of his sonnes *Inheritance* [is] a kind of private *Princedome*.

There were of course many houses designed to more modest plan. The master masons did much that was in the manner of the best London craftsman and their "oblong square houses" (which anticipated developments in the early 1660s) brought together parts taken from a wide range of useful sources. Many of these were English, but foreign architectural books by Serlio, Palladio, and Sir Peter Paul Rubens (his *Palazzi di Genova*, 1626) were combed for ideas. Some houses were given plans and elevations that rivaled in scale the grandest medieval abbeys. This interest in grand form, gathered and displayed with care or abandon, focused itself in the buildings of a gentleman-architect, Sir Roger Pratt (1620–1684). In the "Certain Heads" he set down in his notebooks in 1660, he noted five requirements concerning "the undertaking of any Building": money, a model to work to, availability of suitable materials, workmen at the correct rates of pay, and the situation of the house. Additionally there was need to consider the nature of pasture for animals, what "air" and water were unhindered and near, what fuel for fires, and did the neighborhood have "markets, poor people, Gentleman, Noblemen, the King, or his lands, etc." Pratt took the idea of the small compact plan, which had long been in existence, and modified it to design a warm and convenient house, which he also described in his notebooks,[8] coining the term "double-pile" plan. He wrote that this plan was most useful because it gave "much room in a little compass" and needed very little ground on which to build. Essentially, a rectangular block was divided across its length by a corridor, with rooms to either side of it, thereby giving a house a depth of two rooms. On the short axis, the central staircase hall rose through two storys, rising from a great parlor to a saloon or dining room on the first floor.

Those anxious to build were keen to observe such new thoughts, and these were given a further ingenious twist by the architect Hugh May (1621–1684) when building in 1663 at Eltham Lodge, near Greenwich. In his double-pile plan for Eltham, May had two staircases rise from the east and west ends of the central corridor. A more flexible arrangement of rooms could thus be managed on both the

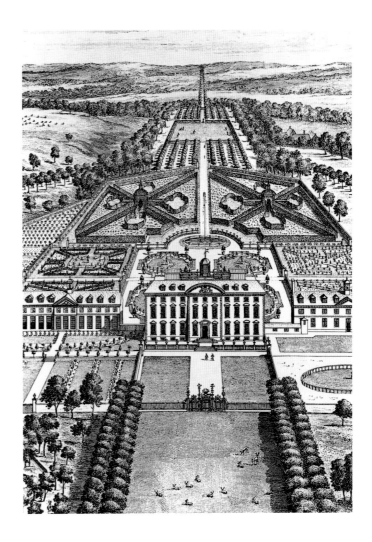

56. *"Wimpole Hall, Cambridgeshire." Engraving from "Britannia Illustrata" by Leonard Knyff and Johannes Kip. 1715.*

The "bird's-eye view" engravings of Knyff and Kip's book show country houses with requisite French-style gardens. For the most part such gardens were swept away by the naturalistic landscapists later in the eighteenth century.

ground and the first floors. It was a pattern that was copied endlessly, even in small manor houses, rectories, farmhouses, and schools. It is possible to summarize a number of improvements made to country houses at this stage of the seventeenth century. Most showed a marked improvement in the quality, style, and detail of plaster-work, carving, sculpture, and other decorative work. Also, as water supplies and plumbing improved, houses were built on elevated sites. This gave more emphasis to the long gallery—best when giving on to a spectacular view—of which there are many important seventeenth-century examples, such as those at Hatfield House, Hertfordshire

57. *Attributed to Jonathan Richardson (1665–1745). "Richard Boyle, 3rd Earl of Burlington." c. 1717–1719. Oil on canvas, 57 x 46". National Portrait Gallery, London*

The identity of the sitter, one of the most celebrated gentlemen-architects, is established by the building depicted in the background, the Bagnio or Casina, which was erected by Burlington to his own designs in the gardens of Chiswick House in 1717.

Opposite: 58. Castle Howard, Yorkshire. The hall. 1708–1710.

Sir John Vanbrugh built Castle Howard, perhaps England's greatest country house, for the 3rd Earl of Carlisle as his first essay in architecture. Its fine Baroque spaces were painted by the Venetians Pellegrini and Marco Ricci. Vanbrugh said that it was so carefully designed and draught-free that the new house would require little more expenditure on candles than the old castle of Henderskelfe it replaced.

(1612), Blickling Hall, Norfolk (c. 1620), and Ham House, Surrey (remodeled in 1639).

English noble society, after the restoration of Charles II to the English throne in 1660, was avid to consider the Continental ideas so many of them had witnessed in exile or on a long-remembered Grand Tour. In 1670 Godfrey Richards had translated into English the French edition of Palladio's *Quattro Libri* (1570) by Pierre Le Muet. As the title page shows, his little work only contained the "first" of Palladio's "Four Books," which dealt with the architectural orders. To this, Richards, from his bookshop near the Old Exchange in London, added "diverse other designs necessary to the art of well building," including designs for doors, floors, and frames of houses. In the 1683 edition, two plates were given of parquetry floors in the French manner at Somerset House, London, where Henrietta Maria, wife of Charles I, had lived as Queen Dowager on her return in 1660 from exile in France. She had presumably become familiar with parquet floors at Versailles and elsewhere and wanted them laid in London. And what she wanted her courtiers wanted. The joiner Henry Harlow installed parquet flooring of cedar, inlaid with walnut, at Ham House, Surrey, in 1673–1674 for the Duke and Duchess of Lauderdale. He worked in the queen's closet (where the duke's coronet and cipher are incorporated in the floor of the arched recess) and in the queen's bedchamber, making a standard charge of 16 shillings a yard (rising to 35 shillings for ornate parquetry sections). His method of parquetry involved inlaying various colored woods, or slivers of the same wood, into shallow grooves cut in the contrasting wood surface of the floor to form elaborate geometric patterns.

Sir Roger Pratt had noted in about 1660, in his views on the "Disposition and Dimensions of Rooms," that each bedchamber should have a closet, a small room adjacent to it. Thus, the queen's closet at Ham House was a grandly furnished cabinet, intended to impress visitors. Harlow's floor was set below walls lined with brocaded satin, bordered with a striped silk, and all within an area of but twelve by nine feet.

The most flamboyant decorations that titled owners sought, however, were those in which most internal walls and ceilings were covered with great oil-on-plaster mural paintings. The ceiling and walls of the "Heaven Room" at Burghley House, Northamptonshire, were painted in the 1690s by the Italian Antonio Verrio (c.1639–1707) for the fifth Earl of Exeter. Verrio had come to England in about 1672. On the ceiling is an "Assembly of the Olympians" attended by spirited creatures of the zodiac. The walls, painted with a trompe l'oeil colonnade of Corinthian columns and a rearing pediment strung with garlands of exotic flowers, are peopled with a host of aerial and muscular figures. A horse and its red-robed rider gallops down from the cornice, and on the north wall Neptune strides toward the onlooker with burning eyes and backed by sharp trident and swirling dark cloak. Most dramatically, the east wall has a lively representation of Vulcan's forge, with a self-portrait of Verrio himself seated nonchalantly among the attendant Cyclops. The colors for the artist's palette are established in a bright, arching rainbow. The accounts for this great room, completed in 1696, show that Verrio received a weekly sum, with many advances and extras for colors, oils, pencils, brushes, and board for his assistants or for his specialist painters of flowers and martial trophies. Additionally he and his wife and children lived within the house convivially with the earl and his wife, and received keep for his retinue, schooling for his children, and the provision of such items of diet as Bolognese sausages, Parmesan cheese, and olive oil.

Verrio was but one talented painter among many in England whose work stretched over vast expanses given to the position of the staircase, grand salon, and richly decked bedrooms. Important houses such as Chatsworth, Derbyshire, had lavishly painted rooms embellished both with painted ceilings and with wood wainscoting with applied carvings in soft fruitwood. But Chatsworth, with its Baroque interiors fitted into rooms given their proportion and arrangement by the plan of the Elizabethan house, was inconvenient for staff access. In a house such as Ragley Hall, Warwickshire, designed in 1678 for Lord Conway, secretary of state to Charles II, the architect Robert Hooke arranged closets and servants' stairs at each of the four corners. This left the center free for the great reception rooms of hall and saloon, flanked by a chapel to the south and a library to the north. As Mark Girouard has remarked in his seminal book, *Life in the English Country House* (1978), there was a point to the careful arrangements of plan in houses like Ragley:

The gentry walking up the stairs no longer met their last night's faeces coming down them. Servants no longer bedded down in the drawing room, or outside their masters' door or in a truckle bed at his feet. They became, if not invisible, very much less visible.

At the end of the sixteenth century a great household might have as many as one hundred and twenty servants. The improvement in plan and servicing of rooms, the better disposition and equipping of the service areas, the laundry, bakeries, stables, and gardens meant some economies were possible. Fewer people could accomplish more, and the social prestige of many offices declined from their Tudor importance.

The great house at the end of the seventeenth century, guarded over carefully in the owner's absence by his steward, was ready for many refinements of its services. The uses made of its series of grand rooms increased, with apartments specifically for eating, resting, dressing, taking audience of visitors, making music, and reading books. The Baroque rooms at Petworth, Sussex, home of Charles Seymour, the sixth Duke of Somerset, were visited by the Archduke Charles, titular king of Spain, in 1703. His progress through them tells much of the early eighteenth-century courtly etiquette that influenced such a visit. Charles Seymour had married Elizabeth, the young heiress to the vast Percy estates on May 30, 1682. She was sixteen, but had already been married twice before—to Thomas Thynne of Longleat, who had been murdered early in 1682, and previously to Henry Cavendish, styled Earl of Ogle, who had died in 1680 in his eighteenth year. His wife's fortune enabled the Duke of Somerset to build at Petworth in a way fitting to one obsessed with lineage and consumed by pride. Nevertheless in his own house, on such an occasion, he took second place to a person of higher rank. The Spanish king was welcomed at Petworth by Queen Anne's husband, Prince George of Denmark, who escorted him to the entrance of his private apartment. After a time, a bewildering series of calls were paid: by the prince to the king, the king to the prince, and the king, prince, and duke to the duchess. After being shown round the house by the prince, all joined together in the saloon for supper. The plan of the rooms, with some apartments more exclusive than others, allowed an elaborate ritual to take place as an ordered and necessary part of power and influence.

While the erection and roofing of an early eighteenth-century house were in progress, the mason and carpenters were considering the stone and timber floors beneath. Payments for paving and marble abound in house accounts, and much information can also be gleaned from an examination of the many manuals of practical instruction. Courts, stables, kitchens, and halls needed to be paved with tiles, bricks, flags, and stones, often bedded on a lime-and-sand mortar to give a utilitarian surface: there was no attempt at pattern in these floors, but the combinations of black and natural stone, or, of course, of colored marbles, lent themselves as readily to pavement patterns as they had done in the seventeenth-century house. This was so in staircase halls (where the staircase itself was often of stone), chapels, halls, and saloons.

From the medieval period on, with a pious observance of the tenets of the established Church, some great houses had their own chapel and resident cleric. Catholic households might be visited by a Jesuit priest but the strong penal laws against this religion in the sixteenth and seventeenth centuries rendered open show of allegiance a dangerous affair. By the early sixteenth century the chapel was furnished with stalls, screen, and pulpit set below windows filled with the fervent imagery of "pictures" in stained glass, often of Flemish origin, and surrounded by linenfold paneling (in which folded linen is suggested by the carved vertical lines of each panel).

Hardwick Hall had two chapels, one being for the use of servants. That at The Vyne, Hampshire, is prefaced by a chapel parlor and an ante-chapel. The Tudor chapel at Petworth, Sussex, was given a Baroque decorative treatment at the end of the seventeenth century. The sixth Duke of Somerset, known as "The Proud Duke" (he is said to have disowned a daughter who sat down in his presence while he was asleep), had his family pew looking down from the west end, with its own firegrate and carved wooden "curtains" held back, as crimson "draperies," by gilded angels, with putti in joyous abandon flanking his carved coat of arms. The late seventeenth-century chapel at Chatsworth with paintings on its walls by the decorative painter Louis Laguerre, godson of Louis XIV, had a towering altar in Derbyshire stone and marble rising through two storys, so that again the first Duke of Devonshire, a little nearer his Maker in his elevated pew, could gaze at Verrio's canvas of "The Incredulity of St. Thomas." If the duke chose to pray, the curious were far below.

All the significant architects in the eighteenth century lavished their skill on chapels, Vanbrugh at Grimsthorpe, James Gibbs at Wimpole (with fine frescoes on "The Adoration of the Magi" painted by Sir James Thornhill), James Paine at Wardour Castle, and Robert Adam, in a variation of the chapel, with the small estate church at Croome D'Abitot. It was part of the process to provide the owner (and patron) of a great house with all the spaces his life-style demanded. This was particularly true of the social rooms, such as the saloon.

At Blenheim Castle, Oxfordshire, the saloon rises through two storys on the south side of the house. It was painted by Louis Laguerre in 1720 after the Duchess of Marlborough declined to accept Sir James Thornhill's price of painting for 25 shillings a yard. There was a grand dining room with marble doorcases carved by Grinling Gibbons, but once the daily need for formal meals seemed at an end saloons became elaborate sitting rooms, with rows of cut-velvet upholstered chairs ranged along the walls like shy guests who have arrived too early. Taste and expense ruled what rooms of state were like. At Holkham, Norfolk, they open on to one from another, a grand enfilade across the south front, damask on the walls, gilded chairs in profusion, and painted gods and goddesses on the ceiling. Whilst "Diana asleep in the arms of Morpheus" might be suitable decoration for the ceiling of the state

59. George Lambert (1700–1765). "Chiswick House from the West." c. 1742. Oil on canvas, 29 x 57".
Devonshire Collection, Trustees of the Chatsworth Settlement

Chiswick House, Lord Burlington's villa near London, was based on Palladio's celebrated Villa Capra (or Rotonda) at Vicenza.
Kent's landscape gardens are already maturing by the time of Lambert's painting.

bedroom, the "Death of Julius Caesar" most certainly was not.

Marble has one disadvantage in that cool air condenses on it, and the architect James Gibbs advised patrons in his *Bibliotheca Radcliviana* (1747) that it was more suitable for "Churches, Porticos, common Halls and Passages than a Library." Nevertheless, all leading architects favored some use of marble in their buildings to give a cool, classical appearance. Charles Howard, the third Earl of Carlisle, approved of his architect, Sir John Vanbrugh, commissioning the marble-cutter John Thorp, of Bakewell, Derbyshire, to fit black marble squares into the stones of the great hall floor at Castle Howard in 1708. It ran to the edge of the flamboyant stucco chimneypiece and scagliola niche created by the Italian stuccoist Giovanni Bagutti (plate 58) and reared up below Pellegrini's painterly depiction of the Sun God, Phaeton, racing his chariot across the heavens in the high gilded dome above.

Through tall windows—equipped with the new sliding sashes and perhaps with frames, also gilded to catch the sun's rays as at Chatsworth—the pacing nobleman could spy his extending gardens. Before the distant tree-laid expanses of his estate—timber was an important economic resource—the king's gardeners, such as George London and Henry Wise, may have set out the precise and ordered lines of a French-styled parterre (plate 56). Hydraulic waterworks could shoot jets of sparkling water high into the sky or tumble it down stepped cascades, while pleached fruit trees, white-painted lead statues set within radiating walks, and fish-stocked long canals stretched almost to the horizon.

The English country house estate seen today, however, preserves little of this formality. It was mostly swept away by the naturalizing efforts of a succession of landscape gardeners: Charles Bridgeman, William Kent, Lancelot "Capability" Brown, and Humphry Repton working across the course of the eighteenth century. Charles Bridgeman, who died in 1738, was the originator of English landscape gardening, in which formality was replaced by less severe schemes of planting. William Kent (1685–1748) took this rebellion against formality forward—Horace Walpole wrote that Kent "leaped the fence, and saw that all Nature was a garden."

A sharp stir by Kent's inventive ideas, set out at

60. William Kent (1685–1748). "The Great Room, 22 Arlington Street, London."

Kent, who had studied in Italy 1709–1719, tried hard to be a painter but succeeded only in fine imitations of grotesque and antique cameos. He is known for his architectural, landscape, and decorative designs. He designed the Arlington Street town house for Henry Pelham in the 1740s using decorations familiar to a Grand Tourist. The room, recently restored, has been rehung with crimson damask.

Rousham and elsewhere, fermented into considerable action in the enormous landscape designs of "Capability" Brown (1716–1783). He is said to have earned his nickname from a habit of referring to "capabilities" of park layouts that he was asked to improve. It is often forgotten that he swept away many late seventeenth-century formal gardens, as at Chatsworth, and when these are tabulated against the perspective engravings of such expanses, as set out by Johannes Kip and Leonard Knyff in their *Britannia Illustrata* (plate 56), the loss is seen to be real. To dwell on this, however, is to deny Brown the success that came

61. *"Architecture." c. 1780. Engraving, 8 x 10". Colonial Williamsburg Foundation*

This ideal view shows the typical raising of a new house. It was inspected frequently and eagerly by the patron and his lady.

as a result of his undoubted ability. The clumping of the trees, the serpentine line of walk and lake, led the eye on a wanton kind of chase and enhanced the already considerable settings. It was left to Brown's younger follower Humphry Repton (1752–1818) to tempt patrons in a novel way. He compiled for them a "Red Book," so known from the color of the binding, in which by moving an ingenious series of flaps the owner could see Repton's ideal landscape.

At the center of all this was the house, "the physical expression of the standing of the family and the tangible repository of its traditions."[9] The proud quarterings of the family's arms were set within the pediment, or in morocco-bound books left lying for all lesser souls to see on the new library writing table neatly designed by William Hallett or Thomas Chippendale.

The patron intent on taking many decisions himself could rely on pattern-books rather than architects. Indeed he may have had in mind the Duchess of Marlborough's constant quarrels with architects and craftsmen over the building of Blenheim Palace. In one particular splenetic outburst to the Duchess of Bedford, on July 21, 1732, after twenty-six years of building, she expressed herself on architects, thus:

I know of none that are not mad or ridiculous, and I really believe that anybody that has sense, with the best workmen of all sorts, could make a better house without an architect than any has been built these many years.[10]

In his *A Book of Architecture* (1728), James Gibbs had warned the intending builder to consult, whenever possible, "an Able artist" and so avoid "the mortification of finding the building condemned by persons of Taste." He expressed the hope that his book would be of use to "such gentlemen as might be concerned in building." The library of a person of quality invariably contained certain standard works that would have assisted him in architectural dabblings. Despite the availability of the main foreign treatises from Serlio on, the English publications, such as John Shute's *The First and Chief Groundes of Architecture* (1563), and Sir Henry Wotton's *Elements of Architecture* (1624), still had their place.[11] However, none could compete with the three magisterial folio volumes of *Vitruvius Britannicus*, which Colen Campbell issued beginning in 1715.

Campbell's three volumes (1715, 1717, and 1725) had superb engravings of English houses and other buildings and must have been particularly attractive to the amateurs and *dilettanti*. There then followed a veritable spate of such books, some no more than carpenters' manuals, measuring and price books, or books on the architectural orders, but additionally, there were editions of Alberti and Palladio, archaeological treatises on buildings at Palmyra, Balbec, Pompeii, and Herculaneum, the antiquities of Athens, Diocletian's palace at Spalatro, and so on. The desirability of being accepted as a "man of taste" tended to encourage striving in many different ways for the accolades of excellence. In fact, John Gwynn, writing in 1749, thought that all men of quality should possess some practical ability in architectural design. The lack of knowledge, he believed, accounted for much of the undistinguished architecture of the period.[12] Nevertheless, Philip

62. Francis Cotes, RA (1726–1770). "Purley Hall, Berkshire, Prospect from the Hill." 1756. Watercolor, 14 x 21".
The Trustees of the Victoria & Albert Museum, London

Purley Hall was remodeled by Francis Hawes into the compleat house, surrounded by a landscape park.

63. *Sir William Chambers* (1723–1796).
"Section of York House, Pall Mall, London." 1759.
Royal Institute of British Architects, London

This is one of the earliest English drawings to show a complete
scheme of decoration. Of the many elaborate elements, the grand
staircase rising to a stuccoed dome is the most theatric. However,
Chambers lost the commission to build this town house for George
III's younger brother, the Duke of York.

64. *Croome Court, Worcestershire. The Tapestry Room.*
Designed by Robert Adam. c. 1760. Re-erected at
The Metropolitan Museum of Art, New York, 1958.
Gift of the Samuel H. Kress Foundation.

Adam's room, for George William, 6th Earl of Coventry,
was designed around a set of tapestries woven at the Gobelins by
Jacques Neilson after designs by François Boucher, 1758–1767.
For style-conscious patrons, such French craftsmanship was in vogue.

65. *Robert Adam (1728–1792). "Elevation, Painted Breakfast Room, Kedleston Hall, Derbyshire." 1760.*
The National Trust (Kedleston). Pen, ink, and watercolor, 8½ x 12". Trustees of Sir John Soane's Museum, London.

This lavishly decorated room was a space only eighteen feet square in the northwest corner of the family pavilion.
The artist was the Italian Agostino Brunias. The room was unfortunately dismantled in 1807 but five landscapes
by Brunias from it are at the Victoria & Albert Museum, London.

66. *Robert Adam (1728–1792). "Section of the Glass Drawing Room, Northumberland House, Strand."*
Demolished 1858, re-erected at the Victoria & Albert Museum, London

The effect of this fine room in a London town house was achieved by putting colored foil behind glass,
over which gilded composition ornaments were applied. The result is as rich as the drawing suggests.

Dormer Stanhope, fourth Earl of Chesterfield, in a letter of advice to his son modeled on those of the Elizabethan years, warned on October 17, 1749:

For the minute and mechanical parts of it (that is, architecture) leave them to the masons, bricklayers and Lord Burlington, who has. . . lessened himself by knowing them too well.[13]

Richard Boyle, third Earl of Burlington, visited Italy for the second time in 1719, intent on absorbing the ideas of Palladio and collecting drawings by him. On his return from Italy he moved gradually into independent architectural activity and was soon in demand by his friends for advice, and even designs. The building of his own villa at Chiswick (1727–1729) was also an opportunity for him to show his patronage of others, particularly of the painter, architect, and landscapist William Kent, whom he brought back with him from Italy in 1719 (Kent had studied there for nine years), together with significant architectural activity of his own. It was not, however, an accomplishment many peers were adept at, hence Lord Chesterfield's remark, noted above, which implied that matters of building construction were best left to mere artisans. What Lord Chesterfield overlooked was Burlington's important role in reviving the ideas of Palladio in a manner appropriate to the early eighteenth century, but owing much to antique rule and precedent (plate 57).

Indeed, William Hogarth's important *The Analysis of Beauty* (1753),[14] which was written "with a view to fixing the fluctuating Ideas of Taste," ignored the theories of the ancients and the Palladian ideas of the group dominated by Lord Burlington and his friend William Kent—Hogarth could not forgive Kent for winning a commission to paint murals at Kensington Palace, over his aging father-in-law, Sir James Thornhill (c.1676–1734) in 1722. But the whole basis of architectural design was broadening to consider the frivolity of what was (as the magazine *The World* noted in 1754) a happy mixture of both Chinese and Gothic motifs.[15] It was a broad and perplexing environment and while there may be a sharp, unconsidered edge of satire from the writer in *The Connoisseur* in 1756, who tried to define taste, there was a certain truth in what he wrote:

The architects, whether Gothic or Chinese, build with Taste, the painters paint with Taste, and in short, fiddlers, players, singers, dancers and mechanics themselves, are all the sons and daughters of Taste. Yet in this amazing super-abundancy of Taste, few can say what it really is. . . . If you ask, What is Taste?—they will tell you that "Taste is a kind of a, sort of a-a-a-a; in short Taste is Taste!"

Several fashionable magazines, which found their way to country house tables, were available to those with fertile or controversial ideas to express. *The World*, *Adventurer*, *Connoisseur*, and *The Lounger* were ready to give space to expose the vagaries of taste, of orientalism, of new vogues in gardening and in dress, and all done with a fine twist of a vast, often pseudonymous and scurrilous, literature, which tested the validity of tradition against the experience and practice of generations. The poet and writer William Whitehead was typical of *The World*'s contributors: he disclosed an anti-medieval sentiment, railed also against things Chinese at the expense of neglecting Grecian architecture, and deplored the present as "an age of license in which every individual is free to play the clown." It was desired satirical reading in every forward-looking country house gathering.

Every patron in England who wished to be up-to-date in stylistic matters wanted to be rid of such styles, which lacked symmetry and were seemingly uncontrollable in format; soon patrons and their architects were to be involved in promoting the new classical revival. The rivalry for patronage was to focus in the architectural careers of William Chambers,[16] who had studied in the early 1750s at the influential French Academy in Rome, and Robert Adam,[17] who had spent four years (1754–1758) in the Eternal City. Chambers, who was sometimes eclipsed by the determination of Adam to establish a reputation that would carry well beyond the grave, was the more significant theorist. Born in Sweden in 1723, he had profited from an English education, but then entered the service of the Swedish East India Company. This is a key to his split career, for traveling out to Bengal and China gave him a unique knowledge of oriental art. With a succession of studies in France, and five years in Italy, he was well fitted to enter architectural practice at a time when, despite the satirical jibes of *The World*'s correspondents, society was involved with great eagerness in the vogue of Chinese decoration. He became architectural tutor to the Prince of Wales. When that young man became King George III it was Chambers (with his rival Robert Adam) who was appointed one of the joint architects of His Majesty's Works. There then followed his significant public works, culminating in Somerset House edging the river from the Strand in London (plate 63).

What Robert Adam set out to do, as he explained in *The Works in Architecture of Robert and James Adam* (1773–1779), was to conceive houses with "variety in the outside composition, and in the decoration of the inside, an almost total change." The overriding approach of architecture, which lasted until the end of the eighteenth century, was to introduce informed adaptations of the essential details of antiquity and infuse them with a personal spirit. Such neoclassicism was avidly adopted in America by architects and builders, notably Charles Bulfinch (1763–1844) and Samuel McIntire (1757–1811). When Asher Benjamin issued *The American Builder's Companion* in 1806, he cribbed liberally from English sources. But by the mid-1820s Greek architectural forms reigned triumphant in America, and they replaced, gradually, all that was Adamitic and spoke only of Rome.[18]

It says much for Adam's achievement that the minds of patrons, as well as of those craftsmen, such as plasterers, carvers, and furniture makers, dependent on fashion, were turned to his version of the antique. In such a precise environment there was little room to indulge in the whimsy of the Gothic style, as Horace Walpole had done at Strawberry Hill, his house at Twickenham, in the 1750s. The eccentric, self-indulgent house had no place in the rigid linearity of great elegance that Adam imposed on all buildings and objects. Such aberrations as Strawberry Hill, if that is what it was, will always thrive despite prevailing fashion, and gentlemanly life and letters have benefited from countless examples of the indulgence of wild eccentricity and dogged temperament. Toward the end of Adam's life—he died in 1792—his younger rivals had built effectively in the Gothic things "medieval" and "castle-like." From the sixteenth century on, Gothic, often eclipsed, may be described as having survived rather than being "revived," and as such was an alternative style.

In England the precise neoclassical great houses, which had atrium-like halls, quadrant colonnades, and classical statues in niches, were replaced by baronial castles with numerous towers, built for prosperous times, by Regency-era and Victorian-era business magnates.[19] The guidebooks were soon lyrical, in the fashion of William Whellan describing Lowther Castle in Cumbria in 1860:[20]

The staircase, sixty feet square which climbs
the great central tower, with the ceiling ninety
feet from the ground is highly imposing.

Lowther is now the grandest of ruins but in its heyday, its oak-paneled and marble-bust–lined corridors opened to many rooms of use, or sheer opulent display.

In his influential book *The Gentleman's House*, published in 1864, Robert Kerr indicated that the skeleton of the house-plan[21] had to be disposed so that rooms were in correct relationship and lines of communication ran from them. Two routes should lead outside (one to the front entrance, the other to the garden), one going upstairs and another "vanishing" on its way to the service quarters. Kerr stipulated that these routes should be short, direct, uninterrupted, well lit, and well ventilated. It was, as one writer has observed,[22] "the skeleton which ensured that the dinner route was noble, the servants invisible and the boiled cabbage kept at bay."

On the ground floor, most house-plans incorporated a hall, dining room, drawing room, library, and study. From the 1870s, when billiards was popular, a room for this activity might flank (or replace) the library. There were, as in most Victorian breakfast menus, many "extras" that could be had—a breakfast room of course, and a music room, smoking room, ballroom, picture gallery, and even a chapel. The central core contained shared rooms, with those at either side for each sex. The men's quarters were used for smoking, playing billiards, drinking port, and talking sport or politics; the women's, in particular, the drawing room, for tea and polite conversation with the card-announced "carriage callers," for working at needlework, the supreme accomplishment of ladies, or for making music at the piano or the harpsichord.

A visitor for the weekend coming in his carriage over the graveled drive between formal flowerbeds would alight, with assistance, under the *porte cochere*, a porch large enough to permit the passage of a carriage in front of the steps to the oak front door. He, or she, would be unaware that the luggage would go into the house by a separate entrance, that there would be a business entrance near the estate office, a garden entrance, and one leading from the detached smoking and gun rooms. And that inside there would be perhaps six staircases to separate the family from its servants. Apart from any staff accompanying him, a guest could expect that his host's staff would consist of upper and lower servants, laundry, bakery, and brewery hands, cooks, grooms, and stable boys, all dispersed to their respective quarters beyond the baize doors, but all available at the tug of a bell handle at any hour the owners chose. And tugged they might well be by, say, any of the forty houseguests. In their waking moments guests were in every room of the house, standing before the roaring fires or in summer strolling through to the drawing room to admire the decoration of gilded, French-

style carvings and to receive a servant-proferred drink.

In consequence of these requirements, in both English and American houses, the drawing-room was placed so that it had the best view and received the southeast or southern sun. The advantage of a southeast siting was that the full glare of the sun had passed by the time favored late afternoon visitors came to tea. It was a room to be treated with some reverence. By contrast, dining in even a moderately sunny room was considered unpleasant until Edwardian times, and Kerr pompously noted: "In as much as where there may be no state whatever in the habits of the family, there will be at least a little of that quality occasionally, in the act of proceeding to and from dinner."

Most hostesses found the pervasive smell of cigar smoke intolerable, and the practice of smoking was often forbidden in many houses. When H. H. Emerson painted[23] Lord Armstrong and even the Prince of Wales (later Edward VII) smoking cigars at Cragside, Northumberland, his subjects were conspicuously outside on the terrace. Smoking

67. *George Garrard (1760–1826). "The Building of Southill." 1803. Oil on canvas, 37 x 59". Private Collection*

A fortune made in brewing allowed the Whitbread family to build Southill Park, one of the finest Regency houses in England, designed by Henry Holland, c. 1796.

96

rooms were thus separated from other parts of the house. As shooting parties became more organized, from the 1860s on, it also no longer proved convenient to clean guns in the butler's pantry. Kerr considered that a gun room was indispensable in a country house of any pretensions. There was a gun room on the second floor at Cragside, but it was usual for it to be easily accessible from the grounds—so much so that Lady Carbery's "Uncle Philip" even made a proposal of marriage there; despite the unusual location for a young lady to be in, the suitor was successful.[24]

The upstairs areas of a house were usually simpler to plan than the ground floor, as bedrooms could be reached from a landing or corridor. The principal bedroom needed a dressing-room and should, Kerr thought, not be less than 24 feet by 18 feet in size. These modest dimensions were frequently exceeded, the size being partly governed by the size of reception rooms and the position of bearing walls below. The ceiling could be as high as 14 or 15 feet in order that four-poster beds should have adequate head space and that the great dressed windows and satinwood wardrobes might be disposed correctly and not dwarf the draped *toilette* and brass-inlaid writing table.

Brooding over the plans for all this expansion were those black frock-coated, watch-chained gentlemen, good husbands all. They gathered money, attended to their estates, coal-mines, or factories, and forced architect and craftsmen to be competent in order to survive, and even to improve their skills. At the end of a busy day in 1880, well might Henry Isaac Butterfield, a Keighley textile manufacturer, sit down satisfied at Cliffe Castle, a "French carpet specially manufactured for the purpose" stretching away under his feet, his family depicted in Elizabethan dress in the stained glass of the staircase nearby, and be left to ponder on the heavily draped opulence of his domain (plate 142)— or his French wife.

All houses of any size relied for their functioning on a host of domestic servants, the denizens of the deep recesses, silent as they went about their duties: padding over the high graveled terraces as watchmen, nudging open doors with their knees as "coal-men, refilling one's bin with pieces the size of ice-blocks," or, as water-men, keeping "all jugs, cans and kettles full in the bedrooms. . .morning or evening." They were always ready too to bring "the hot water for the hip baths."[25]

The servants in a great household could thus be very numerous. At Eaton Hall in Cheshire, home of the dukes of Westminster, in the late nineteenth century, there were 346 servants,[26] divided between inside and outside duties. Apart from a chef, there were two kitchen maids, two scullery maids, a kitchen porter, and a head of kitchen. The housekeeper controlled the head housemaid, nine other maids, the sewing, scullery, and still-room maids, and the Duchess of Westminster's two ladies' maids. In addition, the total included fourteen people who dealt with laundry, three coachmen and twelve grooms keeping the horses and coaches (as well as thirty men and boys working for the head groom), forty gardeners, seventy foresters, forty farm workers, and seventeen tradesmen. The house steward controlled two grooms of chambers, a valet, under-butler, three footmen, a pantry boy, a hall usher, a night watchman, and an odd-job man. It was a mighty team, able to serve and feed their master, his wife, and their family and guests—and to be sure they themselves were housed, fed, and paid. Kerr summed up the running of a great home: "Every servant, every operation, every utensil, every fixture should have a right place and no right place but one."

The journal of Philip Vickers Fithian, a plantation tutor in Virginia in the 1770s, is revealing about the role of master and servants. Edited by H. D. Farish in 1957, its compelling pages are too many for but an odd mention here. The young Fithian "was greatly struck" by the grandeur of Robert Carter's country seat in Virginia, Nomini Hall. It had a "ballroom" thirty feet long, but it was the dinner table that was the focus of ritual in the gentry household. To Mr. Carter's table came not only the heads of neighboring houses and their families, "by particular invitation":

But also, as they had cause to call on the master a succession of persons. . . such as clerks, estate stewards, head overseers and tobacco inspectors. . . About ten o'clock an old Negro Man came with a complaint to Mr. Carter of the Overseer that he does not allow him his Peck of corn a week.

In 1818, William Cobbett, who had lived for a year in America, wrote:[27]

68. *Wightwick Manor, Staffordshire. The cloakroom. The National Trust*

Wightwick is important for its nineteenth-century decoration effected by members of the Pre-Raphaelite circle. As befitting any bustling family house, there needed to be a space for muddy boots and wet cloaks and for someone to restore them to use by vigilant maintenance.

69. *Springhill, Ireland. The gun room. c. 1882. Photograph. The National Trust*

The fireplace, huge sword atop, oriental carpets on the floor, studded leather armchair, and guns on display give every incentive to dream of a fine shooting day.

70. Sledmere, Yorkshire. The Turkish bath. 1913.

After a fire Sledmere was restored in 1911–1913 by W. H. Brierley for Sir Tatton Sykes. One of the improvements was to put in a Turkish steam bath lined with Islamic-style tiles.

What a difference would it make in this country, if it could be supplied with nice, clean, dutiful English maid servants!

But as the nineteenth century wore on, American house-owners found that servants no longer considered all their time to be at their mistress's disposal. As Mrs. Graves wrote in 1841[28]: "After doing the specified work (they) claim the rest of the time for themselves. . . (and) are beginning to demand the right to receive visitors." It would be naive to assume that servants were always proud of the houses in which they worked, but even those built as homes could still be admired—built by those with money and ambition and often admired most by those without either. In 1888 George W. Vanderbilt could easily afford to instruct his architect, Richard Morris Hunt, to see that the staircase at Biltmore in North Carolina was modeled after that at the French château at Blois, and he also knew that he could easily pay to have fifty teams at work hauling away the earth over the eight acres of site in preparation for building it all.[29] New York might be where some of his fortune originated, but he had no real need always to be there. Biltmore satisfied the need that an American millionaire had to re-create "a baronial castle," with his "breeding stable, droves of rare cattle, flocks of sheep, acres of fertile meadow and woodland, his gardens and his orchard," thereby approaching the ideal of the English squire nearly "as such a thing is possible in the Republic that he loves." [30]

In all building ventures it was the attitude and requirements of the owner, however bizarre, that were important. In 1891 Margaret Helen McEwan, of the Scottish brewing family, married the Hon. Ronald Greville, a member of

71. A. de Faxthorn. "T. A. Cook in His Carriage at Sennowe Park, Norfolk." c. 1908. Oil on canvas, 29 x 40". Private collection

The house, built for the travel agent Thomas Cook's grandson, also Thomas, by Skipper of Norwich, was surrounded by a large park and a seven-acre lake. The painting shows the owner driving his family in a four-in-hand past the new house.

famed Marlborough House set. In 1906 she and her husband purchased the Polesden Lacey estate in Surrey and the house was substantially remodeled for her by the creators of the new Ritz hotel, the Anglo-French architects, Mèwes and Davis. Mrs. Greville was a well-known hostess, a clever woman with little time for those of shallow mind. After the death of her husband in 1908, she invited distinguished guests to stay for long periods.

The dining-room at Polesden Lacey was the setting for the fabled creations of Mrs. Greville's French chef, and the carved and gilt paneling, c.1700, in the drawing room had once adorned an Italian palace. In *Down the Kitchen Sink* (1974), Beverley Nichols describes the scene at Polesden Lacey during teatime for a weekend party. In the small drawing room, or "Tea Room," with its painted *boiseries* (carved paneling) in the Louis XVI style, the ceremony was about to take place. The "political house had stopped, for tea and gossip":

> Tea is at 5 o'clock. . . and not 5 minutes past. . . which means that the Spanish ambassador, who has gone for a walk down the yew avenue hastily retraces his steps, and that the Chancellor of the Exchequer hurries down the great staircase, and that the various gentlemen rise from their chaise-longues. . . and join the procession to the tea-room. The tea-pots, the cream-jugs, the milk-pots and the sugar basins are of Queen Anne silver; the tea-service is Meissen; and the doyleys, heavily monogrammed, are of Chantilly lace.

Within the contemporary American world, and in a fictional tale of compelling attraction, F. Scott Fitzgerald desribed a comparable world: "With a tower on one side, spanking new under a thin beard of raw ivy, and a marble swimming pool, and more than forty acres of lawn and garden. It was Gatsby's mansion. . . ."

It could equally, in actuality, be William Randolph Hearst's San Simeon or James Deering's Vizcaya. Nothing in attitude had changed all that much since 1719, when James Brydges, first Duke of Chandos wrote to his gentleman-architect friend Robert Benson, Lord Bingley:[31]

72. Ince Blundell, Lancashire. The Pantheon. 1802–1810.

This sculpture gallery, a reduced version of the Pantheon in Rome, was added to the house from 1802 by Henry Blundell. It housed his collection of antique statuary (now relocated at The British Museum). With its coffered dome, sky-lit ceiling, and giant pilasters, it was a worthy setting in which to remember a classical past.

By the time your Lordship returns I hope my little building will be advanced so far as for one to be able to make a guess what appearance it will have; and if it should be such an one as is displeasing to your Lordship I shall pull it down with more satisfaction than I carry it up.

The Goddess of Taste reigned, as always, supreme.

CHAPTER V

"In All Labour There Is Profit"

"In all labour there is profit."

Proverbs, XIV, 23

*The Plumb Men of the City of London have made most of their Estates,
by which they are enabled to deck their Wives in Velvet and rich Brocades,
while poor Country Gentleman are hardly able to afford their Wives
a Gown of Lindsey Woolsey.*

Gentleman's Magazine, 1733, 450

The business schemes in which many Elizabethan courtiers invested large sums of money were various, ingenious, and occasionally destined to dramatic failure almost from inception. However, if it is assumed that those with enough acumen to prosper had been educated at university, traveled widely, made an advantageous marriage, and newly built a house, they had enough sense also to know it was a way of life that needed adequate financial backing. In any age it is unwise to be dogmatic as to the sources by which money is raised in more than ordinary quantity. In sixteenth-century England there were unusual opportunities for those in the right position to profit from, say, the confiscated property of the Church. But in order to give some balance to the short discussion here, I propose to treat a gentleman's income as arising, usually, from six sources: profit from official positions held; the management of business enterprises and estates; inherited capital or through an advantageous marriage; active involvement in a profession; investments of various kinds; and from indirect rewards such as privileges and monopolies.

The Elizabethan social commentator Sir Thomas Smith (1513–1577), who had been educated at Cambridge and was a doctor of Civil Law of the University of Padua, classified the "gentleman." What Smith did not comment on was whether there was a distinction between a gentleman and one merely rich. In Smith's opinion the major difference was between the titled and untitled, the *nobilitas major* and *nobilitas minor*. However, in 1600, Thomas Wilson added to Smith's statement by including among the *minor* "lawyers, professors and ministers, archdeacons, prebends and vicars." The long history of the argument has never been resolved satisfactorily. Arthur Ponsonby, in *The*

73. Manner of George Gower (d. 1596). "Sir Charles Somerset." c. 1575. Oil on panel, 37 x 27". His Grace, the Duke of Beaufort

Decline of the Aristocracy (1912) wrote that the aristocracy were the "nobled and leisured gentlefolk," a better term than vague phrases such as "upper class" and "the rich."

The variations to any accepted historical position are considerable enough to distort any sweeping statement. The reasoning of judges and lawyers was needed in the House of Lords, and talent, whether applied to land or to business, could be rewarded with a knighthood. Jane Austen, an acute social commentator, noted in *Pride and Prejudice* (1813) that Sir William Lucas was raised to

74. *Marcus Gheeraerts the Elder (1525?–1599?). "William Cecil, 1st Lord Burghley." c. 1590. Oil on canvas, 50 x 40". Trustees of Burghley House Collection*

As Lord Treasurer to Queen Elizabeth I, Burghley enjoyed unique power and exercised it in a careful blend of service to his sovereign and to himself. He entertained her twelve times in his great house at Theobalds with masques, pageantry, and banqueting—at a cost of 3,000 pounds a visit.

knighthood from the level of mere trade by presenting an address to the king. While the church, army, navy, and the law were predominated by long links with the ruling *élite*, considerable mobility between land and trade occurred in the latter half of the seventeenth century. Self-made men of affluence reached the top of society in the late 1680s after the overthrow of the Catholic king, James II: few of them had land to back their speculations. Those who had extending acres closed ranks, and the links between land and commerce, strong enough in Sir Thomas Smith's Tudor boyhood, widened in the eighteenth century and had almost gone by the nineteenth. No healthy bank balance could "buy" a title, but J. V. Beckett has noted that of the 624 baronetcies awarded in 1821 over 62 percent (392) came "chiefly on account of wealth."

The outstanding statesman in Queen Elizabeth's reign was her Lord Treasurer, William Cecil, to whom she had given the title Baron Burghley in 1571. A few days after the queen's accession to the throne, in 1558, Cecil was appointed a councilor and asked to be chief adviser. Within three years, in 1561, the queen had appointed him to the lucrative position of Master of the Court of Wards. With this position went the guardianship of wards who were minors, and leases on their lands (with the right to determine whom they married) were eagerly sought from the Master. Not only could profits be made by exploiting use of the land but marriage to the ward could be offered to the highest bidder. In consequence significant financial inducements came both to Burghley and to his patronage secretary, Sir Michael Hickes.[1] Many were over-anxious to share in the benefits the two could bestow, and a careful sovereign knew that while Burghley's salary as Master of the Court of Wards was only 133 pounds a year, he could receive hundreds of pounds more from importuning suitors.

The management of a careful system of patronage was part of Queen Elizabeth's political strategy. While she reserved giving the greatest offices and gifts to herself, a trusted and well-placed officer like Burghley had enormous influence. Only the powers granted to the queen's favorite, Robert Dudley, Earl of Leicester (and thus Burghley's rival), equaled it in scope. Leicester was given the right to lucrative customs duties levied upon the importing of sweet wines. This privilege passed after his death to Robert Devereux, second Earl of Essex, Queen Elizabeth's last favorite and an opponent to the high offices that devolved on Lord Burghley's son, Robert. (And this despite his having been one of Burghley's own wards: he had succeeded to his title when he was but ten years old.[2] Essex's opposition, with other grave misdoings, led him to the executioner's block.) Known as "Customs Farms"—"farm" signifying the taking of proceeds for payment of a fixed sum—the collecting of duties on silks and velvets, currants, oils, and sweet wines continued to be as widely granted by James I as by Queen Elizabeth. Provided the Crown received its fixed rent in excess of the average of the previous seven years, it was satisfied, and the titled courtier had an assured and steady profit. Particularly successful at this were Lionel Cranfield, first Earl of Middlesex, and his partner, Sir Arthur Ingram. Both had official contacts with Burghley's son, Robert Cecil, who had been created first Earl of Salisbury in 1605. Cecil enjoyed many more perquisites of office after his appointment in 1608 as Lord Treasurer, the lucrative post his father had held for some twenty-seven years (1572–1598). Cranfield doubled his fortune in the five years from 1601 to 1606, exploiting his customs holdings and wine shares, which alone were worth 4,000 pounds a year to him.

The granting of monopolies to unscrupulous people became one of the most virulent grievances of James I's reign. The writer Ben Jonson satirized the practice in 1616 in *The Devil Is an Ass*, in which Meercraft, the prince of monopolists, takes a monopoly on toothpicks![3] Meercraft might well have been Sir Arthur Ingram himself, the bright "gambler" in almost every commodity and a scandalous manipulator of the alum monopoly. For his part, Cranfield, who belonged to the Society of Merchant Adventurers, was one of three merchants controlling cloth in the London textile trade. The insistent demand for imported taffetas and velvets was balanced in Cranfield's books by his export of often inferior cloth, particularly the ribbed wool kerseys made in the north of England. He also dabbled extensively in the growing spice market, particularly importing pepper, cloves, and cinnamon. There were also more profits of office in store when he became Master of the Wards in 1619 and Lord Treasurer in 1624.[4]

Profiting from service in office continued unabated into the eighteenth century. James Brydges, first Duke of Chandos, was Paymaster-General to the Duke of Marlborough's forces, with power to fix supplier contracts and to use "public funds, in his control, for private investment."[5] Daniel Finch, the second Earl of Nottingham made a clear profit of over 50,000 pounds during his tenure as secretary of state at the end of the seventeenth century.[6] Even more remarkable, in terms of audacity, was John Aislabie, who, as Chancellor of the Exchequer at the time of the South Sea Bubble fiasco in 1720, was accused of marking large profits by foreknowledge of stock movement. He had been building a house at Studley Royal, Yorkshire. It has been established[7] that he gained over 32,000 pounds from his privileged position. He was impeached, his estates (reported in 1729 at the colossal sum of nearly 2 million pounds) forfeited, and he was then imprisoned in the Tower of London for eleven years. Work on his house in Yorkshire resumed, nevertheless, in 1729, with many believing that he had buried a japanned tin or two of gold sovereigns at a point only he knew, so that he could alleviate his final disgrace.

The process of creaming ill-gotten gains from office was also endemic to much of eighteenth-century political life. For example, William Pulteney, later first Earl of Bath, spent most of the summer and autumn of 1725 trying to find damning evidence against the prime minister, Sir Robert Walpole. It was reported "that he had sent his brother to Flanders to secure evidence that Walpole had received an enormous bribe from the Ostend Company."[8] But was it ever possible to prove misapplication of, say, secret service funds (with the inevitable secrecy surrounding their distribution) in a society given to regarding corruption as a necessary practice? Walpole was capable of surviving it all, of retaining power for its own sake. The level of corruption in official life by the nineteenth century had declined dramatically. What took its place was the conferring of lucrative sinecures.

The conduct of management of business enterprises and estates could provide or lose considerable fortunes. The most successful Elizabethan exemplars were Sir Francis Willoughby (1546–1596) and "Bess of Hardwick," Elizabeth, Countess of Shrewsbury (1518–1608). Coal had been mined on Francis's estate for his great-grandfather, Henry Willoughby. In the 1490s there were five pits in operation, yielding an annual profit of 200 pounds.

75. *John Michael Wright (1617–1694). "Colonel the Honorable John Russell." 1659. Oil on canvas, 50 x 42".*
The Trustees of the Victoria & Albert Museum (Ham House), London

This portrait is considered to be Wright's masterpiece and one of the greatest of all British portraits. The soldier's career is suggested
by "the sharp, counterbalanced rhythms of flag and sash, the sleeves gently filled by a light wind from the battlefield."

Production had risen to over 10,000 tons a year by 1547, and the annual profits had doubled. During the 1570s and 1580s coal, iron, and glass production remained as the staple contributions to Willoughby's income. He had always invested in improving the processes prudently, and his profits rose as high as 1,000 pounds a year. Willoughby also experimented with growing woad—for the extraction of blue dye—and could with assurance build a great house at Wollaton in the 1580s (plate 50).[9]

Bess of Hardwick, already rich from four advantageous marriages, was also keen to exploit the extraction of many minerals on her own extensive estates. She had blast furnaces and an iron works at Wingfield and a small glassworks (which may have led her to be casual about the use of glass in the very large windows at her house, Hardwick Hall), and there was coal to be mined in plenty. In the 1590s her gross annual receipts were on average 8,300 pounds, "of which an average of 3,000 pounds came from

76. Sir Peter Lely (1618–1680). "Sir Ralph Bankes." c. 1660–1665. Oil on canvas, 46 x 38".
Yale Center for British Art, Paul Mellon Collection

Ralph Bankes traveled abroad during the Civil War and then in 1659 he entered Parliament.
Knighted at the Restoration of Charles II in 1660 he set about building a new house at Kingston Lacy, Dorset, to the designs
of Roger Pratt, which put him seriously in debt by his death in 1677.

the jointure of her Talbot marriage settlement"—the Earl, her husband, had died in 1590, and she was sole executrix of his will.[10]

In the early seventeenth century the wealthy William Herbert, Earl of Pembroke, obtained a royal grant (1612) to erect furnaces and forges at St. Briavels, and in the Forest of Dean he was allowed to take up to 12,000 cords of wood a year for charcoal burning and to dig for iron ore. The charcoal was used as a fuel for ironmaking. After many successive ownerships the ironworks were leased in 1640 to Sir John Wynter, principal secretary to Queen Henrietta Maria.

It has been implicit in this study, although worth constant repetition, that the more land a family owned the

more right it had to assume a governing position, an assured place in an established hierarchy. Writing in 1804 about landed property in England, the agriculturalist and philologist William Marshall (1745–1818) noted that "landed property is the basis on which every other species of material property rests; on it alone, mankind can be said to live, to move, and to have their being." The level of income commensurate with being a peer was secured mostly from land. In the medieval period, apart from the vast wealth possible at sheep-farming, there could be occasional additions from booty and ransoms exacted in time of war, or by quiet speculation in trade or a commodity. But land, especially if acquired by the distribution of appropriated monastic properties, could establish a leading social

77. *Attributed to Edward Bower (before 1627–1667).*
"Francis Rous." 1653. Oil on canvas, 50 x 40".
The Provost and Fellows of Eton College

Rous is in the robes of the speaker of the House of Commons.
He personifies what many gentlemen did—worked hard
at a profession and enjoyed modest success.

78. *Antonio Verrio, finished by Sir Godfrey Kneller and Sir James*
Thornhill. "Sir Christopher Wren." c. 1706–1724. Oil on canvas,
73 x 69". The Sheldonian Theatre, Oxford

Wren, polymath gentleman, is shown holding his plan for
St. Paul's Cathedral.

and political position for a family with enough money to enter the market in the first place. For land was not just a place for sheep and cattle to graze: under its valleys and hillocks might lie substantial mineral resources to be garnered for high profits.

Two enterprises that attracted aristocrats' money and abilities in the seventeenth century were the draining of land to standards fit for arable cultivation and rough pasturing and the more attractive proposition of property development in London. If swampy land in the fens of Lincolnshire, Yorkshire, or East Anglia could be efficiently drained, there was an income to be had. In Lincoln one of the tasks undertaken by Benedictine monks at Thorney Abbey was draining and building causeways. Certain Dutch merchants were specialists in drainage systems, and Sir William Russell had used their services, in 1590, to help with draining near the abbey, which had come into his family's possession in 1549 following the dissolution of the monasteries and dispersal of their lands. In the 1630s a syndicate led by Sir William's son, Francis Russell, the fourth, or "Puritan," Earl of Bedford, was active in draining the fens, an area of 307,000 acres in the counties of Northampton, Cambridge, Huntingdon, Norfolk, and Lincoln, known thereafter as the "Bedford Level." The earl had invested some 15,000 pounds, entitling him to three of the twenty shares, but the return on the reclaimed land eventually produced a third of his landed income.[11]

The earls, and subsequently dukes of Bedford—the fifth earl was created first duke by William III in 1694—also speculated in the development of London estates. The third earl had started to develop property in Long Acre in central London as early as 1612, but the fourth earl embarked on a greater scheme in Covent Garden *piazza* in 1631. Houses were designed for him by the French architect Isaac de Caus, and a great Tuscan-order church, dedicated to St. Paul, was built by Inigo Jones. The earl expended some 13,000 pounds, but it was really the fifth earl's revenues that benefited, rising from rents to some 1,300 to 2,000 pounds a year after 1652.[12] The whole plan, in which King Charles I took a keen interest, gave London new standards in architecture, with a *piazza* on the grand Italian scale and external stucco dressing the houses on its north and east sides.

Throughout the eighteenth century, Parliament met for

longer and longer sessions, ranging over some seven months of the calendar. There was therefore a continual demand by its members for great houses in London. In 1772 John Robinson, Secretary of the Treasury, calculated there were five hundred members of Parliament in town.[13] In consequence, there was good and profitable reason for landlords to develop their property. Lord Burlington, the "Architect Earl," submitted a bill in 1718 to the House of Lords to allow him to grant building leases on land near his London home, Burlington House, in Piccadilly. His own great house (much altered in 1866), lay at the heart of the estate, with a screen wall hiding it from the bustle of Piccadilly. Additionally, the Grosvenor family and the Harleys, earls of Oxford, were actively building and extending their estates north and south of Oxford Street with the combined help of the talented architects James Gibbs and Edward Shepherd and the industrious builder John Prince. In the 1770s both Robert Adam and Sir William Chambers built important town houses for those peers who were not content to live in a row of similarly sized houses.[14]

As with all cities, with their noise and stench, there were times to leave and to pay due attention to the management of land around a country seat. There was usually a busy home-farm to supply food to the household and often very considerable investment in large flocks of sheep. While always foolish, easily led creatures, sheep had been important to every monastic community, and sheep-farming continued to be "the business of big men." For example, Sir William Fermour was keeping sheep in the 1520s on twenty-five different grounds in Norfolk, with the Fermour shepherds charged with the care of over 17,000 sheep; whilst Sir Richard Southwell had over 13,000 sheep on fourteen different foldcourses. Income was derived "from the sale of wool, stock, skins, pasturage and the fold," with wool and stock the biggest earners.[15] Labor costs were minimal, as the shepherd was given much in kind as well as a wage. The extra help needed at washing and clipping time was not significant, and the only other requirements were inexpensive: Baltic tar for dressing scab, hay, and straw, and hurdles made in the estate timber yard. While sheep-farming was no shortcut to great wealth, the returns to the large flock owner were considerable—and almost inflation-proof.

Aristocrats could regulate the benefits of agriculture to many of their number by parliamentary legislation. Laws concerned with limiting imports of commodities, improving drainage, or estate inheritance could be of direct use in protecting an economic position. Particularly this applied to the great advances made by moving from a medieval system of open-field farming, with common rights to the peasantry, to the extensive enclosure of land for private use. Hundreds of private Acts of Parliament for enclosure were introduced in the eighteenth century, by which "the owners of large areas of land could, if necessary, coerce the smaller owners into compliance" with the new territorial arrangements. These "replaced open fields by com-

79. Benjamin Ferrers (c. 1725). "The Court of Chancery." c. 1725. Oil on canvas, 29 x 24". The National Portrait Gallery, London

The Court of Chancery, which heard disputes on debt, property, and other matters, is shown at session in Westminster Hall. The figure beneath the royal arms is the Lord Chancellor, the Earl of Macclesfield. The chancellor's mace and purse of the Great Seal are displayed below.

80. *Thomas Gainsborough, RA (1727–1788). "Mr. & Mrs. Robert Andrews." c. 1750. Oil on canvas, 27 x 47".*
The Trustees, National Gallery, London

This is Gainsborough's most famous portrait. It also exemplifies the maintenance of an estate; woods to fell, crops to gather,
game to shoot. Mr. & Mrs. Andrews (she was French-born) lived near Sudbury in Suffolk.

pact farms." It was a prelude to creating a good environment for agricultural development,[16] even if it denied the easy access of cottagers to keep a cow and a few geese on common land and, combined with a rapid growth in population, thereby increased rural poverty.

The great proprietors played a leading role in the "agricultural revolution," with experiments in improved breeding methods to flocks and herds, the use of lime and manure to increase crop yields, and better machinery. However, it was "the country gentlemen who managed home farms, the large owner-occupiers, and the better tenant-farmers" who effected the greater change. Writing in 1804, William Marshall[17] thought the latter led the technical advance, that they traveled more, acquired new ideas, and put their sons out to farmers who were forward with new ideas. But there had always been a feeling that while

a few good landlords[18] might try out new ideas, it was more rewarding to invest money in the purchase of land, mortgages, or stocks and let tenants instead pauper themselves as entrepreneurs.

I have noted (Chapter III) the significant increase to a fortune that could arise from advantageous marriages. These might be worked at, as Bess of Hardwick did, in marrying "two sons and a daughter to the children of this fourth and last captive"—the Earl of Shrewsbury.[19] Horace Walpole, waspish commentator on events many years before his birth, noted about Bess:

Four times the nuptial bed she warm'd
And every time so well perform'd
That when death spoil'd each husbands billing
He left the widow every shilling.

81. *George Stubbs, ARA (1724–1806) "Reapers." 1795. Enamel on Wedgwood biscuit earthenware, 30 x 40".*
Yale Center for British Art, Paul Mellon Collection

The diligent master of the estate rides out to the full summer's day gathering of the harvest.

Bess's ambitions centered on her second son, William, who later became first Earl of Devonshire, acquiring a great Elizabethan house at Chatsworth from his brother, Henry, in 1609 for 8,000 pounds. From 1584 he had received an annual allowance but was also acting deviously, for his mother and himself, in arranging to hide money from Lord Shrewsbury's acquisitive hands. The earl's death, in 1590, saved Bess from such further harassment and she could devote her energy to her varied estates and to building a house suitable "to the dignity of a dynasty."[20]

Comparable in status to Bess, but living a century later, was James Brydges, first Duke of Chandos. His first marriage, to Mary Lake in 1696, allowed him access to the tortuous paths of acquiring the estate of old Cannons from his wife's uncle. It was to this Elizabethan house that he brought his second wife, Cassandra Willoughby, in September 1713, only five months after Mary's death. A new house was now built, for he was soon to be created Earl of Carnarvon (1714), and his new wife, blessedly, had a fortune of 23,000 pounds. A little later, on enquiry, he revised this to 11,000 pounds in South Sea stock and 20,000 pounds in the hands of her trustees. He further noted, perhaps with tongue in cheek, that if he had insisted on a fortune he "might have found a greater, but wanting not money, how imprudent it would have been to prefer it before the perfections of the mind." At the duke's third marriage, in 1736, to a widow of twenty-two years, Lydia, Lady Devall, *Gentleman's Magazine* reported that she brought with her a fortune of 40,000 pounds.[21] "Perfections of the mind" came a poor second, or third, to that.

The problems of inheriting great wealth always seemed to those without such expectations to be minimal to assuming the responsibility. In March 1803 the unmarried Francis Egerton, third Duke of Bridgewater, died at his London house. He is justly regarded as the founder of inland navigation, for through his enterprise, and the abilities of the engineer James Brindley, he developed the canal system in England. The profits therefrom were enormous, "his return to the income tax being 110,000 pounds a

82. Godfrey Sykes (1825–1866). "Interior of an Ironworks." c. 1850–1860. Oil on canvas, 18 x 24".
Yale Center for British Art, Paul Mellon Collection

England achieved some of its greatness from its iron industry. Those who banged hot metal on the anvil
were as important as the visiting owner.

year." He left his estates, together with the canal property, worth some 15,000 pounds a year, and Bridgewater House in St. James's, including the contents of his picture gallery and plate, to his nephew, Lord Gower, who was a few months afterwards created second Marquess of Stafford and subsequently, in 1833, first Duke of Sutherland.[22]

While the business generated through the canal system was profitable—the Bridgewater Canal approached 80,000 pounds a year profit on an investment a little more than four times as much—the coming contest between the canals and railways was well focused in many minds, including that of Sutherland's astute agent, James Loch. In 1825 he had advised the then Lord Stafford to invest 100,000 pounds in the Liverpool and Manchester Railway, a direct rival to the Bridgewater Canal. The intention was to have a place in the "revolution that is likely to take place in the mode and rate of conveyance throughout the Kingdom." Loch's foresight proved to be yet again an aid to a greater fortune.

It was such investments that were well known to American entrepreneurs in later years. The railroad kings of the Central Pacific at the end of the nineteenth century were Collis P. Huntington, Leland Stanford, Mark Hopkins, and Charles Crocker. Huntington, an accomplished lobbyist, had persuaded Congress to pay his railroad company 16,000 dollars per mile for track laid over footland and 32,000 dollars for that laid in hilly or mountainous terrain. With Hopkins to keep the books, Crocker to keep the railroad workers in line, and Stanford sorting out California's politics, they were an unstoppable quartet. Although, the Central Pacific railway cost some 27 million dollars to build, the foursome were not spending their own money. They merely profited from the considerable outlay.

Opportunities on the eastern seaboard were seen similarly by Henry M. Flagler, John D. Rockefeller's secretary at Standard Oil. On his second honeymoon in 1883—his first wife had died in 1881—Flagler saw the fortunes to be had by building a railroad down to Miami, and eventually the Keys, and by matching the development with hotels and resorts. With his third wife—the second having been declared incurably insane in 1901—Flagler then set up "court" at his grand mansion of Whitehall in Palm Beach—a villa that Henry James likened to "those remembered villas of the Lake of Como or, of the Borromean Islands. . . only to surpass them at every point." Flagler died there in 1913, surrounded by the color-washed mansions of the almost equally wealthy, most erected by Addison Mizner and all within sight of the ever-rolling blue waves.23

Acumen, if coupled with inherited wealth, makes an almost unstoppable combination, and this was true with the Duponts of Winterthur, Delaware. James Antoine Bidermann, a financier from Winterthur in Switzerland, had invested in the early nineteenth century in Éleuthère Irénée du Pont's gunpowder company at Hagley, founded in 1802. Bidermann sent his son, also named Antoine, to Delaware in 1814 to check some defaults in payment. After satisfying himself that they were to be paid, the young man stayed on to marry Evelina du Pont, and he took control of the company at her father's death in 1834. The house they commissioned from the French architect, Vergnaud, in the late 1830s is still "lost" within the present great structure at the heart of the present Winterthur Museum. Successive generations of du Ponts (and particularly Henry Francis du Pont, who turned the house into a museum) contributed to the wide-ranging inheritance. In this way too Collis P. Huntington's great wealth was carefully deployed. It descended to his nephew, Henry Edward Huntington (1850–1927), who added to it and then built the great library and gallery in San Marino bearing his name. Henry Clay Frick (1849–1919), the Pittsburgh coke and steel industrialist, did the same in New York for the amazing assembly of works of art known as "The Frick Collection," and there are countless other examples in America's great families.

It might be argued that such conspicuous wealth had always come from some application to a profession and as a means to an end that had a long ancestry. One of the most significant professions a gentleman could undertake was training for the law. The Inns of Court, centered in London, had originated in the early fifteenth century, but

only came to have a prominent role there by the late sixteenth century. Students entered the Inns of Court just as they attended universities—for a variety of reasons. In a highly litigious age a useful knowledge of the law was sensible as a part of most young men's education. And there were a few who had the aptitude and application to attend the lectures and the disputations and to do the extensive reading (mostly without supervision) that admission to the bar entailed.

That so many overcame the difficulties is evident from the strength of the legal profession in the seventeenth century. Admittedly the Inns had the added attraction that they gave a place of residence near the active life at court, and it was also easier in London to seek instruction in the courtly arts of dancing, singing, and fencing. Members of the Inns could then practice their dancing at the revels held each Saturday night, between All Saints and Candlemas, and in the occasional masques staged by the societies.24 But what did a full legal education entail?

Knowledge of the common law was not derived from any respectable classical pedigree and was therefore excluded from the university *curricula* at Oxford and Cambridge. Students at the Inns needed to take part in oral exercises as a formal requirement of legal education throughout the sixteenth and seventeenth centuries. These were devised so that one of the first formal exercises in which students participated was a *moot*, a case argument in the form of a mock trial. The formulation of a moot case was "the responsibility of the two barristers who were to present it, helped by two students who were to recite the appropriate pleadings, for and against the action concerned." They were heard by three adjudicators, the essential element being the "formulation and elucidation of cases and the participation of junior and senior members, the former doing most of the argument, the latter adjudicating, explaining and commenting on their efforts."25

The rapid expansion of both the universities and the Inns of Court in the early seventeenth century provided variations in oral instruction and in the pursuit of rhetoric and logic backed by the availability of both pious and frivolous pursuits. Many found the learning so onerous that the lament of Sir Henry Spelman was typical. He had been admitted in 1598 to Lincoln's Inn from Cambridge, having been sent by his mother to "learn the law." What he found was "a foreign language, a barbarous dialect, an uncouth method. . . and I confess that my heart sank within me."

The main part of the intended lawyer's training lay in reading and understanding cases and statutes. There were various abridgements that helped in this process and in acquiring knowledge of more specialized areas, such as mercantile law. The cornerstone of common law was Sir Thomas Littleton's *Tenures*, written in the fifteenth century, which had been published in some sixty editions by the 1640s, the most notable being those with Chief Justice Sir Edward Coke's commentaries—*Coke upon Littleton*—first appearing in 1628. Nevertheless, neither was an easy text, and the lawyer and historian Roger North (1653–1734) noted that *Littleton* bred "more disorder in the braine than any other book can." In fact a number of authors had tried, alternatively, to improve the learning techniques of the law student: Abraham Fraunce's *The Lawyers Logicke*

(1588), William Fulbecke's *A Direction, or Preparation to the Study of Law* (1600), and Sir John Doddrige's *The English Lawyer*, published posthumously in 1631, were three such manuals.[26]

The complex process by which the law evolved is not to my purpose, but certainly, by the late eighteenth century the greater number of the judges came equally from landed and professional families. Those who acquired such high office were expected to be able to purchase an estate befitting their station.[27]

In America, many private law schools had been established by the late eighteenth century. These based their studies mainly on Sir William Blackstone's magisterial *Commentaries on the Law of England* (1765–1769), but adapted it to the American scene. The Revolution accelerated the trend for colleges to be founded and for more formal training for a young legal profession. In his observations on American society, Alexis de Tocqueville, writing in

83. John Dobbin (d. 1875). "The opening of the Stockton and Darlington Railway, 1825." 1865. Watercolor, 30 x 40". Borough of Darlington Museum

George Stephenson (1791–1848), the gentleman inventor and founder of railways, was a proud man when on September 27, 1825, the Stockton and Darlington line was opened. He had been the engineer, and Dobbin's watercolor shows all the district came to see his achievement.

1831 in *Democracy in America*,[28] noted that: "The aristocracy of America occupies the judicial bench and bar." The rise of the Columbia and Harvard law schools, against a distinguished group of others (including Jefferson's University of Virginia), to a dominant position occurred during the 1870s, with Harvard becoming preeminent during the deanship of Christopher Columbus Langdell (1870–1895).

Large numbers of gentlemen were attracted to service in the ranks of the navy and the army, the gentler, if similarly hierarchical, categories of the Church, and the rough-and-tumble of a parliamentary career. Since medieval times it had been possible to purchase a commission as an officer in the army. Nevertheless in time of threat of war or invasion the sovereign had the right to demand service. But actual invasion of England had appeared likely only in 1538, when France allied with Charles V of Spain and again when the unlikely formations of the "Spanish Armada" put to sea. Henry VIII's urgent plans to review his navy were set out in the "Device by the King" of February 1539, which needed for its oversight the cooperation of a long list of titled commissioners. Many were veteran soldiers, such as Sir Anthony Wingfield, who had been knighted for his bravery in the French war of 1512–1513, or Sir Anthony St. Leger, who had reported a few years earlier on the defenses of Calais. The shared military experience of the peerage, including a limited knowledge of fortification, was strengthened by the actual builders of round and angled bastions of great strength and by resourceful gunners who occupied them, all aided by books and maps from the pen of such strategists as Stephen von Haschenperg, a Moravian mercenary in the king's service.[29]

The extensive works on fortification and improvement of defenses continued during Queen Elizabeth's reign. Some officers, like Sir Charles Somerset, merely basked in the favors the queen's service could command. Sir Charles, sometime Standard Bearer to the Band of Gentleman Pensioners, may have accompanied his brother William, third Earl of Worcester, on an embassy to the French court in 1573 to act as proxy for Queen Elizabeth at the christening of the daughter of Charles IX. His portrait (plate 73) depicts him in French armor and may have been acquired as a royal gift at that time. The background does also suggest a "specific event in the sitter's military career." Those who had an active command, such as the Earl of Sussex, who held the rank of captain until his death in 1593, were rewarded by the queen for their service in time of war. In 1589 she created Sussex a Knight of the Garter for his work in equipping the fleet to repulse the Armada. The extensive voyagings of Sir John Hawkins, Sir Francis Drake, and others adept at exploring, plundering treasure-ships, and slave-trading brought not only wealth to England and the queen, but gave her redoubtable sea captains in time of war. Others like Sir Humphrey Gilbert and his half-brother, the poet-adventurer Sir Walter Raleigh, attempted to annex parts of Newfoundland and Florida in the name of the Virgin Queen. Unsuccessful as many of the escapades were, they avoided dependence on Portugal for supplies of tropical produce and persuaded the queen to grant a charter, in 1600, to the English East Indies Company, thereby laying the foundation stone for the empire.

Throughout the Civil War and those wars with France and others in the beginning of the eighteenth century, there were a standing professional army and navy. They were regulated by Parliament, rather than by the absolute rights of the monarch, but there was the right, until 1871, to purchase rank, which allowed the aristocracy to place themselves to advantage.[30] But, within the senior service (where purchase was not allowed), the First Lord of the Admiralty in 1733, Sir Charles Wager, before accepting his post, drew Prime Minister Sir Robert Walpole's attention to the fact that the First Lord was normally a peer. Of the twenty-three persons who held the First Lordship in the eighteenth century, one was a prince of royal blood, Prince George of Denmark (Queen Anne's husband), sixteen were peers, one the son of a peer, and one the son of a peeress. The navy thus remained securely within aristocratic control.[31] But in the army, Edward, first Viscount Cardwell's reforming act of 1871 finally abolished purchase of a commission, but not without a struggle. Having been thrown out by the House of Lords, "the Act had to be effected by the use of the royal prerogative."[32] Similarly, in the role of the "diplomatic soldier" in the field, the ambassador to a foreign country, about 60 percent in the period 1689–1789 were peers, while others had close connections to the peerage.[33]

These younger sons had always represented a strain on

84. *Anonymous. "Outside Harrods'." 1909. Chromolithograph. The Trustees of the Victoria & Albert Museum, London*

This animated well-dressed group of men and women throng outside one of the most famous shops in the world.
While the really discerning could order by telephone, there was always a fascination for shopping in person.

a family's economy. Whilst the eldest sons, within the rigid orbit of primogeniture, inherited the title and if possible made an advantageous marriage, younger sons could only turn to commissions in the army or navy or service in the Church. Within a titled family's possessions often lay the ownership of many advowsons, or the right of presentation to a church living (or benefice). The antiquarian Browne Willis (1682–1760), who published many books relating to English cathedrals, established that for the period 1723 to 1730 of 9,800 churches peers had the right to present to 1,200, some 12 percent. Later research has shown 9.6 percent in the hands of the Crown, 26 percent belonging to the Church, and 6.7 percent to foundations such as Oxford and Cambridge.

The largest impact on ecclesiastical patronage was exercised by the ducal families, ranging from the Catholic Duke of Norfolk, awarding thirty-one, to the Duke of Bedford with twenty.[34] That the person so presented could occasionally be less than diligent is instanced by the example

of Lord William George Henry Somerset, a son of the fifth Duke of Beaufort. In the 1820s he held five livings in the Beaufort gift, but it was stated by those who knew him:

> That he never wrote a sermon; but there is a tradition that he preached twice in the Cathedral in the course of twenty-three years. On the other hand he had all the skill of his family for driving a coach and four. . . and the stables he built at Tormarton were much more imposing than was the rectory.[35]

Clergymen could be most useful as canvassers at election times, and they could administer some of the landlord's necessary, if occasionally grudging, provision to the poor of his estate villages. Tenants, for their part, could be browbeaten to vote according to their landlord's whim, on threat of their eviction. However, this did nothing for reputation, and bribery by means of settling debts and fines or outright payment was more usual. The Oxfordshire

85. *Ford Madox Brown (1821–1893). "Work." 1852–1863. Oil on canvas (arched top),*
53 x 77". City of Manchester Art Galleries

This painting was started in 1852, then abandoned and finally completed to commission in 1856–1863. The view is from
the west side of Heath Street, Hampstead. Work in all its muscular forms impedes the leisured on horseback, identifiable
as the artist Robert Martineau and his daughter. At the right the "philosophers" stand, Thomas Carlyle and F. D. Maurice.
The artist used real workmen and poor Irish for his models.

contest in 1754 was said to have cost the Tory party some 20,000 pounds, with the same for the Whigs. The dispute between Sir James Lowther and the Duke of Portland in 1767 at the Cumberland and Carlisle contests cost more than 40,000 pounds. Small wonder that Hogarth's four-paintings series *The Election* (1754–1755; plate 125) depicts rampant corruption. At least part of the series was inspired by the notoriously corrupt Oxfordshire election of 1754, in which the Duke of Marlborough was involved. Hogarth set the election entertainment at the fictitious Guzzletown; the canvassing for votes takes place outside the Royal Oak public house. The corpulent winning Tory candidate is then raised aloft, while nobles and officials gather in a room above for a celebratory feast. Electioneering was thus a major cause in undermining several family fortunes.[36]

What no amount of attention to a profession in the law or being an officer in the army or navy or a bible-clutching black-robed younger son could do was equip a family to avoid conspicuous expenditure. The fevered pursuit of the election, a casual attendance to business affairs, and a liking for extravagance could lead quickly to decline. Only building or gambling were a greater drain on a family's resources. It mattered not that the lawyer Sir Edward Coke[37] had counseled aspiring patrons of builders early in the seventeenth century, "Put not your finger in the mortar," or that Sir Thomas Wroth had warned in his *The Abortive of an Idle Houre* about idle hours:

The world is full of prodigall expenders
The Borrowers are more than the lenders;
Those Prodigalls commit the highest cryme,
Who wast their lives in vaine expence of time.

Those with knowledge of Littleton's *Tenures*, or the formation of a cavalry regiment, were perhaps always to be outnumbered by Wroth's "prodigall expenders," most of whom, by their efforts, and ties of blood, they had long supported.

Careers for American gentlemen followed a somewhat different pattern. There was no natural succession to land,

86. Trade Card of S. & J. Fuller. 1818. Paper. The Trustees of the Victoria & Albert Museum, London

Every polite young lady loved to paint in watercolor and may well have needed to visit Fuller's London
emporium to buy her colors and artists' materials.

only that which arose from tilling it and improving it, growing crops, and building permanent residences. The colonists settling in New England in the seventeenth century had known the cost of trying to own an acre or two in England. However, few of them were gentry in the English sense, and none aristocrats.[38] In the eighteenth century plantation owners flourished. The house at the center of the estate might be a pattern-book copy of an English one or incorporate significant motifs based on English prototypes. But England knew nothing of growing tobacco or cotton, and little of slaves, although several eighteenth-century fortunes were based on their use on far-distant sugar estates in the West Indies. And where there were slaves, in Virginia for example, there was need for a regulating militia and for some commissioned officers. When Edward Kimber, an Englishman, traveled in the Chesapeake region in the 1740s[39] he noted:

Wherever you travel in Maryland (as also in Virginia and Carolina) your Ears are constantly astonished at the Number of Colonels, Majors and Captains that you hear mentioned.

The gentleman as an armed man in a growing population of enslaved blacks was reinforced, and Colonel William Byrd II of Westover was proud to be a commander of county militia.

The clergyman in eighteenth-century Virginia, unlike his English counterpart, did not have an institutionalized patron. He needed to humble himself with powerful persons, and the temperament of the Virginia gentry did not make themselves respecters of weakness.

As "a center of commerce, government, divinity and education," Boston had merchants in plenty, and they dismissed any Puritan austerity they might have have felt (although this austerity has been described as a "nineteenth-century caricature") to surround themselves with not only good silver but "London style joinery and turning, painting, upholstery, printing and the importation of textiles and books."

The summation of these activities in the eighteenth century may be found in the well-established career of George Washington. Acquiring Mount Vernon (which his great-grandfather had been granted in 1674), Washington settled there in 1759 with his wife and two young stepchildren.

87. Anonymous. "Interior of Grand Shop of B. Read, London." 1834–1835. Lithograph fashion plate from "Winter Fashions." The Trustees of the Victoria & Albert Museum, London

Read's shop in Pall Mall, near to St. James' Palace, was the kind of grand establishment that gentlemen and their ladies patronized when shopping for their many material possessions.

He inherited the property outright in 1761 on the death of the widow of Lawrence, his elder half-brother. Within fifteen years he had been elected general to command all Continental forces. He might have been content to resign his commission in 1783 and retire to Mount Vernon, but politics and public service claimed him. He became president in 1789 and held that office until 1797, two years before his death.

In 1760 Colonel Charles Ridgely (1733–1790) gained control of one hundred acres at Northampton in Maryland for the purpose of establishing an ironworks. He already owned eight thousand acres of land in Baltimore and elsewhere. A new house, Hampton, was built in 1783–1790 to befit his status as a "country gentleman." Upon his death in 1790 four nephews were included as principal heirs, and the long descent in the Ridgely family continued throughout the nineteenth century. At the outset of the War between the States in 1861, Charles Ridgely, the fourth Master of Hampton, was elected Captain of the Horse Guards, organized under Maryland's militia laws.

Charles had married his first cousin in 1851. Their eldest son, John, was sent to Europe to continue his education in Paris, prior to going to Trinity College, Cambridge. On his return, he had electricity installed at Hampton, using profits from the sale of the famous Ridgely wine cellar to J. Pierpont Morgan during Prohibition. It was his eldest son, also named John (1882–1959), who finally sold Hampton to the National Park Service as a National Historic Site in 1947.

I have pursued the Ridgelys in some slight detail because they epitomize the devotion of many American families to their own patrimony—admittedly less venerable than an English estate stretching back eight hundred years, but one which owed much to ability, hard work, and professional service in the law, the army, the church, and the more rewarding management of land and of trade. As the *Baltimore American* recorded of a party at Hampton in 1832, it was "most hospitable, amiable and refined," a gathering of an American gentleman and his friends.

CHAPTER VI

Streets Paved with Gold

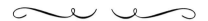

Me-Thinks, already, from this Chymick flame,
I see a city of more precious mold:
Rich as the town which gives the Indies name,
With Silver pav'd, and all divine with Gold.

John Dryden, "Annus Mirabilis," London, 1667

Impecunious peers and their expensive wives and children were keen to swell London's teeming crowds and always wanting to leave the mire of country roads and the absence of a social scene for something more lively, albeit for a few months only. The men were intent on financial and legal matters, ever causes for concern, and on attending Parliament, gambling, or perhaps commissioning a fair half-length portrait from the most fashionable painter, whilst the ladies were more than anxious to enjoy a little of what Sir Richard Wynn called, in 1666, the "pride, pomp, luxury, and treason of this damned place."

Called the "metropolis" for the first time in John Dryden's *Annus Mirabilis* (1667), seventeenth-century London absorbed its surrounding villages and doubled its area and population in less than fifty years. Having reached its maximum development within its walls, extension began outside the old boundaries, and this work coincided with the rise of the professional architect—Inigo Jones being the outstanding example in the first half of the seventeenth century and Sir Christopher Wren in the latter half. After the Great Fire (1666), Wren was given the magnificent opportunity to build a series of new churches, of ingenious plan and spatial complexity, and to crown that achievement with his masterpiece, the cathedral of St. Paul's, which was completed in about 1710.[1]

After the Civil War and the Fire courtiers started to settle in the western quarter of London, with a natural tendency for officers of the court to live near Parliament, at Westminster. A new residential area to the north of Piccadilly became popular in the 1660s—the Earl of Clarendon building a great house on an eight-acre site. The diarist Samuel Pepys went to see it on February 20,

88. *Attributed to Marco Ricci (1676–1730). "A View of the Mall from St. James's Park" (detail). c. 1710. Oil on canvas, 45 x 76".*
National Gallery of Art, Washington, D.C. (Ailsa Mellon Bruce Collection)

89. *Attributed to Marco Ricci (1676-1730). "A View of the Mall from St. James's Park." c. 1710. Oil on canvas, 45 x 76".*
National Gallery of Art, Washington, D.C. (Ailsa Mellon Bruce Collection)

The Venetian artist Marco Ricci here observes courtiers, townsfolk, and visiting foreigners promenading along London's tree-lined Mall.

1665, and thought it would be very noble. He also mentioned that Lord Berkeley was building on one side of Lord Clarendon's house and Sir John Denham on the other. In March 1673 the Earl of Craven petitioned for permission to develop Drury House in Drury Lane and to improve the same by "several streets and regular buildings, which will be both ornamentall and usefull." Sir Thomas Bond built Bond Street and Albemarle Street. Finished early in the eighteenth century, they became at once extremely fashionable, just as the development of houses and streets to the south, around St. James's Palace, had become.

Two of the visits a nobleman needed to make while in London were attending sessions at the House of Lords and examining his bank account. The pomp and circumstance of a state occasion, such as the opening of a new parliamentary session and the speech from the throne, was ever a reason to be in town. Coroneted and robed, the peers crowded into the small chamber that was the House of Lords. There was no space for their ladies, who needed to wait at home to hear how the sovereign was arrayed and who was in his entourage. At his bank a peer had to attend

to the credit or debit to hand, which he had to sign, as "allowing." If he was short of money, his banker, acting also as a goldsmith, could help with loans. The banker could also cash cheques if drawn on other accounts in his care and could undertake many other duties. At the sign of the gilded leather bottle over the door of Richard Hoare's shop in Cheapside there were displayed gold and silver wares, as well as an extensive range of jewelry and precious stones. Though the shop's main business was a lucrative trade in lending money and arranging mortgages, articles of jewelery were made to the order of customers, and Hoare also mended coronets, "new lining the cap with Furr irmin'd round" (as he did for the Earl of Derby in 1694), engraved arms on coffeepots (even on chamberpots), and imported "brilliant rings" from Amsterdam.[2]

Outside Parliament and the somber halls of banks, reportage and discussion, one peer to another, took place in the many coffee and chocolate houses. These establishments had grown up in the seventeenth century to take advantage of the fashion for imbibing tea, coffee, and chocolate. There was time to read the newspapers and hear the latest gossip and to do so in convivial and suitable company. Some of these places became in turn men's clubs. White's Chocolate House for example (becoming White's Club in 1736) was opened in 1693 by Francis White. When he died in 1711 his widow still carried on the business, whose sideline was providing tickets for the opera, balls, and similar amusements. At the noted Garraway's, in Change Alley, where tea was first sold in England and where speculators in the South Sea Company congregated in 1720, it was possible to hear all the foreign and domestic news. Indeed, Jonathan Swift, in his "Ballad on the South Sea Scheme" (1721), specifically mentioned those who:

Meantime secure on Garways cliffs,
A savage race, by shipwrecks fed,
Lie waiting for the founder's skiffs
And strip the bodies of the dead.

Besides the many political clubs there were those concerned solely with social, literary, or artistic matters. The Kit Cat Club was the most famous. There gentlemen could meet over a bottle of wine in the evenings to discuss politics, literature, or news of the town with friends of similar interests and political views. The club grew out of informal meetings arranged by the publisher Jacob Tonson (1656–1736) and by 1700 included most of the

90. Antonio Canaletto (1697–1768). "The Thames and the City of London from Richmond House." c. 1747. Oil on canvas, 41 x 46". His Grace, the Duke of Richmond and the Trustees of the Goodwood Collection

Two views of London from the Duke of Richmond's house (the other looks to Whitehall) were painted within a year or so of Canaletto's arrival in London. In the foreground is the terrace of the Duke of Richmond's town house and, across the river, the spires of several Wren city churches and the magnificent dome of St. Paul's Cathedral.

91. British School, Seventeenth Century. "The Great Fire of London, Showing Ludgate and Old St. Paul's." After 1666.
Oil on canvas, 53 x 43". Yale Center for British Art, Paul Mellon Collection

When fire raged through timber-built London on September 2, 1666, there was little immediate thought of the opportunity it gave to Sir Christopher Wren and others to rebuild the city in an enlightened, grand manner. The artist captured the rare moments of utter destruction.

leading Whigs of the day. Tonson had set himself up as a publisher in 1677, having purchased the copyright of John Milton's *Paradise Lost*. He was associated particularly with publishing many of John Dryden's poems and plays.

Meeting at first at Christopher Cat's tavern and raising their glasses to favorite ladies, members went on to the club for a convivial meeting of equals: the members were bound together further by the fact that most of them were men of wit, taste, and social accomplishment. Tonson was also publisher to three other literary members, the dramatist William Congreve, who affected also to be a considerable man of fashion, the author and politician Sir Richard Steele, and the essayist, poet, and statesman Joseph

Addison, who had been educated at Charterhouse with Steele and with whom he produced in 1711–1712 the influential magazine *Spectator*. The architect member, Sir John Vanbrugh, also a playwright, could talk both of plays and architecture with them, and with two of his celebrated patrons, Charles Montagu, first Duke of Manchester, and Charles Howard, third Earl of Carlisle. The prime minister, Sir Robert Walpole, was a member, too, and there was a touch of practicality in that peers could turn for information not only to him, the skilful manager of the House of Commons, but they could also bargain with the astute member and moneylender Thomas Hopkins, who could advance many a cherished cause at a high rate of interest. All members had their portraits painted by another fellow

93. Attributed to Thomas Smith (d. c. 1691). "Major Thomas Savage." 1679.
Oil on canvas, 42 x 37". Museum of Fine Arts, Boston

Thomas Savage emigrated to America from London in April 1635. Within a year he was a freeman of Boston,
a merchant, and part-owner of the Saugus ironworks. In 1638 he joined the Ancient and Honorable Artillery Company
and rose to be chief commander of the Massachusetts forces.

member, the distinguished painter Sir Godfrey Kneller.[3]

The Scribbler's Club, whose name also appears frequently in the literature of the day, was founded by the satirist Jonathan Swift in 1714, and writers such as John Gay and Alexander Pope were members. Swift was the "Martin Scriblerus" of the group, the name arising from the fact that the fellow member Lord Oxford was wont playfully to term him "Martin" as being the most powerful of the "Swift" tribe. These were gatherings at which women and children were not welcome, although Lady Mary Wortley Montagu recalled later in her life how she had been toasted at the Kit Cat Club when but seven, being taken there on a visit by her father, Lord Dorchester, who was an active member.[4] Some of the resistance to admitting women to the men's clubs was owed to the fact

that their education had been inferior. In the seventeenth century few women could even sign their names to legal documents, with the percentage being but half of their number by its end. However, many could read, a result of the frequent repetition of the words of the scriptures and of the catechism.

When not consorting in the clubs there was some advantage in being seen about town, in the right company, with a silver-headed cane ready to flick away rubbish on the pavement from soiling fine polished leather boots. The prospect of being more interested in human activity than mere topography took more time to develop in England, where artists favored painting the country house and the view across the stretching panoply of its surrounding estate. In his diary, Samuel Pepys, under the entry of June 1, 1665, records what became very popular to him: "To Foxhall in the spring-garden and there walked an hour or two with great pleasure." In the early eighteenth century courtiers, townsfolk, and many visiting foreigners would promenade along the Mall in St. James's Park. It was the nearest equivalent to the country within the city—indeed the Latin motto *rus in urbe* adorned Buckingham House, built in about 1707 by the Duke of Buckingham at one end of the Mall. The Mall, with three avenues bordered by trees for pedestrians and two ornamental pools of water, "became the most fashionable walk in London for the *beau monde*, who came to take the air here from midday onwards" (plate 88).

The gardens south of the Thames in Lambeth, which Pepys refers to, grew still more popular. Addison recorded in the *Spectator* in 1712 that when his "Sir Roger de Coverley" visited them, it had become the haunt of the Cyprians of the town, but all knew that its (eventual) proprietor had to rid it of the strumpets of the town. A dozen years later Spring Gardens is referred to as one of the sights of the City, and it found its mentor in Jonathan Tyers, who obtained a lease in 1728 and subsequently purchased the property. Tyers set about thoroughly reorganizing the gardens, and on June 7, 1732, opened them with what he called a *Ridotto-al-fresco*—an outdoor entertainment with music—limited to four hundred people, each charged one guinea for entry. His enterprise was so successful that he repeated the occasion several times during the same summer. His "Vauxhall" gardens were mostly for pleasure in the summer (whereas Ranelagh, in Chelsea, was largely patronized in the winter). An orchestra, with an organ, had been installed at Vauxhall by Tyers, but in 1749 he built an enclosed concert room (plate 97) in the Gothic style, in which Mrs. Arne and Thomas Lowe sang to *habitués*, including Tyers's ground landlord, Frederick, Prince of Wales. Indeed, in honor of this musically gifted royal patron Tyers built a "Prince's Pavilion," a grand supper-box at the west side of the grove, facing the orchestra. Paintings by Francis Hayman decked all the supper-boxes on the so-called "Grand Walk," and four giant canvases in "four grand elegant frames" on the theme of the recent Seven Years' War, were placed in the saloon.[5]

In due course the pleasure grounds at Ranelagh, opened in April 1742, proved a strong competitor to the older Vauxhall, and as early as a fortnight after their opening, Horace Walpole was writing to Horace Mann: "Two nights ago Ranelagh Gardens was opened at Chelsea; the Prince, Princess and Duke, much nobility, and much mob besides; were there. There is a vast amphitheatre, finely gilt, painted and illuminated, in which everybody that loves eating, drinking, swearing, and crowding, is admitted for twelve pence." Part of the grounds on the east side of Sir Christopher Wren's great Chelsea Hospital had provided the site. Here the fashionable, as Walpole observed, could sport themselves, "where a royal Duke elbowed his shopkeeper," and purses were lost to nimble fingers. After the death of the Earl of Ranelagh, in 1712, the house he had erected on this spot remained empty till 1733, when it was sold to Lacy of Drury Lane, whose object was to open it as a rival to Vauxhall. It was not, however, till eight years later that a definite move toward this was made, when the famous "Rotunda" was erected (plate 98) to the design of William Jones. It was an enormous structure, 555 feet in circumference, with an interior diameter of 150 feet. The roof was supported in the center by a square construction of pillars. Around the area were two tiers of fifty-two boxes, each capable of holding eight people. The interior was elaborately decorated and gilded with innumerable chandeliers suspended from the roof on long ropes. Sixty windows above the boxes afforded light, and an organ was installed. When all the lights were blazing, the floor crowded with an elegantly dressed crowd whose flashing jewels were brash signals of conspicuous wealth, well might a titled lady feel that eight months of gilded slavery to a country life could be forgotten with the meaningful twist of an ivory-boned painted fan.

In the gardens at Ranelagh was a "Chinese house," in the middle of a long narrow sheet of water; in fact, devoted readers of Tobias Smollet's *The Expedition of Humphry Clinker* (1771) will recall that Lydia Melford thought, "Ranelagh looks like the enchanted palace of a genie." Within two years of the opening, Walpole had told Mann "nobody goes anywhere else," but its continuing popularity made it, as Walpole thought, "disagreeable"; much of the enjoyment of being there seems to have consisted in walking the circular promenade of the rotunda—to use a contemporary's words, "following one another's tails in an eternal circle, like asses in an olive mill, while the other

94. *Charles Philips (1708–1747). "A Tea Party at Lord Harrington's House." 1720. Oil on canvas,*
40 x 49". Yale Center for British Art, Paul Mellon Collection

Doubts have been expressed as to whether the party was at Lord Harrington's London house, but the assemblage is typical.
The ladies on the left (5th & 6th from left) taking tea include Lady Betty Germain and the Duchess of Montagu.
To the right of them, the Duchess of Dorset and Lady Suffolk are playing cards. There is even perhaps some mild flirtation
between the ladies and one or two of the men.

half are drinking hot water under the trees."

One of the rival attractions to such places was the Pantheon in Oxford Street, designed by James Wyatt and erected in 1771–1772. It was to be "a winter Ranelagh" with a great cathedral-like hall or "rotondo." Horace Walpole wrote to Horace Mann in May 1770 that the

"winter Ranelagh" was "the most beautiful edifice in England." The artificial lighting highlighted the architecture, with friezes and niches accented with purple and green lamps, "and the dome swam in a heathen twilight," reflected from gilt vases. Walpole took the French ambassador to see the progress of the work, and he also told his friend Mann that it was so glorious a vision that he thought he was in Rome in the old Pantheon, or in the Temple of Delphi at Ephesus. Dr. Johnson and Boswell, on the contrary, thought it was not as striking as Ranelagh, but in letters, plays, and novels of the period frequent references are found—for example, Goldsmith refers to it in *She Stoops to Conquer* and Fanny Burney in *Evelina* and *Cecilia*. It became immensely popular during the time when the masquerade was one of the principal forms of entertainment. The Reverend Dr. Campbell recorded in 1775, in his *Diary of a Visit to England*, that he saw at the Pantheon, among many notable persons, "the Prussian Ambassador, Lord Stormont, the Duke of Cumberland, and Lady Grosvenor, a fine woman, lost to all sense of modesty, Lord Lyttelton, and Lady Archer, painted like a doll, but handsome with her feathers nodding like the plumes of Mambrino's helmet." On January 4, 1792, the Pantheon was totally destroyed by fire, and, although rebuilt in 1795, it had lost its earlier eminence, being "but a fancy large room for music, masquerades, etc." It was demolished finally in 1937.

One of the delights of visiting London, or for that matter any large city, was the variety of tradesmen's shops, and the range of goods sold. A collection of trade cards[6] easily shows that temptation could be mildly encouraged. Whether it was for "new invented Water Colours in Cakes," "Curious Canvas for Window Blinds" or "Cotton, Thread, Silk and Worsted Caps, Silk Mitts and gloves, Silk Purses, etc." Everything was "made after the Newest Fashion, at Reasonable Rates." It was also possible to order furniture, curtains, wallpaper, beds, new coaches, and almost every imaginable item destined to confer opulence and comfort on the purchaser. Other shopkeepers were ready to mend broken items or, in the case of silver, to change it for a more fashionable style of surface decoration.

Many quarters of London became associated with certain trades. Cabinetmakers gathered in Clerkenwell, the silk-weavers in Spitalfields, and in Artillery Lane, off Bishopsgate, a splendid Roman Doric shopfront of c.1756 of a silk-weaver's shop survives. However, the designed shopping street belongs to the Regency period and after, and one particular important development of this period was the creation of shopping arcades, a Parisian idea. In

95. *Francis Hayman, RA (c. 1708–1776). "The Artist and His Friends."*
c. 1745–1748. Oil on canvas, 44 x 55".
Yale Center for British Art, Paul Mellon Collection

This has traditionally been called "Lord Chesterfield and His Friends." The only figure with a certain identity is the London artist himself, seated at the lower left.

96. *Francis Hayman, RA (c. 1708–1776). "Grosvenor Bedford and Hayman in His Studio." c. 1748–1750. Oil on canvas, 28 x 36".*
National Portrait Gallery, London

Grosvenor Bedford (deputy to Prime Minister Horace Walpole at the Exchequer a few years after this portrait) was one of Hayman's most consistent patrons. He commissioned several family portraits. Hayman used the setting of his London studio for sitters with whom he was on friendly terms.

London, the Royal Opera Arcade of 1816–1818 by John Nash and George Repton and the Burlington Arcade of 1815–1819 by Samuel Ware became justifiably famous among the wealthy. In such a setting, comparable to the best of the shopping malls of today, were gathered the perfumers and wig-shops, the jewelers, and those selling wine, tea, and coffee—all shopfronts were reduced to a disciplined regularity, protected from the weather in a top-lit vault, but delighting with their varied merchandise set out in classical mahogany-lined interiors.

The use of cast iron for columns and large sheets of plate glass made it possible, from about 1850, to achieve interesting spatial complexes without sacrificing strength. Additionally, the abolition of the tax on all forms of glass in 1845 encouraged the use of great 8 x 14–foot sheets of plate glass for shop windows and indeed for the complex

magnitude of the greatest display of things to buy, the Crystal Palace Exhibition of 1851. But soon department stores began to appear alongside arcades. There was, in the West End of London, a desire to "create a drawing room atmosphere for leisurely shopping," with elegant tall show-cases ranged between decorated pilasters (plate 111) and ample carpeted space from which to inspect the table cases; patrons might even take a cup of coffee from a delicate cup, "the whole service being available in three different colours." One of the reasons, apart from stock, that the department store thrived was the ease with which it could be approached in horse-drawn cab. The arcades were for walking in, having left the conveyance at one end; unless one retraced steps, a long circuitous route was necessary by the coachman to reach the opposite end of the arcade. For those less fortunate, the capital had to be reached for

The Inside of the Elegant Music Room in VAUX HALL GARDENS. Le dedans du Concert Elegant aux Jardins du VAUX HALL.

97. H. Roberts after Samuel Wale. "The Inside of the Elegant Music Room in Vauxhall Gardens." 1751.
Line engraving, hand colored, 10 x 16". Yale Center for British Art, Paul Mellon Collection

The "Rotunda" or Music Room was a fashionable gathering place for the cognoscenti in the late 1740s. The Rotunda was extended eastwards to a saloon in which the four large frames (here empty) were later filled with pictures by Francis Hayman.

98. *Antonio Canaletto (1697–1768). "Interior of the Rotunda at Ranelagh Gardens." c. 1751. Oil on canvas,*
20 x 30". The Trustees, National Gallery, London

The great Rotunda, 150 feet in diameter, was ringed with two tiers of boxes where one could take tea.
It was the most fashionable place to be seen: the eight-year-old Mozart played there in 1764.

most of the latter half of the nineteenth century by train. The imposing train sheds near the city center were the real "monuments to commerce,"[7] or at least to its "movement" in things and people. Art as usual could well record the stories of great incident. William Powell Frith's *Paddington Station* (plate 112) shows the excited bustle in 1862 on the new gaslit platforms, as does Philip Hardwick's drawing of the scene in the adjacent hotel coffee-room.

Leaving the train, it was by horse and cab that one was taken to the pinnacle of shopping perfection at the great emporium of Harrods in the Brompton Road. Beginning as a small family grocery business, Harrods expanded rapidly to become a limited company in 1889. The present building, by the architectural firm of Stevens and Hunt (1887–1905), is faced with Doulton's yellow terracotta culminating in a dome worthy of a public monument. The crowds thronged daily through its many rooms and spilled out on to the pavements (plate 84). When they tired of it they could move off, albeit slowly, in a long line of horse-drawn cabs through Hyde Park to see the new Selfridge's department store in Oxford Street, the first ten bays of which opened in 1909. Only after the First World War did shoppers try to come a little nearer to their destination in their own slow popping motorcars, for which, then as now, there was little provision to leave them whilst one mounted the first public escalator in Harrods to the crystal glass displays.

It is easy to forget, with the dominance of London life represented in fact and in a wide literature (even if the novels of Charles Dickens and Arthur Conan Doyle do render it as fog-bound and hazardous), that other cities and towns thrived too. This was particularly true of those blessed with a constant supply of steaming sulphurous "spa water," calculated to ease all ailments, even imagined ones. Such from Roman times were *Aquae Sulis* (Bath) and Buxton in Derbyshire.

Bath, a small insignificant place but with a fine situation, was chosen by the leaders of fashion to be a summer retreat. Following them came "all those possessed of rank or fortune" with the excuse that they could regain health from the waters, their minds untroubled by the simple rustic life around them. It is known from surviving inscriptions that visitors came to Bath in the Roman period from Chartres and Metz in northern France and from Trier on the German border. The hot springs have given the town a European importance out of all proportion to its position on the navigable river Avon in southwest England. It acted as a local market center, a trading center for the region, but was renowned as "an international religious, medical and probably recreational centre, based on the cult focus at the hot springs."[8] All the world flocked to Bath in the belief that its waters had special curative powers, and the city prospered.

Much of Bath's preeminent position as a spa town in the eighteenth century was owed to the attention and facilities provided to visitors and to its Master of Ceremonies, Richard "Beau" Nash (1674–1762). He had come to the city in 1705 as a professional gambler, his predecessor as Master having died in a duel. Nash succeeded in imposing order on all those activities that were held as harmful. He drew up a code of conduct for public entertainments that banned, among other things, the wearing of swords at the card table and dueling in the city streets. He also banned prostitutes from wearing the "white aprons," a commonly worn emblem of their trade, and he tried to protect the aristocratic young from the card-sharks and to extract money for charity from those on a winning streak. Goldsmith described him as having "an honest, benevolent mind, with the vices which spring from too much good nature." Nash managed even to extract money from Sarah, Duchess of Marlborough, towards the fund for building the city's Mineral Water Hospital, incorporated in 1739, and he held sway over Bath "before the nobility and even in the presence of royalty." Yet he could also make a sharp personal profit when it suited him, particularly from the gaming tables.[9] In 1739 Parliament passed a law that was calculated to stop private lotteries and fraudulent gambling. Certain card games with such wondrous names as "Hazard, Pharoah and Ace of Hearts" were banned, and while others were being frantically thought out, a further act in 1740 made it illegal to take part in games of chance involving the throwing of dice and use of numbers.

It was inevitable, with large numbers of the aristocracy visiting Bath, that many professional gamesters and those seeking out wealthy heiresses and widows came too. Cutting a dash at the gaming tables drew attention to what a desirable young companion you could make to all those, described in an anonymous pamphlet of 1700[10] as the "celebrated beauties" cavorting in the hot waters of the Cross Bath: "ladies with their floating Jappan bowls" of essences and perfumes, wading about "like Neptune's courtiers" ready for amusement, sexual provocation, or both. Pornographic literature was readily available, particularly in many editions of Thomas Stretzer's *A New Description of Merryland* (1740s). Under its guise as a serious study of topography, all manner of sexual attractions were discovered, with Merryland represented as a woman's body, a "Paradise of Pleasure, a Garden of Delight."[11]

The great building enterprises in Bath by the architect John Wood and his son, also John, namely the famed King's Circus (1754) and Royal Crescent (1776)[12]—a circle (one thousand feet in circumference) and a crescent of town houses, respectively—encouraged many noblemen to take leases on houses with the intention of settling for some months in a year, or as long as the liver was troublesome without the dosing of the therapeutic waters. But the social life of balls, theater, gathering in the Pump Room to drink the waters and gossip, or taking out the latest novel from the subscription libraries slowly declined. No adequate successor as Master of Ceremonies had followed Nash, and there were the rival attractions, by the 1830s, of going to such developing seaside towns as Brighton or taking a Regency villa for a time at Leamington or Cheltenham. The celebrated painter Thomas Gainsborough may well have lived in Bath's King's Circus before he left in 1774 for London, and the town was certainly mentioned by every writer of note, including Pope, Fielding, Sheridan, and Jane Austen. What it could not be regarded for any longer was the daily announced arrival of every national figure, and the sick, the frivolous, the obese, and the slim all sinking in rapture in the healing springs.

A similar but less dramatic story attended the rise and fall of the Derbyshire spa town of Buxton. Elizabeth Willoughby (plate 38), whose husband, Francis, was busy building at Wollaton in the 1580s, was one of the many who claimed that her poor health required her to take the waters frequently at Buxton. The town had been made a fashionable retreat of the Elizabethan court, with Bess of Hardwick's fourth husband, the Earl of Shrewsbury, and others, maintaining houses there. In 1572 John Jones had published his tract *The benefit of the ancient Bathes of Buckestones*, drawing attention to the discovery of its healing waters by the Romans. It did no harm to his sales that as well as Lord Shrewsbury, guardian captor of Mary, Queen of Scots, Queen Elizabeth's favorite, Robert Dudley, Earl of Leicester, also made use of the springs.[13] However, Buxton's principal development as a spa did not begin until about 1780, when the fifth Duke of Devonshire, as lord of the manor, conceived the idea of making Buxton into a second Bath. So, using the services of the talented northern architect, John Carr of York (1723–1807), he built a great crescent close to the original St. Anne's well. It contained a fine Assembly Room, as well as extensive stables at the rear for visitors' horses and a circular courtyard for riding exercise. Access to the hot waters was readily available, with later hospital developments giving greater comfort to use them. These were designed by the sixth Duke of Devonshire's London architect, Henry Currey, and they still survive.

Two hundred miles north of London, with a great concentration of noble families, lay the vast reaches of Yorkshire, with its center at York. In consequence York became a second metropolis with an extensive aristocratic life: horse racing, music, assemblies, theater, worship at a major cathedral, and several town houses. The administrative and ecclesiastical center for the north of England,

99. *After Sir Joshua Reynolds. "A Group of Members of the Society of Dilettanti." c. 1780. Line engraving, 15 x 12". Colonial Williamsburg Foundation*

Sir Joshua Reynolds's great canvases of the society's members (now at Brooks's Club) were finished in 1779. The engravings were popular immediately as mementos. All the members are known supporters of travel and archaeological inquiry in the eighteenth century.

York, or *Eboracum*, had great prominence in Roman times. It had a Christian community by the fourth century, for in 314 Eborius, Bishop of York, was one of three British bishops to attend the Council of Arles. The Vikings, Saxons, and Normans all plundered, built, and restored in York, with the greatest positive contributions coming from the Norman archbishops. The Benedictine abbey of St. Mary at York was by 1364 a mitred abbey—in other words, its abbot sat in the House of Lords as a peer of the realm. Towering over all of York was the great central tower of the Minster, a cathedral many times remodeled,

100. Edward Edwards, ARA (1738–1806). "An Interior View of Westminster Abbey at the Commemoration of Handel's Centenary, Taken from the Manager's Box." c. 1793. Oil on canvas, 48 x 40". Yale Center for British Art, Paul Mellon Collection

101. *Sir Joshua Reynolds, PRA (1723–1792). "Frederick Howard, 5th Earl of Carlisle." 1769.*
Oil on canvas, 95 x 59". The Castle Howard Collection

Lord Carlisle is wearing the robes of the Order of the Thistle, the highest order of chivalry in Scotland.
He had been invested with them, however, by the King of Sardinia at Turin in 1768 so that he could make a spectacular
appearance at its court. He resigned the Thistle on his elevation to the Order of the Garter in 1793. Reynolds shows
how grand the earl would be in London or Edinburgh circles.

with the present one dating to 1407–1410. It was the soaring creation of the master mason Hugh de Hedon, working to the glory of God and for the satisfaction in his ancient art.[14]

When St. Mary's Abbey was dissolved in November 1539, the Council of the North, set up to govern the northern part of England, with its appointed members under a president, settled comfortably into the palace of the abbot. The presidents, successively the second Earl of Rutland, the Earl of Sussex, the Earl of Huntingdon, and Lord Sheffield, all had the office, power, and resources to make their stays in York fruitful, too, for their own depleted coffers. And so it was for a hundred years, until the council was abolished in 1641.

102. Trade card of Peter Langlois (c. 1718–1767; French ébéniste resident in London). Paper, 8 x 6". The British Library, Heal Collection

Langlois provided fine ormolu decked marquetry furniture to affluent clients. Such a shop was a necessary port of call in London.

As befitted a city with an extensive business in the wool and cloth trade, York's Company of Merchant Adventurers was active with overseas contacts. A great timbered Cloth Hall, known as Trinity Hall, Fossgate, served as their center of activity. But it was an activity of merchants alone, with little involvement by the Yorkshire gentry. They were content to administer the stretching folds of pasture over which their flocks roamed and to send wool to market at the appropriate shearing times.

As with Bath, York became an important county town in the eighteenth century. It attracted the local gentry for its social life and entertainment, and they could also seek out craftsmen for their building enterprises. Their town houses reflected the general national trend for precise Palladian proportioning, but look confused: backward because of the conservative taste of the populace and advanced because of the presence of the work of Lord Burlington and other fashionable architects.

Richard Boyle, the third Earl of Burlington, was a major patron of the arts. He had extensive Yorkshire estates at

Londesborough and was himself an architect, albeit in the more gentlemanly aspects. In May 1730 the earl was asked for a design for the Assembly Rooms in York, which he completed by November. It consisted of a great Egyptian hall, reminiscent of the work of Vitruvius and Palladio. The foundations were laid in March 1732, and the main building was finished by August that year, although work was still being done as late as 1736.[15] With its Corinthian columns, elegant chandeliers and large free central area, the rooms attracted all the many gatherings of the aristocracy—those intent on an evening's drinking and gossiping after a day at the horse races.

This might well have been true of the Viscount Fairfax, one of many anxious to escape the rigors of a harsh winter on his east Yorkshire estates, for he built a lavish town house in Castlegate, York, in 1762. At its opening in 1763 various parties were arranged to coincide with the viscount's birthday. John Moyser, a local brewer, had been brought in for five weeks previously to brew up an astonishing quantity of ale and beer. Fairfax's friends ate their way through some sixty-four dishes in three courses.[16]

In order to avoid returning to their country houses over wet, mired roads late at night, most noblemen with Yorkshire country houses had a town house. This was usually set within the confines of a street frontage but characterized by the distinction of a pediment over flat classical pilasters, with a small iron-railed forecourt over the entrance gates of which there was an elegant curving overthrow, also in iron, with a lantern at its center. There are handsome town houses in both York and Bath—the Mansion House for the Lord Mayor in York, and Ralph Allen, the exploiter of the use of Bath stone, had one near the south front of the Abbey, in Bath. But however fine, they could not compare in grandeur of frontage or opulence of decoration to those in London. Many of York's important seventeenth-century houses have disappeared or been much altered in subsequent years, but those of the eighteenth and nineteenth centuries have fared better.

Particularly impressive survivals incorporate the work of William Kent, fresh in the 1730s from completing Kew Palace for Frederick, Prince of Wales. In 1740 he started to build a house at 22 Arlington Street for Henry Pelham (c.1695–1754), who was to rise in office to the Treasury, eventually becoming First Lord and Chancellor of the

103. *Johan Zoffany, RA (1735–1810). "John Cuff and an Assistant." 1772. Oil on canvas, 35 x 27". By gracious permission of Her Majesty, Queen Elizabeth II*

Cuff was an optician whose shop was at the sign of the "Reflecting Microscope" off Fleet Street. He sold microscopes to George III and Queen Charlotte, as well as to every scientifically-minded gentleman.

Exchequer. The exact process of its building is minutely recorded.[17] The principal rooms lay on the ground and first floors, with the great room (plate 60) occupying the full width of the front of the house and hung with crimson damask. When it was completed, Horace Walpole, observant and faithful recorder, noted it as one of three examples of Kent's "admired" architecture.[18]

The next important phase of London town houses started with John Vardy's Spencer House (1756–1787) for John, first Earl of Spencer. The west front overlooked Green

104. Sir Joshua Reynolds, PRA (1723–1792). "Dorothy, Lady Worsley, 1772." Oil on canvas, 94 x 57". The Earl of Harewood

This full-length portrait (there is another by Reynolds of Lady Worsley's sister Lady Harrington at Harewood House) shows Lady Worsley in a red riding habit. She was however an habitué of town life, having had countless lovers and many amorous escapades in London. Lady Worsley was the stepdaughter of Edwin Lascelles, for whom Robert Adam built Harewood.

TIGHT LACING, or FASHION before EASE.
From the Original Picture by John Collet, in the possession of the Proprietors.

362   Printed for & Sold by Bowles & Carver, at their Map & Print Warehouse, N°169 in S¹Pauls Church Yard London. ── Published as the Act directs

*105. Bowles and Carver after John Collet. "Tight Lacing, or Fashion before Ease." c. 1770–1775.
Hand-colored mezzotint, 12 x 9". Colonial Williamsburg Foundation*

*Bowles and Carver had a print shop in St. Paul's churchyard in London. This popular mezzotint draws attention to the fashion of contorting
the figure into laced stays (a corset stiffened with whalebone) and to the compleat gentleman's unfortunate dalliances in town.*

Park in central London and Arthur Young noted in 1768, "I do not apprehend there is a house in England of its size better worth the view of the curious in architecture. . . . I know not a more beautiful piece."[19] But it was one of many, for Horace Walpole wrote to George Montagu in November 1759: "I stand today at Piccadilly like a country squire, there are twenty new stone houses; at first I concluded that all the grooms that used to live there, had got estates and built palaces."[20]

And in these "palaces" a great variety of entertainment, music, dining, political talk, looking at the possessions of others, and mere gossip took place. When Lady Mary Coke attended the opening of Spencer House in 1767 she found that "the hangings, chair and window curtains of the Great Room are of the three coloured damask, but I think the finest I have ever seen. The glasses are magnificent. Four rooms were open, but not many people; three tables however at loo. . . ."[21] At Lichfield House, 15 St. James's Square, which James Stuart (the brilliant, but lazy designer of the early [1759] neoclassical decorations at Spencer House) designed for Thomas Anson in 1759–1765, Stuart recorded what no lady wished to witness. He told Lord Anson that when the first floor was completed there was the grand function of "wetting it, performed. . . when upward of 50 men had their bellies full of Beef pudding and Ale. Your health was drunk with very cheerful huzzas."[22] Similar scenes must have taken place when Robert Adam's "regiment of artificers" created his many elegant town houses. Elizabeth, the Duchess of

Northumberland, whose husband, the first duke, was Adam's significant patron at Syon House on the Thames and in commissioning the opulent glass drawing room for Northumberland House in the Strand (plate 65), wrote to her son, in 1772, about the "vast number of private balls this winter. The French Ambassador has given four very fine ones, and a fifth for children."[23] But, she continued, "Lord Stanley gave one (at Derby House) a fortnight ago, which surpassed them all." Again Walpole's description of this helps to show the rich variety of aristocratic London life. Writing to the Countess of Ossory on April 3, 1773, he noted:

In the hall was a band for French horns and clarinets in laced uniforms and feathers. . . in the ante-room was a bevy of vestals in white habits making tea. [Lord Stanley] had burst open the side of the wall to build an orchestra, with a pendant mirror to reflect the dancers. . . the musicians were in scarlet robes. In six rooms below were magnificent suppers.[24]

It was a conspicuous display of wealth, only outdone at the celebrations for his wedding the following month and the final fitting-up of Derby House, with its complex ceilings, Etruscan dressing room, and stylish marquetry furniture.

106. Philibert Debu Court (1779–1843). "The Gamblers." c. 1810. Pencil and ink drawing, 5 x 7". The Trustees, Victoria & Albert Museum, London

Cards and eight figures round a gambling table: a fatally flawed combination that racked society across the seventeenth and eighteenth centuries, ruining families and spoiling lives.

Adam's neoclassical decoration was popular, but his death in 1792 saw its inevitable decline into a thin pastiche and its replacement by robust and gilded displays in the nineteenth century. The building magazines were able to use phrases like "conveniently and sumptuously" without feeling in any way untruthful. Devonshire House for the Cavendishes, Dukes of Devonshire, vied with the new rooms at Northumberland House for the third Duke of Northumberland. Disraeli immortalized Holdernesse House of the Londonderrys as "Deloraine House" in *Sybil*: "The saloons. . . blazed with a thousand lights to welcome the world of power and fashion."[25] And finally the grandest was fittingly that for England's wealthiest peer: Grosvenor House, re-created in the early 1870s for Hugh Lupus Grosvenor, the first Duke of Westminster. The Marquess of Westminster had toyed with ideas in the 1820s of improving Grosvenor House to designs by Thomas Cundy and his son and by Robert Smirke. However, Lady Grosvenor liked the old house "with its sunlit, bow-fronted rooms on the south, and could not face the idea of the upheaval involved."[26] So little, except for work on the picture gallery, was done and it was left to the first duke to employ Henry Clutton to remodel the house in the Italian Renaissance style. Clutton, who had been working for the duke's father-in-law, the Duke of Sutherland, at Cliveden, Buckinghamshire (a seventeenth-century house remodeled by Sir Charles Barry in 1850–1851), worked on seven rooms in particular: the saloon, drawing room, dining room, corridor, anteroom, the picture gallery, and the Rubens Room.

Each summer the duke and his family left Eaton Hall, his Cheshire country house, and settled in at Grosvenor House for three months. The house was entered through wrought-iron gates, which gave boundary to a courtyard, the paved drive of which was sprinkled with sand to prevent coach horses from slipping. A flight of low steps under a covered porch led to the front door. In the entrance hall stood a sedan chair and a liveried hall porter was on duty. An inner hall led to the drawing room, where there were the two canvases of Gainsborough's "Blue Boy" and Reynolds's portrait of "Mrs. Siddons as the Tragic Muse" (both now in the Henry E. Huntington Art Gallery, California). An anteroom led to the magnificent picture gallery (plate 113), also used as a ballroom. Great French windows looked out on to a wide balcony with steps leading down to the spacious, immaculate lawns.

The first floor was given over to the duke and duchess's own quarters, their bedroom, dressing rooms, his study, her boudoir, a wardrobe room, and one for the use of the duke's secretary. The floor above was used by the children, their noise and laughter remote from the gilded rooms beneath, and it contained a schoolroom, day and night nurseries, and six other bedrooms. Eight maids slept in separate rooms in the attics. In the basement they spent much of their long day, part of an indoor staff of twenty. These included the housekeeper, who presided over the serried rows of preserved figs, jams, and chutneys in her stillroom and the arrays of china, many with armorials, in the china room; the butler with his pantry and pantry scullery; the steward with his neat room and office; and the cook and head housemaid, each with their own rooms. A hall and sitting room was used by the other lesser servants, with the men having their own dormitory. Near to the kitchen, with its glowing array of copper vessels and busy game-cooking fires and ovens, were vegetable and meat larders, a bakehouse, and, smelliest of all, a lamp-room, where oil lamps needed the whole-time attention of a manservant. There was a brushing room for clothes, a boot room, a carpenter's shop, and a hot furnace room given to providing the house with its hot water and radiator heat.[27]

Grosvenor House was a fine setting for balls, huge dinner parties, garden parties, and for all the "royalty and all the rank and fashion" who were the guests of the duke and duchess. The picture gallery opened onto the Rubens Room and, through an enfilade of coffered and stamped leather rooms, onto the saloon. There amid thirty-five paintings, including five Rembrandts, the duke and duchess could sit down, as their daughter Lady Helen Seymour noted:[28]

For the huge dinner parties. . . .The dinner table. . . was a lovely sight. The snowy table-cloth was lit by candelabra and ornamented by my father's racing trophies. . . .The flowers were usually pale pink Malmaison carnations grown at Eaton. The fruit, also from Eaton, was delicious: grapes, peaches and nectarines.

107. Sir George Hayter (1792–1871). "The Trial of Queen Caroline." 1823. Oil on canvas, 41 x 64". The National Portrait Gallery, London

After her disastrous marriage to the Prince Regent, Princess Caroline gave way to a life of casual debauchery
conducted throughout Europe. This led to divorce proceedings when she returned to England at the death of George III in 1820.
The "trial" in the House of Lords was something of a farce, but it was a grand social occasion for the aristocracy.

For the Grosvenor House ball in 1886 the duke's ten-year-old granddaughter noted in the diary:

Everybody was beautifully dressed. . . .Mr. and Mrs. Gladstone were there and the Grand Duke of Mecklenburg. The garden was all lit up with Chinese lanterns and there were tables inside the tent for people to eat at. Then the band played "God Save the Queen" and the Princess of Wales came in and down the middle of the Ball Room. She looked very pretty in a mauve gown.

And for those whom the duke would send home in his own carriage, a pair of heavy bay horses and footmen in full livery aggrandized it all, with the coachman wearing a wig and tricorn hat. Late they might all be to bed, but last of all, turning down lights to a soft glow, was the housekeeper. Servants slept when it was late and woke all too early.

So it was across the years of the second duke, who succeeded in 1899. With four marriages there were changes enough in house and household, but by October 1927 the vast spaces of Grosvenor House were of little use to the

108. William Holman Hunt (1827–1910). "The Awakening Conscience." 1853–1854.
Oil on canvas, 30 x 22". The Tate Gallery, London

Hunt's attempt to codify the redeemed fallen woman displays a keen interest in prostitution as a pressing metropolitan problem.
The canvas has many allusions: the girl's lack of a wedding ring, the lover's discarded and soiled glove (the "cast-off" mistress).
The web of intrigue is further symbolized by the tangled embroidery in the right corner and the music "Cross Purposes"
on the piano. Yet the bird being tormented can escape. . .

duke. With the crashing of the demolition gang's iron ball the way was clear for the new Grosvenor House Hotel in Park Lane, "the first in London to have a separate bathroom and a separate entrance lobby to each bedroom and running iced water in every bathroom." And a new generation of peers and plain "misters" soon found the convenience of all that.[29]

Great Britain had close links with the colonial towns that grew up during the seventeenth century. In fact the royal officials who journeyed to Boston in the late 1680s and 1690s brought with them "the ostentatious life-style of Restoration England." There was a considered demand for luxury articles, which Boston's many silversmiths did their best to supply. By the early years of the eighteenth century many in Boston were making large profits from "the production and shipping of war materials," but there were hard economic times ahead.[30] In 1767 the Townshend Acts increased duties on certain goods exported to the colonies. This encouraged many American manufacturers to be innovative, and improved standards of living could

109. *"London, The Reform Club." Steel engraving, from "The Pictorial Times," August 29, 1846. By permission of The Reform Club, London*

*In an issue of "London Interiors" (1840) it was noted that "the general effect of the dark blue drapery and furniture
is that which a library should convey, viz, therefore a rich and quiet solidity." Here the gentleman could escape from his family
and read newspapers, take coffee, talk, and sleep.*

110. *"The London Skating Club, Regent's Park." 1891. Oil on canvas, n.d. Bath Museums, Costume Research Centre*

*The morning coat, smart without being too formal, was considered appropriate dress for skating in the 1890s. This group includes the Prince
of Wales (bearded in the right center), whose presence guaranteed full attendance at a leisured pursuit.*

111. *R. L. Roumieu (1814–1877). "Design for the Interior of Mr. Breidenbach's London Perfumery Shop, 157 New Bond Street, London."*
1853. Pen and watercolor, 20 x 27". Royal Institute of British Architects, London

Roumieu has been castigated as an architect: "An architectural criminal whose wild fantasies are hardly worth considering."
However, for the queen's perfumer and distiller of eau-de-cologne, he designed London's most fashionable shop, complete
with Italianate arches, mirrors, upholstered chairs, carpets, and lavish light fittings. He had learned early that luxury helps
to convey an atmosphere conducive to conspicuous expenditure.

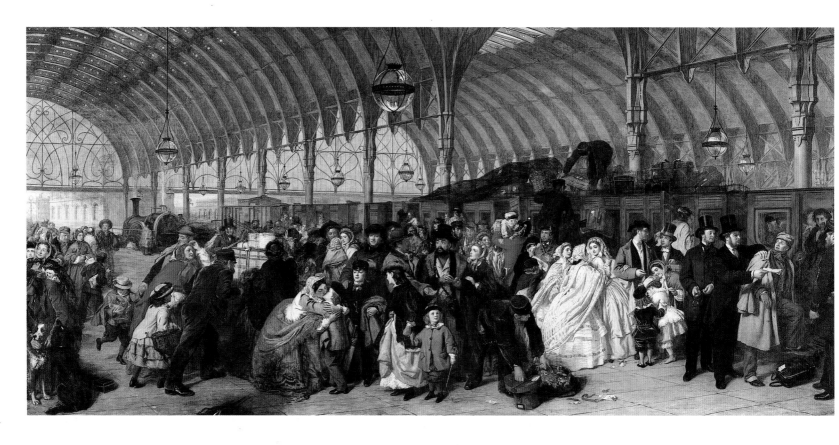

112. *William Powell Frith, RA (1819–1909). "The Railway Station." 1861.*
Oil on canvas, 38 x 60". Royal Holloway College, Egham

Frith captures well the bustle, human drama, and excitement of coming to and going from town in this painting
of the great structure at Paddington. The station had been constructed in 1852–1854, with Brunel being assisted
by the architect Matthew Digby Wyatt.

soon be found in those towns, such as Charleston, that had an active port to encourage coastal trade. Charleston grew from the 1720s, and the arrival of many English artisans and a burgeoning wealth brought about the creation of much fine rococo interior decoration. The foreigners found themselves "readily assimilated into the Low Country gentry which was exceedingly well established through mercantile pursuits and the cultivation of rice and indigo."[31]

Preeminent for some was life in Williamsburg, where the elegant and imposing Governor's Palace[32] served as the official residence of seven royal governors and the first two governors of the Commonwealth of Virginia, Patrick Henry and Thomas Jefferson. But many native-born Virginians devised stratagems that gave them the unofficial means to pursue their own objectives, regardless of the governor's wishes. They were part of a colony that in sixty years, between 1716 and 1775, grew to have a population of half

a million residents (from over eighty thousand). Members of the Council, their families, and other prominent citizens in Williamsburg could have a life that in part was a long round of parties and balls. The *Virginia Gazette* reported in 1738:

Last Monday being the Anniversary of His Majesty's Birth Day, was observ'd in this City. . . In the Morning the Public Flag was hoisted on the Capitol; at Noon the Cannon at the Governor's House was trebly discharg'd; at Night most of the Gentlemen's and other Houses of Note were illuminated. His Honour the Governor was pleas'd to give a handsome Entertainment for the Gentlemen and Ladies together with a Ball.

The general run of storekeepers, craftsmen, and people

*113. Bedford Lemere. "The Gallery, Grosvenor House, London." c. 1872.
Photograph. Royal Commission on the Historic Monuments of England*

*The rich art collections of the Dukes of Westminster had a fine setting at their London town house. The architect Henry Clutton
created a suite of state rooms in the Italian Renaissance manner, including the Gallery and the Rubens Room (1872–1873). Ten years later
electricity was installed, the better to see a collection that included five paintings by Rembrandt.*

of lesser substance, who had provided some of the finery, the food, and service could press to the glass or the fence, and, eschewing a fine punch, go home, happy, to a glass of beer. They tried to believe, as Thomas Sheraton stated in his *Cabinet Dictionary* (1803):

The grandeur then introduced. . . is not to be considered, as the ostentatious parade of its proprietor, but the respect he pays to the rank of his visitants.

But in America of the mid-1770s and France of 1789 there were many who soon overturned all parades of gentility—and they were then gone for many long years.

CHAPTER VII

"Changing the Town for Rural Happiness"

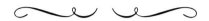

And blest is he, who tir'd with his affairs, Far from all noise, all vain applause, prepares To go, and underneath some silent shade, Which neither cares nor anxious thoughts invade, Do's, for a while, himself alone possess; Changing the Town for Rural happiness . . .

René Rapin, "Of Gardens,"
translated by John Evelyn (1673)

Gentlemen had long an obligation to manage their country estates. Horace (65–8 B.C.), the Latin poet, wrote one of his *Satires* (II, vi) on the difficulties of living in Rome. He told of the country mouse who invited the city mouse to dine at his dwelling in the woods. The city mouse extended a return invitation to his luxurious abode. But as they both lounged on their ivory couches there was a great banging on the doors "and the hall was filled with terrifying hounds." The country mouse beat a hasty retreat, saying that he preferred his frugal cave and his weeds. The Roman satiric poet Martial (A.D. 43–102), accustomed, like Horace, to the simplicity of country life,

tells in his *Epigrams* (XII, 57) of the noise of city life disturbing his sleep and how he longs to be back on his rural farm. Juvenal (A.D. 60–130), the satirist and poet, also amusingly records in his *Satires* (III, 160) the simplicity of country life, where "no one wears a toga until he's dead."[1] In contrast to such simple examples of a rural estate were grander ones such as the important garden of the Emperor Hadrian at Tivoli, erected between A.D. 118 and A.D. 138. On a site between two valleys the emperor reproduced a considerable array of buildings and sites he had visited in his travels, such as the Lyceum near Athens. It required only a fertile imagination to transfer this ideal to the

114. Charles Hunt (1806–d. after 1870). "The Meet" (detail). c. 1840. Colored aquatint, 12½ x 17″.
Yale Center for British Art, Paul Mellon Collection

115. Jan Wyck (c. 1640/5–1700). "A Hawking Party." c. 1690. Oil on canvas, 20 x 27".
Yale Center for British Art, Paul Mellon Collection

With the hawks high above riders on prancing horses, a little of the thrill of the chase is apparent in this imagined view.
The sport was the essential raison d'être; like shooting game, the food obtained was of secondary importance.

Augustan gentleman sprinkling the lush rainswept reaches of an English estate with an array of classical temples.

During the late sixteenth century, at a time when gentlemen knew their classics as well and better than many who came after, the maintenance of the estate was an all-consuming task. At the center of the stretching acres of land, in which all wealth and power rested, was the great house itself. From the table on the dais in the great hall, with the crackling parchment surveys set out before him, an owner's finger could trace every measured field of his domain. In the bowels of the house, behind a great iron door, were shelved all the settlements, wills, inventories, rentals, and leases to withstand the perils of living in a litigious age. Equally stored there and given to frequent scrutiny were the records of expenditure (and income) kept by the various officers of the household, the steward, the clerk of the kitchens, the gentleman of the horse, the country and London agents, those in charge of the home farm and of "His Lordship's Personal Ledger," in which the purchase of every gun, waistcoat, petticoat, fan, and dancing slipper were set out on inked and sanded pages.

Many peers, nevertheless, still had great difficulty in establishing, from a plethora of vouchers and crabbed entries mixed in Roman and Arabic numerals, what their financial state of affairs really amounted to. This led to the employment in great households of able young men from other, but minor, noble households as treasurers, receivers, and stewards. They lived in the house, could meet frequently with an owner, and ride out with him to farms, timber felling, or crop gathering (plate 81). Such service was a useful way for a young man to begin his career and to advance, either in the same household or to move to a greater one or even to royal service.[2]

A good, well-managed estate was able to satisfy many needs. From its rent-roll came the manpower required for a variety of tasks. Each day laborers provided food and fuel for the great house and journeyed over the spreading acres, maintaining cattle and sheep, tending to the growing trees, culling the deer, and harvesting the various crops. And on an extraordinary day, if three new lead statues needed to be reared up on to their plinths, servants, their horses, and devices of Renaissance complexity were ready long before His Lordship trod across the morning dew to the site.

The great stretches of English woodland had been an important source of revenue since medieval times. While the stocks of oak had been severely depleted by building needs and an incessant demand in using it in building the wooden ships of the Tudor navy, an owner normally regarded growing trees as money "banked" against hard times. In fact, Samuel Pepys described woods as "an excres-

116. *Hans Holbein. "Robert Cheseman (1485–1547)." 1533. Oil on oak panel, 23 x 25″. The Mauritshuis, The Hague*

Robert Cheseman, son of Henry VII's cofferer, was Henry VIII's falconer and a man of considerable position and influence.
The king supported his courtiers' love of field sports.

117. *John Wootton (1678?–1765). "Preparing for the Hunt." c. 1740–1750. Oil on canvas, 47 x 49".*
Yale Center for British Art. Paul Mellon Collection

This finely balanced composition in an overwhelming classical setting shows strong interest in the forthcoming hunt
expressed by a lady, who, riding sidesaddle, joins the men and the retainers for a day's sport.

cence of the earth created by God for the payment of debts."[3] Their continuing importance for revenue may be instanced by the later example of George, Lord Lyttelton, building in the 1750s at Hagley Hall, Worcestershire. Writing to his architect, Sanderson Miller, in October 1754, Lyttelton implied that his income as Cofferer of the Household was substantial:

A good £2,200 per annum, all Taxes deducted, and if I hold it three or four years will build my new House with the help of my Falls of Wood without my being obliged to borrow any money.[4]

The care of woodland, over the long, perhaps 150-year

cycle for hardwood maturity, was not every landowner's concern. It was of course possible to thin out the weaker trees every fifteen or sixteen years and to sell that timber. Nevertheless, those who persisted with tree-planting often found a more immediate "return" in the cover given to game, which could be flushed out and proceeded against in "great shoots," which provided meat and sport in even measure. There was, perhaps, a greater need for an owner to decide the scale of farming that could be undertaken. Widespread acreage could put an absentee landlord at the mercy of dishonest stewards, bailiffs, receivers, and auditors. Therefore many farmed on a lesser scale and leased their far-flung demesnes to tenants. The popularity of sheep-rearing and the returns therefrom in a time of rising wool prices had shored up incomes of both monastic communities and private landlords. Furthermore, the value of sheep as mutton contributed significantly to feeding a growing populace.[5] Income usually could be further improved by taking rent in kind. Not only did this provide the household with much of the produce it needed, but the surplus could be sold to advantage in a time of, say, rising grain prices.

The landlord usually had a right to the tithes payable to rectories he owned. A tenth of the annual amount of agricultural produce was conceived as due to God and hence payable for the support of the priesthood. Owners were compensated for loss by the commutation of tithes, "obtaining more than one-tenth of the land in return for exonerating the rest in perpetuity."[6]

It is easy to conjure up an unfair picture of an imperious owner, corpulent at his table, ordering his cowed officers to oppress those on his estates and to extort more in rent and kind. Something of this might well have been true in considering the fifteenth-century chief minister, William de la Pole, Duke of Suffolk. He made many enemies by his greed in amassing land and offices, leading ultimately, not only to his beheading but to a rebellion against the government. But most house-owners recognized the duty they had to the community at their gates, giving to the needy, with themselves, or their wives, visiting the sick, not raising rents, and seeing to it that there was enough fire kindling, vegetables, dead rabbits, and pheasants to light fires and fill all the stew-pots of Christendom. Many owners died in debt but with a fine reputation as generous landlords. Cynically, it was cheaper to be so than risk a general rise in the poor rate, but it is fair to say that this was more a concern for an occupier of property rather than for its owner. Poor rates were paid by occupiers, which usually meant the tenant farmers, rather than the gentry. The Poor Law, a form of welfare system that did little against dire need and the threat of starvation, had been set up at the end of the sixteenth century. Problems arose when the costs of maintaining the system had risen to nearly six million pounds by 1815.

The assumptions society usually made, however, were those that many novelists also portrayed. The virtuous benevolence on hereditary principles of Henry Fielding's Squire Allworthy in his *Tom Jones* (1749) was based on Fielding's own benefactors, Ralph Allen of Bath and George, Lord Lyttelton of Hagley. Tobias Smollett's Don Quixote-type hero, Sir Launcelot Greaves, in the novel of that name (1760–1762) was also benevolent, if a Tory, to Allworthy's Whig persuasion. The Tories equated to the Conservative (or Republican) party and the Whigs to the Liberal (and, perhaps, the Democratic) party. Equally there were those novelists who preached of the dire effects on the poor of rapidly changing agricultural patterns, and Oliver Goldsmith's *Deserted Village* (1770) painted the starkest picture of rural depopulation.[7] One of the problems of this was that a landowner received less in rents. Only with the advance of more effective systems of land management could prices rise and rents regain their importance.

Nevertheless agricultural problems did not attract everyone, and many peers, intent on a parliamentary career, were away in London for much of the year. They spent their money there and could take leisure at the sea, the waters, or horse racing rather than returning to their country estates. Almost any diversion seemed preferable to the long, slow-measured days in the depths of the country, where every track was deep in brown mire and deeper puddles. In fact the novelist John Cleland, in his entertaining *Memoirs of a Coxcomb* (1751), likened the owner visiting his country house—a "temple of dullness"—to an annual "funeral procession." The estate worker at his tied cottage door, however, might delight at catching a rare glimpse of his lordship's new coach, coat of arms quartered brightly on the gleaming painted doors, and perhaps even a blurred image of his master and his lady. He would be at work in the kitchen garden many hours before they arose to view its serried rows through drawn-back festoon curtains.

One focus of attention in country life was the election campaign for a favored candidate for Parliament, at best a corrupt process. John Trusler wrote an amusing play in 1768, *The Country Election: A Farce in Two Acts*, in which, picking up scenes well portrayed in Hogarth's paintings (plate 125), he drew attention to playing court to all: "fawning on, kissing and flattering the women all day, smoking, boozing, and licking the very spittle of the men, all night." The political influence lay with the possessor of a country estate, and the demeaning conduct which

118. Sir Godfrey Kneller (1646–1723). "Frances Pierrepont, Countess of Mar, and a Page." c. 1715. Oil on canvas, 93 x 57".
Scottish National Portrait Gallery, The Earl of Mar and Kellie (on loan to the Scottish National Portrait Gallery)

Lady Mar, in a magnificent pink and silver riding outfit, represents all those titled ladies who had enough money and time to ride in style.

119. Dean Wolstenholme (1757–1837). "Lord Glamis and His Staghounds at St. Paul's, Waldenbury, Hertfordshire." 1823. Oil on canvas, 51 x 81". Yale Center for British Art, Paul Mellon Collection

Surrounded by attendant hounds, the riders, all of the same social level, pause in their chase across the unyielding countryside.

120. Charles Hunt (1806–d. after 1870). "The Meet." c. 1840. Colored aquatint, 12½ x 17". Yale Center for British Art, Paul Mellon Collection

The hunt gathers, ready to follow huntsmen and hounds to the trumpeting kill. Bloodsports, then as now, attracted some disquiet, but the activity has remained a staple aristocratic pastime.

121. *Francis Hayman, RA (1708–1776). "George Rogers with His Wife, Margaret Tyers, and His Sister, Margaret Rogers (at right). c. 1750–1752. Oil on canvas, 41 x 39". Yale Center for British Art, Paul Mellon Collection*

Margaret Tyers was the daughter of Jonathan Tyers, who owned Vauxhall Gardens, the fashionable meeting spot in London. George Rogers delightedly holds aloft a pheasant he has shot. The use of guns for sport began in the late 1690s.

122. *Detail of double-barrel flintlock gun, the stock inlaid with chinoiserie scenes of a huntsman and hounds in pursuit of a stag. Made by William Bailes of London, 1766. The Armouries for Her Majesty's Tower of London.*

Expenditure on a fine gun was increased if elaborate decoration was incorporated.

123. *Johan Zoffany, RA (1733–1810). "The Drummond Family." c. 1769. Oil on canvas, 41 x 63".*
Yale Center for British Art, Paul Mellon Collection

The evident nervous delight of the young girl being helped onto her horse is well captured in the caring faces around her,
accurately painted by Zoffany, a master of detail and of the pose of the privileged.

Trusler wrote of has many other exponents. In 1784 William Godwin[8] noted:

> It is he, most noble patron, who can swallow the greatest quantity of porter, who can roar the best catch, and who is the compleatest bruiser, that will finally carry the day. He must kiss the frost-bitten lips of the greengrocers. He must smooth the frowzy cheeks of chandlers-shop women. He must stroke down the infinite belly of a Wapping landlady.

As Trusler further had it, "at elections all condescend to hug the greasy rogues and shake hands with every dirty fellow."

In addition to mixing with the pressing crowd, the payment of bribes was widespread and could easily get out of hand. The most notorious example was in an election at Northampton in 1768, where over 160,000 pounds was spent to sway votes. As a result both candidates were seriously in debt. One, Lord Northampton, sought permanent exile in Switzerland, and the other, Lord Halifax, withdrew from Northampton politics.[9] Novelists saw good material in such episodes. In *Ralph, The Heir* (1821), for example, Anthony Trollope tells the story of Sir Thomas Underwood campaigning to represent Percycross but insisting no bribes were to be given. Percycross's citizens, used to living in a corrupt borough, avidly accepted bribes from the standing member, one Mr. Griffenbottom.[10]

124. *Frances Wheatley, RA (1747–1801). "George and Mary Browne with Their Five Elder Children." c. 1773–1774. Oil on canvas, 27 x 35". Yale Center for British Art, Paul Mellon Collection*

Repose in sketching for the husband and a careful casting of the fishing line for Mrs. Browne and her children exemplifies the leisured life on the country estate.

There were too many offices of responsibility, the holding of which was considered proper for gentlemen, for all of them to be avoided. At the head of each county was a lord-lieutenant, a post invariably held by a peer.[11] Many did not wish to be appointed to the next ranking position, sheriff, because it was expensive to sustain and demanding of time, as it still is. Being lord-lieutenant, the sovereign's representative, meant also being head of the magistracy in a county and was demanding in ceremonial and official duties. The sheriff was the chief executive officer of a county, charged with keeping of the peace by administering justice under the direction of the law courts and presiding over elections. Many of the gentry were anxious to be justices of the peace, playing their active part as magistrates and in regulating local prices and wages, overseeing the repair of bridges and highways, and administering the Poor Laws. To be eligible for office they needed to own property. Many were anxious to hold office in order to hold power, although most saw the office as a means to serve the community. This was particularly true of those justices who had qualified as magistrates. Those the wrong side of the law might have wished them to be less conscientious, but there were many times when not enough justices were available. Until the accession of George III in 1760 there were too many cases of dismissal by Whigs of Tory magistrates.[12] The new king appointed many new magistrates, and this helped in implementing long-overdue reconstruction. But like many good things, the reforms did not last, and enthusiasm for them waned until the nineteenth century.

When zealous magistrates returned to their country houses their minds turned to estate matters. While poaching of game may have come before their courts, there was equally a developing antagonism to many country sports, particularly that of fox hunting. A sensitivity to the suffering of animals had already arisen by the late eighteenth century, so if young Lady Mary Palliser, keen on her botanical researches and anxious never to hurt a moth—but avid enough to look at them when they were fixed by pins in a mahogany case—posed, hypothetically, to her father—he who was Trollope's "Plantagenet Palliser, Duke of Omnium"—"Father must you hunt foxes when the hounds will kill them and they will suffer grievously?" What should he answer? Dressed in his pink with white stock and shining black boots and standing before the

toasting fire at Gatherum Castle, they could both hear his gray hunter restlessly pawing the ground below and the baying hounds circling the paved forecourt. Could he say anything other than, "It has a long history, me dear?" And of course the duke was entirely correct, as a duke should be, even if he did not answer his daughter's question. It was vastly different from the great and uneventful history of riding out for pleasure (plate 118).

Stag hunting, fox hunting, and hawking had long been favorite pastimes for kings and their courtiers. It was while out stag hunting that King Edmund I (939–946) almost plunged over a precipice to his death. The letting out of land to tenants frequently carried terms allowing hunting and falconry, and those of high rank had their falconers (plate 116) and huntsmen in ready service. It was not thought possible in Tudor England to be a gentleman if one did not like hunting or the sport of hawking. Henry VIII and Anne Boleyn rode out frequently to hunt, using bows and arrows. Anne, an indifferent shot, might well

125. *William Hogarth (1697–1764). "Chairing the Member." 1754–1755. Oil on canvas, 40 x 50".*
The Trustees of Sir John Soane's Museum, London

Political tomfoolery is an ancient aristocratic tradition. This canvas is the fourth of a series inspired by the corrupt Oxfordshire election of 1754. The other canvases show the election entertainment, canvassing for votes, and the polling. The winning Tory candidate is carried through the streets in triumph, hedged around by all those invented in Hogarth's fertile satiric mind.

126. Richard Wilson, RA (1713–1782). "Wilton House from the Southeast." c. 1758.
Oil on canvas, 36 x 56". Yale Center for British Art, Paul Mellon Collection

This limpid view of the Earl of Pembroke's great house is indebted to Wilson's years of training in Italy.

have felt the occasion more enervating to have the king to herself. She was mindful, nevertheless, that the king had also gone hunting with her predecessor, Catherine of Aragon.

Most fine houses had licensed deer parks. And high above the parkland would be a stone hunting lodge or tower from which the chase could be observed by the company, often the ladies, while they had a polite "banquet." The simplest form of hunting stand was a temporary balustraded structure similar to those illustrated in George Turbervile's *Noble Art of Venerie* (1575). But the best were built in stone. An excellent example, both banqueting house and viewing tower, is Weston Hall in West Yorkshire, dating from the late sixteenth century. A variation of use informed the Triangular Lodge at Rushton, Northamptonshire, built by Sir Thomas Tresham in 1594–1597. It was of course symbolical in its plan of the

Holy Trinity, and symbolism pervades every aspect of the façades. However in the Rushton accounts it is invariably called "The Warryners Lodge" and was used to keep rabbits and pigeons in, both being valuable sources of food. The lodge was a fine place at which to gather and set out to take part in the killing of both.

Bess of Hardwick's late sixteenth-century tower on the skyline of the present park at Chatsworth is similarly impressive. The lodge in the New Park at Sherborne, Gloucestershire, erected for Sir John Dutton in the early 1630s was described about 1634 as being "richly furnish'd to entertain them [his friends] to see that kingly sport. There I spent a full houre in viewing that neat rare Building, the rich furnish'd Roomes, the handsome contriv'd Pens and Places, where the Deere are kept, and turn'd out for the course."[13] The lodge's roof was used as the platform for viewing the deer and the hare coursing.

127. *Frances Vivares (1709–1780) after Coplestone Warre Bampfylde (1719–1791). "Stourhead, the Lake and Pantheon." 1777. Engraving, 17 x 21". Yale Center for British Art, Paul Mellon Collection*

Henry Hoare's Wiltshire garden offered this splendid view, taken from the west end of the lake looking toward the Pantheon. This garden was expanded in the mid-1750s, and the valley was flooded to form a large lake surrounded by an attractive walk.

In 1697 Charles Lennox, the first Duke of Richmond, bought Goodwood Park in Sussex for use as a hunting lodge. He was already a member of the Charlton Hunt, whose kennels were situated about two miles away. The Charlton was the first formal foxhunt in England. The Duke of Monmouth, a son of Charles II and half-brother to the first Duke of Richmond (born to the liaison of the King with Louise de Kerouaille, Duchess of Portsmouth) hunted with the Charlton. Ladies, as well as watching, took a greater interest in hunting when Queen Anne took it up in 1703 and made it her principal recreation. Even when Anne became an invalid, she rode in the hunts in a small chariot pulled by two horses.[14] John Wootton's painting *Preparing for the Hunt* (plate 117) and his *Lady Mary Churchill at the Death of the Hare* are splendid portrayals of an almost daily ritual.

In 1671 a law was enacted that prevented indiscriminate hunting of hares, pheasants, partridges, and moor fowls except by those freeholders paying 100 pounds a year. It was a device that favored persons of "higher degree" and excluded those who did not themselves own land, even if they had wealth from other sources. From the early eighteenth century, interest in stag hunting and hare coursing declined as interest grew in pursuing the cunning fox. Hunting allowed the aristocrat to show that he was a leader of social gatherings, since the gentry and the whole of county society often rode together. The hunting fraternity widened, for it seemed sensible when riding at full gallop across a farmer's field not only to have one's wife alongside, but also the farmer himself. In fact it was stated that "the number of smartly turned out tenant farmers who hunted with one hunt, the Brocklesby, exceeded

128. *Winslow Homer (1836–1910). "Croquet Players." 1865. Oil on canvas, 16 x 24".*
Albright-Knox Art Gallery, Buffalo, New York, Charles Clifton and James G. Forsyth Funds, 1941

the total number of hunters in any other county." At one time sixty or seventy farmers, all clad in scarlet and all beautifully mounted, followed the Brocklesby hounds. Lord Willoughby de Broke noted further: "If it [hunting] ever presents the appearance of exclusiveness the whole fabric will dissolve."[15] The rector, solicitor, and village blacksmith would not be far behind. The services of all might be needed, although as Trollope's Dean of Brotherton said in *Is he Popenjoy?* (1878): "A clergyman in my position would be wrong to hunt often."

While fox hunting in England dates from the end of the fifteenth century it took its modern form in the nineteenth century and developed into an upper-class activity. The scarlet uniform, with white stock or cravat and black velvet hat was worn by the master, huntsman, and whipper-in of the hounds. Followers of sufficient prestige were also invited to wear "pink" and the individual buttons of the hunt, along with a black top hat (the velvet cap being the prerogative of those engaged in managing the hounds). Other followers wore top hats or bowlers.

The formation of the great hunts, such as the Beaufort,

the Heythrop, and the Belvoir, each with its own distinctive livery, began in the eighteenth century, and every effort was expended by them in breeding foxhounds. From the late eighteenth century and throughout the nineteenth century one could not venture far on a crisp autumn morning's country walk before the distant thundering of hooves announced the imminent flash of brown fox and the baying hounds swept into view with forty heaving men in pink horse-leaping at every shaking hedge (plate 119).

The expense of hunting was considerable. When the fifth Duke of Rutland succeeded to his title in 1798 the outlay each year leapt to 2,000 pounds. It has been shown[16] that the Belvoir hounds consumed 34 tons of oatmeal in 1798–1799, as well as quantities of horseflesh. To this expense there needed to be added the wages, housing, and part-keep of the several servants, coal to heat the kennel areas in the winter, and a large amount of expensive work in maintaining the hunting territory, mending gates and bridges and creating new rides through the coverts. Additionally there was the need to see that there was suitable cover for all-too-elusive foxes to rear their litters and be "safe," until their time to run.

Apart from the overall expenditure to his estate, when the Master of Foxhounds was a landed owner there was the added expense of the necessary string of hunters. They cost as much as the kennels, hounds, and hunt servants together, and an owner might find it less painful to his accounting mind, or his steward's, to sweep their cost into the general maintenance of the stables, each with their many carriage horses and carriages. It became more usual from the start of the nineteenth century to share the hunt's expenses by taking a good subscription from all those participating: it also meant those who paid were not averse to the packs of foxhounds racing over their own fields.

Despite Lord Willoughby de Broke's insistence on a non-exclusive hunt membership, the great cost of maintaining the meet in the nineteenth century led it to be a sport simply for those who could afford it. The expanding railway system allowed many wealthy Londoners, keen on social advancement, to join the country hunts. As for the balls and dinners, arranged as necessary adjuncts to something only slightly more active, they became an important part of both local life and its economy. Pirouetting the dance floor until dawn was good business for those who

provided the hot silver-dished components of many breakfasts. But it still must be owned that many a prospective son-in-law blanched at the direct question, "do you hunt?"

A greater expense than hunting, excluding that of owning horses at all, lay with entering them to race meetings and the large wagers that had to be laid on their foam-flecked performances. In the 1720s Daniel Defoe, journeying on "A Tour Through the Whole Island of Great Britain"—as his two books of 1724–1726 are so titled—wrote of "a great concourse of the nobility and gentry, as well from London as from all parts of England" at Newmarket racecourse. The origins of horse racing are in ancient warfare, chariot racing, and hunting. Organized races took place in the twelfth century, and in 1377 the Prince of Wales, who later became Richard II, raced his horse against the Earl of Arundel. The first permanent racecourse was not established at Chester until 1540. As Charles II grew older his enthusiasm for hunting was turned to horse racing. While it was still a sport in the mid-seventeenth century, racing had been banned during the Civil War years as giving opportunity for the seditious to gather. By the end of Charles II's reign in 1685 racing was thoroughly established as an integral part of British

129. Sir John Lavery, RA (1856–1941). "The Tennis Party." 1885. Oil on canvas, 30 x 72". Aberdeen Art Gallery, Scotland

The ladies are in improbable dresses and hats; the men hot in breeches and stockings. Lithe athleticism was not easy to sustain in such clothes.

163

130. Sir John Lavery, RA (1856–1941). "Maidenhead Regatta." c. 1890. Oil on canvas, 40 x 62". Glasgow Art Gallery and Museum

The eager throng of well-dressed spectators watches the flash of the two crews skimming the dark waters in a regatta near Henley, where in 1829 the great annual rowing and social occasion had first begun.

social and sporting life. Many horses were trained on the heath at Newmarket. Racing also started at Ascot in the late seventeenth century and became popular when Queen Anne established the Royal Ascot races there in 1712. The Monmouth races were under the patronage of the Duke of Beaufort in 1717 and those at Goodwood under the Duke of Richmond from 1802.

While Queen Anne had started horse racing at Ascot, it was not taken up seriously there until revived by William Augustus, Duke of Cumberland, the third son of George II. He kept his stud at Cumberland Lodge at Ascot, and the races were attended regularly by the king, the queen and the Prince of Wales. The races became a great social and dressing-up occasion during the late years of Queen Victoria's reign. While the queen herself took little part, her fun-loving son, the Prince of Wales (who waited until he was fifty-nine before ascending the throne as Edward VII in 1901) took bevies of his lady friends, in their resplendent feathered hats and sweeping gowns fresh from the Paris couturiers, there each June.

High wagers on a likely winner caused the government

to attempt control by outlawing stakes above 10 pounds in 1710 and making it an offense to hold a race if the prize was for less than 50 pounds in 1740. The large meetings attracted great crowds and the named races, the St. Leger (1776), the Oaks (1778), and the Derby (1780), were established in the eighteenth century. At Epsom, on its opening day, it was said that half the male peerage might be visible in the saddling enclosure.[17] Netherteless those who watched from the rails were from all classes, eager to be part of a great social scene—though with many there just for illicit gain from theft and picking pockets. Many races were for significant plates and cups, and those at Doncaster, York, and Richmond, in particular, led to some fine examples of the goldsmith's and silversmith's art. Particularly attractive is the Richmond Race Cup of 1770, designed by Robert Adam (and now in the collections of Colonial Williamsburg).[18] This silver-gilt cup, nineteen inches high, was made in 1770 by Daniel Smith and Robert Sharp, who had made an earlier version in 1764 for Hugh Percy, later first Duke of Northumberland. The cup relates closely to the Adam drawing. Two cast handles are in the form of winged female figures, and the cup is decorated both with a frieze of horses and riders and two applied oval medallions, with beaded edges, of racing scenes. The cup and its cover are further embellished with palm and acanthus leaves. The prized cup was first won at the Richmond Races in 1770 by the horse *Denmark*.

The investment in horse racing was as considerable as that in hunting. Each sport needed stables, horses, food, and men to tend them. Many ambitious persons also sought to import Arabian stock. The most famous was the Darley Arabian, one of the three Arabian horses from which all English racehorses are descended. The entrance hall at its owner's house, Aldby Park in Yorkshire, was designed in the 1720s to incorporate a great painting of the horse. The painting is still *in situ*,[19] as is that of the Godolphin Arabian at Godolphin in Cornwall. The Lowther family, later earls of Lonsdale, had a stud at Lowther in northernmost Cumbria in the 1690s. They sold horses to King William III, almost certainly for "racing purposes."[20] Necessary control over the complexities of the sport developed with the founding of the Jockey Club in the 1750s. Its titled "stewards" could arbitrate disputed results, as they still do.

A large income was essential for maintaining racing stables. Lord Grosvenor could be regarded as wealthy in that he had a gross income of 20,000 pounds a year in the 1770s. However, with the upkeep of his houses, maintaining the support of the Chester electorate for his candidates, paying alimony to his estranged wife, an annuity to his brother, and interest on his debts of 151,000 pounds, the 7,000 pounds he needed each year for racing was not easily available. By 1795 almost the whole of his estate income was taken by payments and interest charges. His lawyer commented, "We have nothing but the mines and coalworks to look to for support of your lordship's immense establishment at Newmarket." Fortunately, the rental income from his London estates rose rapidly, and when Lord Grosvenor died in 1802 his family could enter "on its great period of nineteenth-century magnificence."[21]

Three other considerable pastimes for the country gentleman—though his peers perhaps thought it more seemly to be better versed in fencing, dancing, and "elegant horsemanship"[22]—were shooting, cock fighting, and fishing. Shooting had become popular in the seventeenth century, although many, like the fourth Earl of Chesterfield in the mid-eighteenth century, believed that the "rustick, illiberal sports of guns, dogs and horses" characterized "our English Bumkin Country Gentleman." The gun, advancing in technique as well as aesthetic appearance, had replaced the falcon as the sure means of felling game for the table. Many a fine portrait—Gainsborough's of "Mr. and Mrs. Robert Andrews," for example (plate 80)—shows a master not only with a fine gun under his arm but a brown and white gun dog quivering at his feet and ready at an instant to retrieve the red flush of feathers fallen from the sky. As a corollary to this the organized preservation of game became a ready preoccupation, needing some necessary time from other activities. Riding the estate with the gamekeepers may have given good exercise: equally, and especially in the nineteenth century, it drew attention to the elaborate and expensive measures necessary to ensure that large bags could be obtained by the swinging, cracking guns of a group of friends. National records for the single day's bag were set and broken. On January 17, 1823, some 525 pheasants were recorded as shot at Ashridge by twelve guns. At Eaton Hall, Cheshire, seat of the Duke of Westminster, the season's bag in 1891 totaled more than 5,000 pheasants, 400 partridges, nearly 600 hares, more than 7,000 rabbits, 100 snipes and woodcock, and over 200 wild duck. It was good sport for the lavish house parties, with grand shoots organized when the Prince of Wales chose to visit.

The morocco-bound game books, making their appearance at the end of the eighteenth century, are still one of the minor wonders of house archives—the precise mathematics of so much slaughter. It was all an easier target for a government bent on extracting revenue by game-license duties. In 1784 a duty was imposed on granting a game license, the number of which, by 1827, had risen to 51,375. An increase in the duty in 1839 caused some decline in the sport of shooting; but from the 1850s in England and Scotland, numbers of licenses and numbers of gamekeepers in employment rose steadily.[23] Shooting for sport was not braked until the outbreak of the First World War, a fact explored, poignantly, in Isabel Colgate's splendid novel *The Shooting Party* (1988).

There were always those gentlemen who took their ability to shoot into the wider world of exploration and safari.

Big-game shooting became a particular obsession in the late nineteenth century (plate 136). The fascination in many to explore for its own sake had been fanned into action by reading about the exploits of Sir Richard Burton (1821–1890). In 1853 he had made the pilgrimage to Mecca (forbidden to Christians) by adopting various disguises and assuming the name of Al-Haj ("the pilgrim") Abdullah. After Mecca, Burton, often accompanied by his wife, Isabel, made many tours into unexplored territories, in Africa and elsewhere, discovering the sources of the Nile and Victoria Nyanza.

Cock fighting was a Tudor obsession whose origins were probably lost in the middle of the fifteenth century. There was a cockpit at Greenwich, constructed in 1532 with a gallery over the bowling alley for the queen to watch the cock fighting. There was another at the King's Palace in Whitehall that had "battlemented parapets, standard-bearing heraldic beasts and a leaded lantern, unusual elaborations for a building devoted to a raw sport."[24] John Smyth recorded in his seventeenth-century history of the Berkeleys[25] how Henry, the seventeenth Lord Berkeley (1534–1613), one of the greatest of Elizabethan gamblers, spent many hours at cards, dice, and the cock-fighting pit. There was money to be made or lost on the ferocious staying power of each preening cockerel, with its steel spurs poised to strike. It remained a degrading sport across three centuries, until outlawed in the reign of Queen Victoria.[26]

While fox hunting, shooting, and cock fighting were

131. James Tissot (1836–1902). "Holiday: The Artist's Garden at 17 Grove End Road, London." c. 1875.
Oil on canvas, 30 x 39". The Tate Gallery, London

Tissot has captured a lazy picnic by still waters, but with the correctly mannered degrees of studied nonchalance and flirtatious interest.

132. *James Tissot (1836–1902). "The Ball on Shipboard." 1874. Oil on canvas, 40 x 50". The Tate Gallery, London*

For this daytime event at the Henley Regatta both formal and informal day dress were allowable. The men wear straw sailor hats,
the women full braided chignons with forward tilted straw sailor hats. The tight jacket bodices with basques are worn with draped
fronted overskirts. Some of the men have two-tone brogue shoes.

activities pursued by groups of people, fishing for pleasure was for the most part a solitary vigil. Many owners had, of course, constructed fish ponds as one of the improvements to their grounds. This continued a monastic tradition, then also providing a source of food, but the idea was stimulated later less by thoughts of cooked fish than by thoughts of Classical and Renaissance examples, of bright Italian skies and shimmering and sparkling waters surrounded by statuary.[27] It was a suitable indulgence for wives and even for young children and also for the many tenants who were granted fishing permits. The skillful art of casting a line across dark green unfathomable waters had been first described by Izaak Walton in *The Compleat Angler*. King Charles II was a keen fisherman. He also loved swimming. On occasion there may have been some correlation. Queen Catherine would often join him in early morning fishing expeditions on the Thames, out from Hampton Court. The king was also keen on yachting, and

apart from costume the scene was perhaps little changed from those recorded by painters such as J. J. Tissot in the late nineteenth century (plate 132). Then it was an aristocratic pursuit to own a steam yacht involving a large crew. The astute New York banker J. P. Morgan was accustomed, aboard his yacht *Sea Wolf*, to conduct business deals and entertain society ladies, not necessarily at the same time.

Many noblemen, abroad on their Grand Tours, learned to play tennis. Dudley, Lord North, did this at Antwerp in 1605, as well as participating in much gambling and sightseeing—and the sport was very popular in France. In Paris tennis courts were counted in the hundreds, and at Fontainebleau and the Louvre Francis I had large covered tennis courts.[28] At Whitehall and Hampton Court, Henry VIII had open courts as well as a small closed one intended for a form of hand—as opposed to racket—tennis. By the early seventeenth century the number of courts there had increased to four, two open and two closed. Interest did not wane, with Charles II adept at the sport, and the game has survived into the twentieth century, with a gradual liberalization in dress that was far from present even as late at the start of this century (plate 129). In contrast to the long-held interest in tennis by many from the sovereign down, croquet became fashionable only in the 1850s. There are many views of overdressed men and women, the ladies in long dresses, bending politely to the task (plate 128).

In 1870 the national championships in croquet were transferred to the All-England Croquet and Lawn Tennis Club (as it then was) at Wimbledon. New rules were agreed on but little could alter the decline of the game as lawn tennis gained in popularity. The establishment in 1896 of the Croquet Association regularized the rules and settings, as it still does, from its headquarters at the Hurlingham Club.

Many men learned to row at university, but it was in the nineteenth century that better, lighter boats could be propelled with greater ease and as part of a competitive sport, rather than as an exercise of commerce or utility. The oldest rowing regatta in Europe was set up in 1839 at Henley-on-Thames in rural Oxfordshire. This was due to interest locally in the first Oxford and Cambridge University Boat Race, which took place in 1829 at Henley. With the Grand Challenge Cup (1839) and the lesser event of the Thames Cup (1868) as well as a Ladies' Plate to compete for, Henley became the leading place not only to row but to disport themselves in fine clothes in the accompanying launches and houseboats.

The only setting and also the best for the game of cricket was the country house pitch with its ideal backdrop of cut-stone façades quivering in a heat haze. Played out in whites to polite applause and across an immaculately mown grass pitch and outfield, the scene might even have been far away at public school or university. Eton, Winchester, Westminster, and Harrow schoolboys played cricket by the eighteenth century. The Gentlemen *versus* Players fixture, first staged at Lord's cricket ground in 1806, became a major amateur event, with an emphasis on style and graceful playing. The owners of great houses vied with each other to attract the game's first popular hero, W. G. Grace, to come to such friendly matches as "Lord

Lyttelton's XI against the Duke of Norfolk's XI." Indeed, the Lyttelton family, all adept cricketers, were said to practice on wet days in the Long Gallery at Hagley Hall, to the peril of its carved and gilt-wood rococo mirrors.

Ladies, of course, may have preferred lazing in a hammock in the shade of trees, while their loved ones played cricket. But many did engage in the ancient art of archery. This, like horse racing, had grown from the use of the long-bow in war. Roger Ascham in his book *Toxophilus* (1545) had supported the retention of the bow, and Bishop Latimer had urged its use in a sermon given before Edward VI. But by 1595 the Privy Council had declared that archers should no longer be enrolled in the army. Inevitably its popularity declined, only to be revived by the many societies of archers which grew up. The Toxophilite Society was founded in 1781 (although it was given the appellation of "Royal" in 1847). The Prince of Wales, later George IV, mindful that when he visited Scotland he was protected by the Royal Company of Archers (1676), gave the sport a push by being a patron of several societies and awarding prizes. There are many attractive engravings of the toxophilists, in profile, the string of an elegantly shaped bow pulled hard back, with the target somewhere distant, but seen by bright, youthful eyes.

The Persian poet Firdansi described a polo match in about 600 B.C., and there is evidence that the game spread across Asia to China and Japan. By the nineteenth century it had almost died away but was discovered by visiting British officers on the northwest and northeast frontiers of India. They established polo clubs at Calcutta (1862) and elsewhere. The first match in England was played in 1871 between the Hurlingham Club and officers of the 9th Lancers and 10th Hussars. The game was imported into America in the late 1870s and was soon everywhere where space, sun, and horses were abundant, including India, Argentina, and South Africa. For the most part it remained a pastime for the very rich and their friends and for those in the armed services. It is still played before the Elizabethan ruins of Cowdray Park in West Sussex, as aristocratic a setting as could be imagined by any bronzed player on his small, racing-fit thoroughbred horse.

Something of the social life lived in the great country

house and the responsibility of the owner for the welfare of his estate workers is shown by an account of the New Year's Day celebrations of 1847 at Eden Hall, Cumbria[29]:

> About one hundred and thirteen of the labourers and their families, together with other dependents and friends of the worthy baronet sat down to the feast. . . . The hosts were Sir George Musgrave and his wife Charlotte, and heir Philip, a younger son and their three daughters, Caroline, Agnes and Sophia. Their health on this happy occasion, was proposed by the estate steward, with the support of his brother, the land agent, and the butler.

Those who served a good estate over long years might expect, in the nineteenth century, a pension, a cottage to retire to, and perhaps some simple employment still. The landowner paid for repairs to the church and the parish hall, gave to local charities, sent food and other provisions to the needy, and made generous donations to the cricket club. Many great estate walls were built by the otherwise unemployed in the Napoleonic Wars, a workforce always greater than common-sense economics normally allowed. There were, alas, exceptions, although the most famous case has been severely overstated. As A. Mackenzie noted in 1883, "To give a proper account of the Sutherland Clearances would take a bulky volume."[30] Clearance of population on the Duke of Sutherland's Scottish estates had taken place in the late eighteenth century, encouraging large-scale emigration to the American colonies. What happened in the early nineteenth century was a larger-scale removal of the population from the hills to the coast, and many again went abroad. The scheme had as its aim trying to achieve some chance of a reasonable livelihood for the many, which the density of population concentrated in the glens of the high interior did not otherwise allow. But it was a policy, including some burning of houses to prevent reoccupation, that was never fully understood—correspondents in the London *Times* railed against it—and it secured for the duke's family a deep and continuing

acrimony and for the factors (or stewards) near universal condemnation.[31]

As a contrast to the alienation of the estate tenants, one could instance the annual feasts given in the 1820s and 1830s at Petworth for his tenants by the third Earl of Egremont (1751–1837). The third earl was both a patron of the arts, particularly of the painter J. M. W. Turner, and a prominent agriculturist. His hospitality was famous, and Edmund Burke spoke of him as "delighting to reign in the dispensation of happiness." The painter Benjamin Robert Haydon ingratiatingly wrote that the earl's "greatest pleasure was sharing with highest and humblest the luxuries of his vast income. The very animals at Petworth seemed happier thán in any other spot on earth." In his progressive farming methods there was always concern to improve the lot of the small tenant. In his role as patron Lord Egremont found support in the lady who long bore the courtesy title of Mrs. Wyndham. For some reason Lord Egremont did not marry her until after the birth of six children, and on his death the earldom passed to a nephew and became extinct.

But life in the country house was usually conducted between two titled persons who had been married in a flush of conspicuous and well-publicized magnificence. They taught their children to ride, shot at everything, rode energetically at every meet, visited the poor, and wrote letters to friends—who never replied—opened fêtes and events—smilingly, in heavy rain—and inspected buildings, from parish halls to sewage works. They wielded the silver spade at tree-plantings as dexterously as though they had been born to a life of manual labor, and they provided for all their children, who perhaps would do little of what they had done. For those same children, astute and better calculated than their parents, might know all too well, as they lazed in wicker armchairs, cigarettes in long yellow Fabergé holders, the lines in Shakespeare's *The Merchant of Venice* (IV. 218–219):

'T' will be recorded for a precedent,
And many an error by the same example.

CHAPTER VIII

"The Chiming Clocks to Dinner Call"

But hark! The Chiming Clocks to dinner call;
A hundred footsteps scrape the marble Hall:
The rich Buffet well-colour'd Serpents grace,
And gaping Tritons spew to wash your face.

Alexander Pope, "Epistle IV. To Richard Boyle,
Earl of Burlington," 1731, 150–154

From the fourteenth century on there was a continuing search for comfort and privacy within the thick walls of the country house. The rooms beneath the great chamber and adjacent to the chilly hall of the medieval manor were soon turned into small living areas, where the family could dine or retire to from the "high table." With a wall fireplace, a less chilly room could be devised, and the great hall could be kept for festive occasions and for the entertainment of visiting lords and their entourages. Langland, in *The Vision of Piers Plowman*, (c. 1362), noted that the lord and his lady no longer liked to sit in the hall, but "eat by themselves. . . in a private parlour" and "leave the chief hall, that was made for meals, for men to eat in." It was a pattern set to continue.

The 1601 inventory for Hardwick Hall, Derbyshire,[1] shows that "Bess" (Elizabeth, Countess of Shrewsbury) was able to sit beneath a canopy, on "a chare of nedlework with golde and silke frenge," with her feet on a footstool, surrounded by company seated on six forms and sixteen stools. They would all eat at "a long table of white wood," covered with a table carpet and a damask tablecloth, and were served by a rigid hierarchy of servants. At the end of the meal they could relax and listen to music or watch the sun set over the forbidding façades of Old Hardwick Hall nearby, before attending family prayers in the chapel below. Both Old and New Hardwick Hall had two great chambers. In New Hardwick the Low Great Chamber was far from both Bess's bedchamber and those of her son and granddaughter beyond. It was part of a sprawling domestic suite and was used for family dining, for play-

133. *John Nash* (1752–1835). *"The Banqueting Room, The Royal Pavilion, Brighton," from "Views of the Royal Pavilion,*
Brighton" (detail). 1826. Brighton Museum and Art Gallery

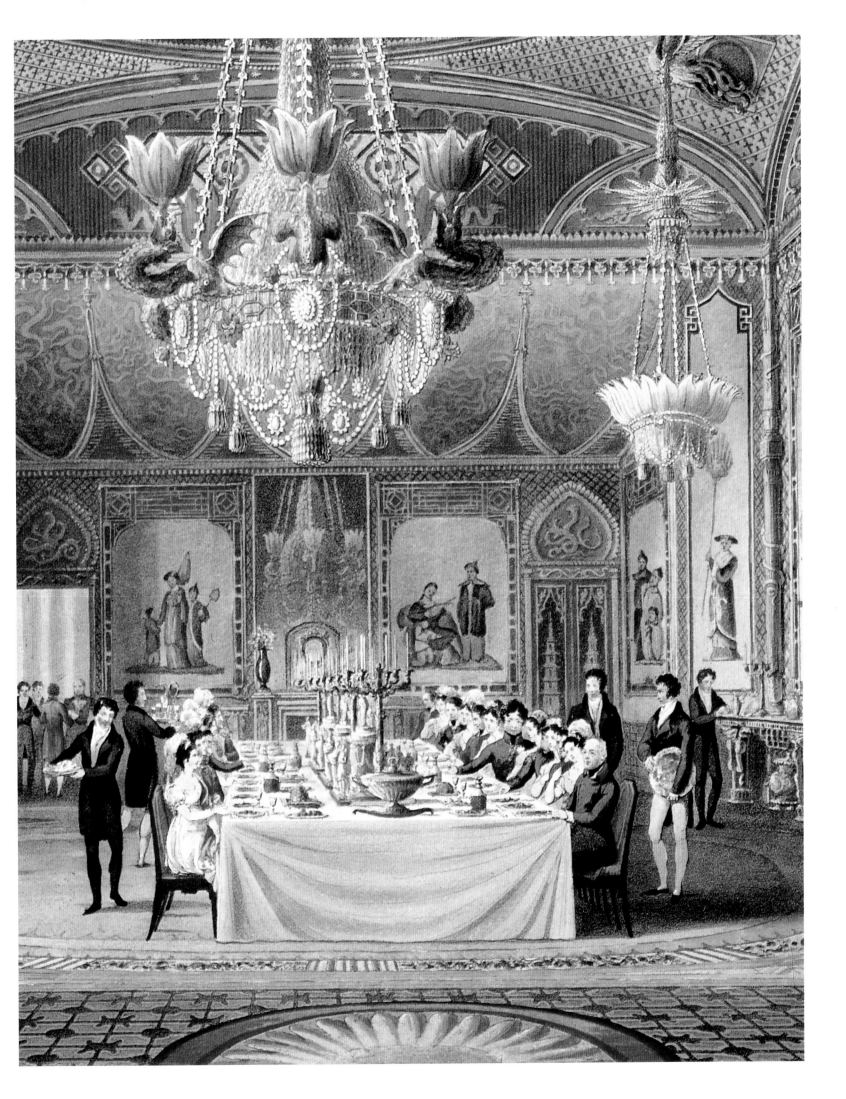

ing table-games, and even for the common room of the upper servants.

The expenditure on everyday living in any household could be considerable, but a period of expansion or of many persons bent on affluent living could soon cause financial trouble. In 1637 Lord Middlesex drew up a paper on how he might meet his very considerable obligations at Copt Hall, Essex. It was titled "Reformations and the improving my Estate": "Fewer Servants; Fewer Horses; Fewer Deer; Fewer Houses; Fewer Jewels, Fewer Rich Stuffs, Carpets, etc."

But still he had thirty-seven servants, herds of deer roamed in his park and forest (their inclusion in his list as an economy had doubtful merit), and the number of houses he owned stayed the same. As part of this exercise, perhaps undertaken to encourage righteous feelings of austerity, Middlesex had estimated in 1636 that his household expenditure was 2,120 pounds a year, of which 1,000 pounds was allocated to food and 400 pounds to clothes. His estimate, as with so many, excluded what he preferred to forget; there was nothing allowed for living in London, for "gifts, extras" and for collecting monies due to him, which remained, as sterile debts, unpaid.[2]

The records available about life in two ducal households, one Scottish, one English, reveal much about the grandeur of the daily routine. Anne, the third Duchess of Hamilton (1632–1716) in her own right—she succeeded to the title at the death of her father at the Battle of Worcester (1651)—married Lord William Douglas, Earl of Selkirk, in 1656, after a courtship of three years. Finally, at the duchess's request, Charles II created Lord William as Duke of Hamilton. William and Anne settled at Hamilton Palace, their Scottish border home. Their married life bore them seven sons and three daughters, all living into adulthood, and Hamilton Palace was also filled with the chatter of many sisters and cousins of both husband and wife.

The young members of the family ate in the nurseries, but the fickle remainder had the choice of two dining rooms. The "Great High Dining Room," paneled and hung, unusually, with tapestries—they were said to retain cooking odors—had a long table that had leaves to extend it and rush-seated chairs around it. The three main meals of the day were breakfast, dinner, and supper. Breakfast differed little from that of many today: rolls, bread, eggs,

and milk, but with one or two meat dishes. The milk and butter came from the dairy, and rolls and bread were made each week in the Hamiltons' bakehouse. Considerable quantities were needed: "thirty dozen" oatmeal loaves, twenty of wheat, and several hundred wheaten rolls. They went well with the house specialty: quince marmalade. The meat dishes for breakfast were unusual to twentieth-century taste, consisting of fried chicken, roast pigeon, and mutton collops.

Dinner, served in the middle of the afternoon, was the time the family gathered for this, its main meal: usually it began with barley broth, thickened with mutton or chicken, and several fresh vegetables gathered in from the extensive kitchen gardens. Then other meat dishes, hot and cold, gave even keen appetites plenty to savor: roast leg of veal, salt beef almost every day, *fricassé* of chicken, lamb, and capons. Fish was in plentiful supply, trout and pike, and there was game and poultry in profusion. The extensive repast was followed by a sweet pudding and fresh fruit. Many biscuits had been made, with wondrous names or contents, followed by marchpanes and plum-almond. At day's end, sleep could not be considered before a light supper of a kind of porridge, or bread and milk, eggs, chicken, and perhaps a pigeon or two.

Supplies of food tumbled in profusion, almost as if from a gilded baroque cornucopia. The dairy made about three hundred pounds of butter a year, and a further large amount was offered from tenants, together with eggs—some four hundred were consumed each week by the hungry household. The carefully controlled killing of livestock meant that the several hundred rabbits and hares that were there for the gun or snare finally came to the kitchen table. Falconers brought in the multicolored plovers, duck, and partridge, and teeming numbers of pigeons could come from the large octagonal dovecots.

There were many goods that could not be grown on the estate, such as sugar, and these came in from Hamilton, Glasgow, and Edinburgh merchants, together with Spanish salt, vinegar, nutmeg, ginger, pepper, and—from a greater distance—cheese, drinking chocolate, coffee, and various green and black teas. And the duke, if he were so convivially minded, could ask his butler for one of the several wines from a Bacchus-like plenty—five hundred bottles of claret and canary and several dozen of Rhenish and

Madeira lay dusty in his cellars. Even his children each took a regular glass of wine. It needed to be supplied in a few hogsheads—each containing fifty-two and a half imperial gallons—and necessitated careful tasting before being drunk by the duke or by the duchess.[3]

In the 1720s the teeming, thriving household of the first Duke of Chandos at Cannons, Middlesex, had an even more exacting routine. The clerk of the kitchen, who was also the cook, one Mr. Pearce, was paid a salary of eighty pounds a quarter, out of which he had to provide all the butter, eggs, poultry, ducks, teal, geese, turkeys, and rabbits the hungry ducal family needed.

The duke's dining room had several tables, ordered by rank, starting with his own table, and descending to that in the servants' hall, six in total. On Sunday, July 16, 1721, a special party was held that allows us to observe the rank-

ing. At the duke's table were the dukes of Newcastle and Kingston, Lord Cadogan, and Lord Carteret. At the chaplain's table were Lady Cadogan and her second daughter. Next in dignity was that of the Gentleman of the Horse, at whose table sat the gentlemen attending the two visiting dukes and Lord Cadogan. There was then an "officer's table" for the upper members of the household staff, a "strangers' table" for visiting craftsmen, and the "servants' hall table" for lesser retainers.

A record of another ducal meal at Cannons in 1725 tells us what a dozen people were served. First there was a "brown and white soup" of mushrooms and cream, then a *fricassé*, pudding, brown ragout, and collops. Relief was provided by the carrying in of two cooked salmon, lamb, and chicken accompanied by artichokes and spinach. A silver epergne in the center of the table was filled with fruit.

However, when the duke dined by himself, or with one or two friends, he was content with a "little broath and a piece of roast mutton, a couple of chickens and some peas, between 3 and 4 o'clock."[4] The records are, alas, silent on the great parties that must have taken place when Chandos's *Kapellmeister*, George Frideric Handel, conducted the performances of his *Acis and Galatea* and *Esther* in the house chapel in 1719–1720.

The Duke of Chandos's baker looked after two of the six tables in the dining room—the Gentleman of the Horse's and the officers' tables. An usher in the hall saw to it that six gallons of small beer a day were available in the servants' hall. After meals he had to lock up any food capable of being served again and have the unfit put in baskets and given to the poor at the gates.[5] The eating of large meals was not of course confined to any period. It continued, and continues to the present day. On the birthday of Viscount Fairfax in April 1763 his friends gathered at his new town house in York. Dinner was to be served at about 4:00 P.M. It took the form of sixty-four dishes presented at the table in three courses. The service was appallingly inefficient, being done by the footmen. Thirty-four bottles of wine were consumed, as well as at least forty-eight pints of ale. Such quantities of wine were not excessive, in fact the normal daily quota for the viscount and his daughter was one bottle of sherry and two bottles of port.[6]

Conspicuous consumption could move along other defined routes, each calculated to cause a worried frown when looking at the quarter's accounts. Many Elizabethan portraits, by George Gower and others, copy those of the queen herself, in showing patrons in elaborate hats, dresses, and jewels. Whilst Lady Elizabeth Willoughby may have quarreled frequently with her astute, sharp-faced husband, all could see his wealth in the opulence of her costume (plate 38). Considerable effects were possible by the use of sharp color contrasts; in this case, black and red, with attention drawn to the sleeves by the slashed panels and bows, and with a fine, feathered hat surmounting the almost irrelevant portrayal of the face. Such paintings were "costume-pieces," in which a concern with character or likeness was incidental.

Dr. Andrew Boord, one-time physician to the court of Henry VIII, had railed against the preoccupation with fine clothes of many at court. In words he composed to accompany a woodcut of a nude male figure, wearing only a large hat, he noted:[7]

I am an Englishman, and naked I stand here,
Musing in my mind what raiment I shall wear,
For now I will wear this, and now I will wear that;
Now I will wear I cannot tell what.
All new fashions be pleasant to me;
I will have them, whether I thrive or thee.

Clothes announced wealth and status as surely as any cut-stone façades rearing up to the sky. Even so, there was often little care in choosing personal adornments, so that Petruchio, in Shakespeare's *The Taming of the Shrew* (IV.iii), speaks sharply of those:

With silken coats and caps and golden rings,
With ruffs and cuffs and farthingales and things;
With scarfs and fans and double change of brav'ry,
With amber bracelets, beads, and all this knav'ry.

To attend court in the reign of any monarch in anything other than garments of the latest luxurious fashion might be regarded as an insult to the sovereign. Conversely few would dare to outshine Queen Elizabeth. Indeed, as it was the custom at New Year for courtiers to show their indebtedness to the queen by bestowing gifts, Bess of Hardwick used the queen's tailor to make up elaborate cloaks and dresses, "fantastical things," that allowed her sovereign to shine supreme. While on a visit to court in 1590, Bess used the royal tailor for herself and her ladies, yet she still joined her cousin, Mary Scudamore, in presenting a much finer garment to the queen.[8]

The buying of necessary materials for fashionable clothes meant many profits for those who imported the exotic stuffs and for those who profited merely from the privilege of farming the duties. In 1608 additional taxes were levied on silk, and this caused Robert Cecil, Earl of Salisbury, to renegotiate his tax farming of velvets, silks, and lawns. Some of these were of dress and doublet weight, others of heavy velvet, cut in intricate relief patterns suitable for upholstering day beds and chairs. Lionel Cranfield, Lord Middleton, who was anxious for a share of Cecil's silk

135. *Attributed to Henry Walton (1746–1813). "A Gentleman at Breakfast." c. 1775. Oil on canvas,
30 x 40". Toledo Museum of Art, Ohio; gift of an Anonymous Donor*

*Still wearing his riding coat and boots, the young man has sat down, oblivious of the mud he leaves on the handsome fitted carpet.
The case-cover protects the chair, the cheval fire screen is before the fire, and the gate-leg table is pulled near to it.
Time for the newspaper, and for coffee in the country house. . . .*

duties, had equipped his wife with enough clothes to give him respect in all eyes, if not hers. When Lady Cranfield died in 1617, she left many gowns of velvet and satin in green and carnation color, as well as "one cloth of silver petticoat and a doublet of the same."[9]

The clothes bought by the first Duke of Hamilton and his wife from 1660 have been well recorded in a study by Rosalind Marshall. The duke made many purchases in Edinburgh, including "dogskin gloves for hawking, white kid gloves and purple gloves, black Spanish leather shoes, a fine beaver hat . . . and striped stuff suits and breeches

trimmed with silver looping." But when he attended court in London in 1689 to celebrate William III's birthday, it was in a "new suit with gold buttons and brocade waistcoat." As well as such fine clothes, the duke needed sets of mourning clothes, his rich velvet robe denoting him a Knight of the Garter, the oldest order of English knighthood. He wore as a Lord of the Session, "a rich black flowered velvet gown lin'd with black taffeta, garnished with rich gold loops and buttons and edged with a rich gold and black lace." Additionally, he had richly lined velvet cloaks, shirts, nightshirts, wigs, waxed boots, and cockaded hats—

and many closets in his palace to house them all.[10]

There was no decline in dress standards in the eighteenth century. By 1700 men's suits had taken on the three-piece style still worn in the twentieth century, although the components differed in appearance. Eighteenth-century suits "had long coats, waistcoats that corresponded to the vest and were worn beneath the coat, and knee-length breeches buttoned at the centre front." Elaborately embroidered suits, with the silk embroidery usually on figured velvet, were worn by wealthy men on formal occasions, particularly for attendance at court. It was not until the nineteenth century that formal clothing for men substituted dark, conservative colors for the bright hues and elaborate trimmings popular earlier,[11] although the fashion for black had been established in the era of Puritan values at the end of the sixteenth century. The less affluent had always been forced into drab colors because the exotic dyes, such as those producing scarlet, were expensive, and Castiglione's *The Courtier* (c. 1508–1518) stated that a gentleman should dress in black. The idea spread to the Protestant North, and John Calvin stated in his *The Institutes of the Christian Religion* (1535) that a Protestant's clothes should be sober, pious, and humble. The long association of black clothes with decorum and sobriety was continued at the Spanish court, which decreed in 1623 that black apparel was compulsory. Black has continued to be a color denoting these values, so that when Lord Ribblesdale asked John Singer Sargent to paint him in 1902 (plate 46) what emerged was a dark portrayal, but in hunting costume. As Albert Boime has stated, writing of this superb canvas: "Lord Ribblesdale, who measured his friends by their fashions and was fastidious about his own clothing,"[12] as befitting his position as Liberal Whip in the House of Lords. This post carried with it the duty to maintain discipline among members of his political party and brought him into contact with many who dressed equally fastidiously. The confidence from being well-dressed touches deep philosophical feelings. When the Charleston gentleman Peter Manigault was in London in 1751 he sat for his portrait to Allan Ramsay. In a letter to his wife[13] he recorded the experience and concluded: "You see my taste in Dress by the Picture, for everything there is what I had had the Pleasure of wearing often."

Women's dress was perhaps at its highest degree of elaboration within the Elizabethan period, but it was almost equally opulent in the eighteenth century. Worn over many layers of underclothing, with corsets stiffened with whalebone, the gowns "were often made with the skirt open at the front to reveal a matching or contrasting petticoat. Many gowns had wide skirts that were held out by hoops constructed of cane and wire, or whalebone held together by tapes or sewn into a petticoat. Wearing wide hoops required careful thought before a woman entered a doorway or carriage or even before she sat down. In cold weather, women wore full capes of varying lengths that frequently had a hood to pull up over the head."[14] The Countess of Mar, as painted by Sir Godfrey Kneller (plate 118), is in a silver and pink riding costume and thus stands equally alongside the grandeur of her husband's portrait (c.1715) in the distinguished green robes of a Knight of the Thistle.

Many dresses were made from silk that had been woven in France or by Huguenot weavers at Spitalfields in London. This was particularly so in the rococo period of the 1740s and 1750s. While English silks were exported to the American colonies, they formed but a small quantity against worsted and cottons. It was silk that affluent families wanted. Several lengths were woven from the designs of Anna Maria Garthwaite (1690–1763), who produced and sold an average of eighty designs each year. She observed the sinuous principles of Hogarth's "Line of Beauty"; (1753) although she had anticipated it and became an outstanding designer in the rococo style. Over a thousand of her dated silk designs survive.[15]

Apart from the use of black cloth for some costumes, dress for men and women from the sixteenth century on was usually rich in color. A variety of surface decorations, pearls, badges, beads, and gilded and raised motifs was set over fine embroidery. Warm colors advanced the subject, cooler ones made them fade shyly into the background, especially if in the presence of someone as redoubtable as Jane Austen's Lady Catherine De Burgh. Owen Jones, in his *Grammar of Ornament* (1856), noted that no "composition" could be perfect if one of the three primary colors was missing. Nevertheless much fashion in the nineteenth century in particular was in subtle pastel shades, and many effects were toned down. As late as 1884 Oscar Wilde complained, "I find an ever-growing difficulty in expressing my originality through my choice of waistcoats and cravats," in a piece he wrote on the subject of reforming men's dress in the *Pall Mall Gazette*. One of the *Gazette*'s readers had written in to suggest that Regency dress should be revived. Wilde thought such costumes too tight-fitting and preferred a "Cavalier look," with a wide-brimmed hat, cloak with a colored lining, and loose knee breeches. The last Wilde wore on his American tour, despite their being derided in *Punch* as clothes for intellectuals.

A major influence in determining what men and women's suits could look like was the invention of the sewing machine in the early 1850s. This enabled some hand-sewing to be dispensed with. Nevertheless careful measuring and hand work in the cloistered workrooms in Savile Row and elsewhere saw the emergence of dress coats, morning coats, and frock coats. The dress coat with tails was worn on formal occasions both in the day and evening. The coat had its origins as a morning coat for horse riding and eventually replaced the dress coat in day-time use. The frock coat, popular after 1815, had front edges cut straight and fell to the knee. It became the principal coat for daytime wear on less formal occasions. Across the single-breasted waistcoat could be a gold watch-chain, an "Albert" (made popular by Prince Albert, consort to Queen Victoria). The high-collared shirt had double wrist cuffs, which, from the end of the nineteenth century, were fastened with jeweled "cuff links," as opposed to the ties or covered buttons of earlier years.

With his top hat set at a rakish angle and, within the Edwardian years, a monocle on a black braid tie, a young man of breeding might well feel that any young lady of similar station should notice him. He had gone to great trouble with his new trouser press (they were available from the 1890s) to give his trousers, with a turned-up hem, a sharp center crease. Heaven forbid that she should choose to perch on his knee and make the trousers "bag" at the knee. Her own tweeds would remain crease-free even if they were announced on the label as "thorn-proof" and looked it. Edward VII was much concerned with sartorial elegance and sometimes changed clothes half a dozen times in a day. His two valets were always busy. It was the king who encouraged the use of lounge suits on social occasions, but to those of his subjects who daily attended an

136. Henry Sargent, NA (1770–1845). "The Dinner Party." c. 1821. Oil on canvas, 40 x 30". Museum of Fine Arts, Boston. Gift of Mrs. Horatio A. Lamb in memory of Mr. and Mrs. Winthrop Sargent

After working with Benjamin West in London, Sargent returned to Boston in 1797 and started to paint unusual interiors and somewhat stiff portraits. The group, all men, severe in black, exemplifies over-serious conversation among society's regents.

office, the morning coat with striped trousers was obligatory wear. Its cut was important—the trousers narrow—a "uniform" that defied change until the relaxation in dress that came from the 1920s onwards. The frock coat then disappeared into cavernous wardrobes, the morning coat was less used, and the lounge suit came more to the fore, to be varied by a flannel blazer or a sports jacket and flannel trousers. The final fillip to informality was given by the Prince of Wales (briefly Edward VIII, then abdicating to become Duke of Windsor). The prince visited America in 1921 dressed in a gray double-breasted suit. The lapels were wide, the shoes tan suede. Sir Max Beerbohm has been noted as questioning the prince's fitness for office

137. David Allan (1744–1796). "The 4th Duke of Atholl and His Family." c. 1785. Oil on canvas, 47 x 61".
His Grace, the Duke of Atholl, Blair Castle. Perthshire, Scotland

The duke is shown in Highland dress with his first wife, the Hon. Jane Cathcart, and their three children. There has been stalking
of deer as well as shooting of game: innocent hands reach for the plumed silent bird. Blair Castle, the duke's house, is white in the distance.

after he had appeared for Sunday lunch in an Italian hotel dressed in shorts.

The last word might be given on ladies' fashions in the early 1900s to Cynthia Asquith. In her *Remember and Be Glad* (1903), she gives a revealing glimpse of her uncomfortable and inconvenient "country tweeds":

> Our vast hats which took the wind like sails were painfully skewered to our heads by huge ornamental hatpins. . . the high choking collars with boned supports that dug red dints in my neck. Country house visiting—a large fraction of our time was spent in changing our clothes, particularly in winter when you came down to breakfast ready for church in your best dress. . . After church you went into tweeds. . .

With a different gown and a different dinner dress each day, no wonder that in some portraits of Victorian and Edwardian fathers the monocle has dropped out of a raised eyebrow, perhaps at the sight of the season's dress bills. There would be no correlation in a father's mind to the expenses he incurred when buying a new soft trilby hat (made popular by Edward, Prince of Wales) at James Lock in St. James's, or at Doré & Sons for his court dress and militia uniform, or at Ede, Son & Ravenscroft for his official robes as Chancellor of Oxford University. All of these advisers were able to prevent their customers committing indescribable errors, for as Mrs. Humphry noted in *Manners for Men* (1891): "If he commits flagrant errors in costume he will not be invited out very much, of that he may be certain."

In the seventeenth century it was sometimes difficult to tell what sex a child was, as boys frequently wore girl's frocks (plate 11) or scaled-down versions of adult clothes (plate 4). The practice of swaddling infants was discon-

138. *John Nash (1752–1835). "The Banqueting Room, The Royal Pavilion, Brighton," from "Views of the Royal Pavilion,"*
Brighton. 1826. Print, 14 x 20". Brighton Museum and Art Gallery

The table is set for dessert. The forty-five-foot-high dome is occupied by the representation of the foliage of a gigantic
plantain tree, some of it in three-dimensional copper. The lotus flower gas chandelier and smaller gasoliers cast their yellow
light in mirrors, on stylized serpents, and on the privileged diners at a party given by the Prince Regent.

139. *Eastman Johnson (1924–1906). "The Hatch Family." 1871. Oil on canvas, 30 x 40".*
The Metropolitan Museum of Art, New York. Gift of Frederic H. Hatch, 1926

This group portrait shows the size of the typical American upper-class family unit: grandfather, his wife, father,
his wife, three boys, three girls, and five children of indeterminate sex—a total of fifteen.

140. *"Mount Vernon, Virginia, The Mansion, from the West." 1858. Lithograph. Mount Vernon Ladies' Association*

In 1858 the Ladies' Association purchased Mount Vernon from John Augustine Washington, a great-grandnephew of George Washington, under a charter from the Commonwealth of Virginia. This lithograph was issued to be sold to raise funds for purchase and preservation of the mansion.

tinued early in the eighteenth century, although young children of both sexes were clothed in dresses with close-fitting bodices fastened at the back. There was also a fashion to paint adults and children in the costume of an earlier age. The celebrated example is Thomas Gainsborough's *Jonathan Buttall*, "The Blue Boy" of c. 1770 (Huntington Art Gallery). The picture, as with others, in costume, pose, and even paint handling is based on the 1640s models of Sir Anthony Van Dyck. Gainsborough's copy of Van Dyck's *Lord John and Bernard Stuart* (c.1639; plate 31) survives (St. Louis) and is a spirited work. George Romney's *The Clavering Children* (plate 1) is a further example attesting to the artist's study in Italy of antique Roman bas-reliefs and wall paintings.

Many aristocratic patrons, keen on displaying the long line of their ancestry, commissioned immense family trees (plate 34). The fascination continued in heraldic display on funerary monuments. In painterly terms, a portrait of Sir Thomas Holte (1571–1654) was commissioned in the 1740s by Sir Lister Holte to complete the array of family portraits.[16] The Leighs of Stoneleigh Abbey, some thirty miles away, also filled their house at the same time with newly painted "portraits of that fallen family"—"fallen" when their loyalty to the Stuart cause brought them, as it did Charles II, into eclipse, with the imprisonment of William Leigh at Gloucester Gaol.

The long spectral finger that traced the passage of most family's lives, swinging inexorably from time to time to the darkness of death itself, had many messengers in the form of mysterious ailments and crippling illness. Frequently the attempts to cure were worse than the illness itself—the prescribing of, say, "extract of Jesuit's bark" washed down with Bath or Bristol water, the application of leeches, taking essence of amber for cramp or "snayle water" and antiscorbutic drinks of gill and scurvy grass.

In July 1742 the first Duke of Chandos feared that he was going blind. The duke's physician, Dr. Wilmot, thought it safe to put a little Portuguese snuff in the corner of his eye. But the duke favored a remedy shared by his wine merchant, Mr. Taunton, who had lost the sight of one eye, and his secretary, Pudsey, whose mother had recovered her sight. Both used snuff, but there was also their recommendation that the duke first wash the eye in urine and then anoint it with viper's fat. With this and snuff, the old duke, obese and a confirmed invalid, did what he could. Perhaps his ears could still detect the high ethereal notes of Handel's "Chandos Anthems," even if he could no longer see the folio score, but had merely to follow it, with his trembling fingers finding the black notes deeply printed on the creamy handmade paper.

The less exalted Nicholas Blundell had, in his early eighteenth-century recipe book, some twenty-nine prescriptions for sore eyes. A doctor who was called to treat Blundell's elder daughter had the idea that improvement would take place if her hair was pulled out by the roots; as it seemed to work, Blundell tried it on his younger daughter.[17] Even toothache, a trivial ailment, could bring great distress to a weak child, and dreaded diseases like smallpox exacted a swift toll. Given the overriding lack of medical expertise, it was the long vigil of many faithful servants that brought some back to weak life in a darkened room. Servants' illnesses are merely recorded in relation to contamination of, or at best inconvenience to, their employers. They suffered in "influenza-type" epidemics of 1733, 1736, and the grievous one of 1741, after particularly severe winters in 1739 and 1740. In February 1733 nearly sixteen hundred people died in London in one week of violent colds, coughs, and fever.

In respect of smallpox relief seemed possible with inoculation. Lady Mary Wortley Montagu had not known that this had been described in the 1714 and 1716 issues of *Transactions of the Royal Society*. She had seen its efficacy in Turkey, and in a letter in 1716, addressed to Sarah Chiswell, she announced herself patriot enough "to bring this useful invention into fashion in England." It was to save her son, in March 1717, and she had her daughter inoculated in 1718. Princess Caroline, impressed by its success on Lady Mary's children, pushed forward the campaign—six condemned prisoners in Newgate volunteered for the operation, and after it proved successful they were given their freedom. The medical establishment railed against it. Lady Mary advocated the correct method in an essay in *The Flying Post*, but the editor suppressed her sarcastic attack on the College of Physicians. The gradual acceptance was not complete until the mid-1720s, and Lady Mary was extravagantly eulogized, in 1754, for "bringing into her own country a practice, of which ages

to come will enjoy the benefit."[18]

One of the popular conceptions of eighteenth-century aristocratic life, although it was as true earlier and later, is that everyone had gout. Dr. George Cheyne, who weighed thirty-two stone (448 pounds) was a prime victim. He described in 1720 how he cured himself in *Observations Concerning the Nature and Due Method of Treating Gout*. Gout, like many other English disorders, Cheyne stated, was due to "immoderate diet, lack of proper exercise, and an uncertain climate that closed the pores, making normal perspiration impossible." His book ran to eight editions in seventeen years. He then conducted a four-year experiment with a vegetarian diet. The result was so successful that his *Essays on Health and Long Life* (1724) ran to nine editions within thirty years of publication and was still being published in the nineteenth century. Cheyne reiterated the assault that had been made on eating beef by the seventeenth-century vegetarian Thomas Tryon. Physical culture had also been advocated by Francis Fuller in *Medicina Gymnastica* (1705). Since Cheyne "was well-known to most of the distinguished neurotics of his day: Pope, Arbuthnot, Swift, Gay and Young," his ideas received adequate publicity. In 1734 he told the young David Hume, the philosopher and historian, who was suffering from scurvy and vapors, that his ailments arose "chiefly from want of exercise, too much hard work and great plenty of food."[19] Portraits abound of the physically corpulent, who practiced, in Hume's phrase noted above, hard work, eating, and little physical movement with apparent ease, albeit occasionally with a gouty foot on a stool.

Many great households relied for the simple purgatives most of its occupants needed on various dubious recipes "filed" in a worn copy of Gerard's *Herball* or John Ray's *Historia generalis plantarum* (1681–1704). Among the 18,600 plants in 125 sections, which Ray described, there were some with remarkable curative properties. The letters of Lady Blois in the early eighteenth century record an old recipe from the seventeenth century for "Lady Brooke's purging beer." Its ingredients included scurvy grass, watercress, liverwort, rhubarb, red dock roots, raisins, and oranges.[20] There is little reason to doubt its effect, and such treatment was no respecter of the status of the patient, or of the person having the noxious duty of carrying away the chamber pot. If a patient needed spectacles, false teeth, wooden legs, or steel trusses for ruptures, all could be supplied from London. Hypochondria was a more frequent "support" to many than wood or steel. The sixth Earl of Pembroke entered all forms of notes on his health in a notebook. He abused his doctors, who found little wrong with him, and gave instructions for his burial and autopsy, "the whole interspersed with mundane business dealings":

My feet on fire, my legs and thighs the same
and mad by pains and fire in my head.
Pay'd for cheese, £2.8.0.[21]

Unless carefully maintained, the water supply and sanitary arrangements in a great house could be a cause of minor illnesses. Nevertheless, medieval monasteries (and royal palaces) had controlled and comparatively efficient systems of bringing in water from a spring, on higher ground, through conduits to the kitchen and *lavatorium* and of sluicing it through the complex drainage systems. The majority of Tudor houses had some such arrangement, but many had to rely on the gathering of rain water, on wells, or even on water brought in from a distance and stored in lead cisterns. The privies were connected by vertical shafts to sewage pits, and if water could run through the smelly shafts, it was helpful. The privies were often grouped on a cool, northern or western side of the house, in a privy tower, with parallel vertical shafts connecting to each floor, and they required constant maintenance. The recent exposure of the great drainage system at Wollaton Hall, Nottingham, shows how elaborate this had become by the end of the sixteenth century. Built on a hilltop, Wollaton had immediate problems with its water supply, and a brick-vaulted tunnel brought water from an underground spring to the basement of the house. At Hardwick Hall, water was pumped to a high cistern near the Old Hall and fed by gravity to the north side of the New Hall.

Elizabethan houses often relied on the use of close-stools, and there are many listed in the 1601 Hardwick inventory. Sir John Harington's new water-closet, which he pioneered in the 1590s, remained a mere curiosity: it may have satisfied its inventor but no imitators followed his lead. Servants still had to do much for their lords and masters without grumble and at some personal distress.

What Mark Girouard has called "The Social House"[22]—all those ready at a moment's notice for political parties, weekend breaks, and sheer relaxation—encouraged architects, surveyors, and "ingenious gentlemen" and their craftsmen to provide more facilities. Cannons was a house that from its completion in 1720 became a great showplace. Visitors were taken over the house and gardens, paying for the privilege, and the money so earned paid for mending lead pipes and for extra cleaning of brass and silver doorlocks. In 1728 the money taken for showing the gardens was used to buy more garden tools, and the house fees equipped those born to sweep and bend with brooms, mops, brushes, and sand to help in effacing visitors' footprints. It could be argued that with such houses as Cannons open to the calling public in the early eighteenth century, the "museum house" was born. The best known example of this was Horace Walpole's villa, Strawberry Hill. In 1784 he even issued a single sheet, "Rules for Visitors to Strawberry Hill." Further, each visitor needed a ticket of admission, and note was kept of those who did not finally attend. The extra demands made by visitors on a house's services caused some amendments and extensions. A water tower was erected at Carshalton House, Surrey, in 1719–1720, which consisted of a water-wheel powered by a mill stream. This turned a pump to send water to a lead cistern, which was then connected both to the house and to a bathroom at the base of the tower. It was a long step forward from Sir Francis Willoughby's plunge bath of the 1580s deep in the sandstone beneath Wollaton Hall, but comparable in convenience to a hot-and-cold water service to the early eighteenth-century "*bagnio*" at Blenheim Palace. This was under the Duchess of Marlborough's bedroom, and she could descend to it by a back staircase. The first Duke of Chandos could also boast the provision of four water closets at Cannons, with "a wainscot bath lined with ledd," as well as a bathing room with "marble cistern and marble lineings to the room."[23] However, the technological capacity to raise water—so well understood by the hydraulics experts of French formal gardening—was little used in the English country house and "running" water above ground level remained rare. Cheap labor was available to carry water to all parts of the house, with cold baths popularly regarded as effi-

141. Robert Huskisson (active 1832–1854). "Lord Northwick's Picture Gallery at Thirlestane House." c. 1846–1847. Oil on canvas, 32 x 42". City of Bristol Museum and Art Gallery

The fashion for ranging pictures high upon walls, recently revived, has a long pedigree. Against the red damask walls the gold frames are well presented. The windows have both shutters and curtains to control harmful rays of sun.

cacious to good health. There was little improvement to the system for another thirty years, and families clung to the environs of the fireplace for warmth, or stood near the various stoves popularized by smiths. Hogarth's painting of *The Assembly at Wanstead House* (1729; plate 134) shows the company taking tea and playing cards near the fireplace. The recently married couple in his *Marriage à la Mode* (National Gallery, London; c.1743) sprawl at the breakfast table drawn up close to the lighted fire. Even the nineteenth-century comforts of a cloakroom, such as that at Wightwick (plate 68), might not be sufficient on a winter day, and the tiled wonder of the Turkish bath at Sledmere (plate 70) was not for everyone.

In 1778 Joseph Bramah (1748–1814), an inventor who had worked first as a cabinetmaker in London, patented a water-closet that was a significant improvement on its gurgling predecessors. A flat trap at the bottom of the pan

was operated by a pull handle at the side and water flushed as long as this was raised. An S-bend, filled with water, had been used in a patent of 1775 by Alexander Cumming, but Bramah's trade was particularly successful because of his willingness to install his necessary devices. He was at Audley End, Essex, for this purpose in 1785, drawing the water supply from tanks placed in the roof, one at each end of the upper story of the gallery.[24] Outside privies continued to be used alongside inside conveniences, and there are many payments to joiners and others in house archives for providing new seats and doors to these, as well as for the unpleasant task of cleaning them.

Bells in houses to call servants were in use by the late seventeenth century, and the "whitesmith" (or tinsmith) Maurice Tobin of Leeds included their maintenance in his overall services to Edwin Lascelles of Harewood House, Yorkshire, in the 1770s. Tobin installed bells in the "State

142. "Herbert Butterfield in the 'French' Reception Rooms
at Cliffe Castle, Keighley, Yorkshire." c. 1884.
Photograph. Bradford Art Galleries and Museums

Mr. Butterfield was a Keighley textile manufacturer married to a French wife.
The rooms he surveys are a tour de force of the upholsterer's art.

Bed Chamber," the dressing-room, and the two drawing-rooms at Harewood in 1774.[25]

A cabinetmaker of the eminence of Thomas Chippendale only occasionally installed bell systems, but was always ready to provide the fine silk tassels and lines for the bell pulls, as well as fixing up hall lanterns with weighted pulleys, which allowed them to be lowered for servicing. Chippendale's other commissions included installing fabric roller blinds, which he obtained from a specialist; supplying painted pine or wainscot attic furniture, deal coal boxes, washing mangles, kitchen tables and chairs; fixing up battens for meat hooks; and even providing for Nostell Priory, Yorkshire, on December 24, 1768, in time for Christmas Day, "A Large strong Elm Chopping block for the kitchen," charged at 10 shillings.[26]

In two volumes on house architecture, published in 1880, J. J. Stevenson had much to say about the drawing room, which he thought should be designed for conversa-tion. The young Augustus Hare, staying in 1851 with his tutor and many other pupils in an "ugly brick villa. . . in the pretty village of Southgate, some ten miles from London," noted that: "a dinner-bell rings at half-past one, and the others come in from the drawing-room whither they adjourn before dinner, with the penalty of a penny if they lean against the mantlepiece, as they might injure the ornaments."[27] In her novel *The Diamond and the Pearl* (1849), Mrs. Catherine Gore wrote that the family spent their mornings in the library and that there were "half a dozen work tables and writing-tables being in play in various nooks of the room, with a praiseworthy activity of small-talk and Berlin wool-work."[28]

The library, scene of so many fathers interviewing nervous prospective sons-in-law, was, as Robert Kerr noted in his book on planning the gentleman's house (1864), "a sort of Morning Room for the Gentlemen." It housed all the richly gold-tooled bindings and often had a smell "as odorous as a private chapel." What the owner and his wife wanted, as they surveyed a model of their intended house, was domestic efficiency: central heating from clanking radiators and gurgling hissing steam pipes, colza oil lamps to light the array of ferns in hall and conservatory—and every other room of use, too—and Mr. Bramah's water closets. However, these innovations existed in large rambling interiors, which still required a host of domestic staff. Jane Austen's writings often stressed the word "comfort," and whilst all levels of society enjoyed it in varying measure, one might recall Benjamin Disraeli's words, in his novel *Sybil* (1845): "I was told that the Privileged and the People formed Two Nations." The domestic world of the American home, from 1750 to 1870 in particular, was one in which society tried hard to find a tenuous happiness. But Thomas Jefferson, when in Washington, found himself too worn down with "pursuits in which he took no pleasure," and he pined "for home and that society where all was peace and harmony, where one was genuinely loved and was loved by all."[29] But in the early nineteenth century many visitors to America noted that its ordinary family life seemed to be lacking in closeness and warmth. The development of the public school and the emergence of Sunday school in the first half of the nineteenth century drew attention away from the home. However, in 1855 Philip Schaff, in his *America*, published in New York, asserted that "table prayer was almost universal; and daily family worship the rule—at least in religious circles." But this was not to be for long, with the urgent forces of a new social order turning life away from the home, toward which the seventeenth-century Puritans had originally directed it.[30] And yet there were always those families with a long distinctive descent from the early colonists. Hugo Munsterberg, writing in his *Americans* (1904), noted that among the seven trustees of Harvard University there was not one "whose family has not been of service to the State of Massachusetts for seven generations." They built grand homes, occasionally complaining that it was costing them a fortune, and perhaps much of their true power, political and economic, lay in the past.

Something of what this past was really about can be observed by concentrating on the rise of life in the capital city, Washington, D.C. In 1800 Margaret Bayard Smith wrote, "I look in vain for the city and see no houses." Until the 1830s Washington was but a collection of villages located near the principal public buildings. In the late months of each fall and through the winter months the city was thrown into a whirl of social activity by the arrival of congressmen and their families. While many lived in boardinghouses or hotels, a few leased houses. People tried to gather around those of similar regional origins and to abide by a firm schedule: breakfast in the house of Lewis Machen (1790–1863), Clerk of the Senate, was at seven, dinner at two, and supper at seven.

Many choices of food were available if there was money to purchase it. By 1822 Washington had at least seven professional pastry chefs who supplied not only elaborate desserts for parties, but more ordinary food for those households of boardinghouses with no kitchen or an inadequate one. By the 1820s large evening teas were fashionable, and Thomas Cosnett's *The Footman's Directory*, published in London in 1826, was meant to assist with advice on its serving. Ceramics, glass, and silver were ordered from England or France, with use of new three-pronged forks betokening a concern to be up-to-date: the 1801 inventory of the White House included "18 French forks." Every anxious mother must have hoped that her son or daughter was not one of those castigated in John Moore's *The Young Gentleman and Lady's Monitor*, issued in New York in 1792. "An uncouth diner was one who: eats with his knife. . . picks his teeth with his fork, rakes his mouth with his finger, and puts his spoon which has been in his throat a dozen times into the dish again." Many city houses were so designed that sliding doors between adjacent public rooms could be opened to create the setting for large parties. A cold supper would be laid out in buffet fashion in the late evening and on the white napery cloth would be a silver mirrored plateau in which dishes were reflected as they sat in a ring around the centerpiece. There would be additional groupings of figurines and flowerpots placed amid the array of cakes, puddings, and jellies; and if the party was grand, there would be ice cream, which was available by the early nineteenth century in every fashionable home.

The Washington social scene, with its emphasis on appearance and on manners, centered around the president's house, with its grandest receptions on New Year's Day and the Fourth of July. Foreign representatives could meet members of the government, diplomats, and other visitors, and be invited on to regular drawing-room parties and even to the occasional spectacle. The young Baltimore belle Betsy Bonaparte was much fêted after her marriage to the younger brother of Napoleon, and even more so when the marriage was annulled in 1806. Her appearance at the Madison White House in a fashionable but transparent Grecian-style gown shocked many of the female guests. It was a far remove from the *Canons of Etiquette* Thomas Jefferson had issued in December 1803: "In social circles all are equal," he wrote. "No precedence . . . of any one over another, exists in either right or patience, at dinners, assemblies, or any occasions."[31]

The approbation of neighbors was best secured by the latest furniture, carpets, and curtains being "from London" or created by craftsmen who had received a London training. It was a short step to copying the best articles and investing them with regional variations. Eliza Wainwright noted in 1831, after a visit to Manhattan, that the furniture in New York was "too shiny and showy for my taste" and inferior she felt to that of her native Boston.[32] It was a judgement as fitted to any American lady as to her English counterpart: the decoration of houses in both countries was at its most successful when, by collaborative effort, it produced a comfortable and enduring home.

CHAPTER IX

"Forward to Posterity"

People will not look forward to posterity,
who never look backward to their ancestors.

Edmund Burke, "Reflections on the
Revolution in France," 1790.

By 1897 Queen Victoria had reigned for sixty years, a long tenure that could not have been foreseen even by her Golden Jubilee in 1887. The prime minister at that time, the Marquis of Salisbury, remarked how the queen had "bridged over that great interval which separates old England from new England." The transition to the new England throughout the century was a process that had been continuous, had quickened pace toward 1900, and had separated, inexorably, each generation more completely from the preceding one. Traditional authority, awesome in its wide-ranging complexity, was being set aside by the force of new observations and opinions. And yet there was still hesitation, an uncertainty, that characterized the start of the twentieth century. As Anthony Trollope[1] had asked in 1868:

The roar of our machinery, the din of our revolutions, echoes through the solar system; can we not, then,

make up our minds whether our progress is a reality and a gain, or a delusion and a mistake?

The English gentleman, perhaps fresh from a tour of duty in the far sultry reaches of the empire, was dimly aware of some of this uncertainty. As a young blood he had been part of the challenge expressed in Rudyard Kipling's well-known poem of 1889, "The White Man's Burden:"

Take up the White Man's burden,
Send forth the best ye breed
Go, bind your sons to exile
To serve your captives' need

But at least he was home, his tropical whites abandoned, and already weary of his father's nostalgic talk of the day

134. John Singer Sargent, RA (1856–1925). "Sir Frank Swettenham." 1904. Oil on canvas, 50 x 40".
The National Portrait Gallery, London

when Queen Victoria had been pronounced Empress of India. He was ready more to overuse the town house, have his portrait painted by Mr. Sargent, and sing such patriotic songs as "Land of Hope and Glory" at the top of his voice in his mahogany-lined bathroom. Mr. Elgar, who might have come to dinner once or twice, had also composed the stirring "Pomp and Circumstance" marches to which his feet were ever tapping in time. Yet he still found some difficulty in understanding why his sister wanted to join movements concerned with emancipation and seeking the vote, and why there was so much talk of heavier taxation for the rich. He would also have to suffer a well-written leader in *The Times* by an old school chum titled "The Sun Is Sinking on the Empire," which followed with very disturbing views on the indigenous nationalism rising swiftly in all the white dominions. Certainly he had grandparents who "quelled" Africans or with difficulty brought Christianity to them, all too often on the orders of zealous, if misguided, superiors.[2] An old order was changing.

The story of imperial expansion is, however, not to my purpose here except to record many a gentleman's energetic part in it all. Everyone, including the aristocracy, was changing as they tried, from the 1870s on, to come to terms with the "Great Depression." "Class" asserted itself selfishly and stylishly, with the most advantageous circle that of the Marlborough House set, the friends surrounding Edward, Prince of Wales at his London house off St. James's.[3] They gossiped, talked of clothes, holidays, and horses, and perhaps even smiled at the prince's voluminous Inverness tweed cape and tweed knickerbockers made by his tailor, Henry Poole of 33 Savile Row. Beatrice Webb commented on the strain—albeit a lighter one than perspiring in Africa or India—of being at court, "the riding in the Row, and attending the lunches and dinners, the dances and crushes, Hurlingham and Ascot, not to mention amateur theatricals and other sham philanthropic excrescences."[4] Commerce held sway, even if at times precariously, and by 1896 over a quarter of the peerage held company directorships. Titles went to bankers, ironmasters, brewers, or those making armaments, so broadening the makeup of "society." And they, "society," moved as such, deserting London at the end of July, after the Marlborough House ball—to Cowes for the yachting and to the grouse moors of Yorkshire and Scotland for the beginning of shooting on the "glorious twelfth" of August. The new word of the 1870s was "the weekend," and the growth of the railways (plate 112) made the rounds of country-house visiting possible, with, as H.G. Wells later noted, only two rules: "No subsequent reporting of the free speech that was customary, and no attempts to profit later from the friendly contacts that were made."[5]

On the evening of January 22, 1901, Queen Victoria died at Osborne, surrounded by all the children and grandchildren depicted so often in canvases by Winterhalter and in daguerreotype photographs in London salons. The queen and the nineteenth century had gone hand in hand, and the country looked with unease to her successor, to King Edward VII, then fifty-nine and too long the Prince of Wales. He was instantly recognizable: a bearded and stout figure. He had traveled widely, spoke at least four languages, and enjoyed a cosmopolitan life. Married in 1863 to Queen Alexandra, the daughter of Christian IX of Denmark, he nevertheless retained complex associations with at least ten other women, a fact Alexandra accepted with silent detachment. The king loved the company of women: he was a regular country-house visitor. Few of his liaisons may have had a really serious side to them, although they were as ill-advised and raffish as his racing losses, his late-night traveling in hansom cabs, or his penchant for tossing his crested dice on every green baize table. "The Prince of Wales is not respected," condemned Mr. Gladstone, and it was a penalty he paid for his pleasure. As Wilfred Blunt succinctly put it in 1920:[6]

> Both King Edward and Solomon had that knowledge of women, which, as we know, is the beginning of wisdom, or at least which teaches tolerance for the unwisdom of others.

Nevertheless, with the grudging admiration of all those who could not do likewise, at least openly, the king came to the throne, with authority and free from his mother's outbursts against him. Before the knee-bending audience of the ermined peers of his realm, he opened Parliament in 1901, driving there in George III's state coach, a horse-snorting, creaking spectacle of great magnificence not seen in the forty years since the queen and Prince Albert had commenced their reign in 1861. And yet he was easily

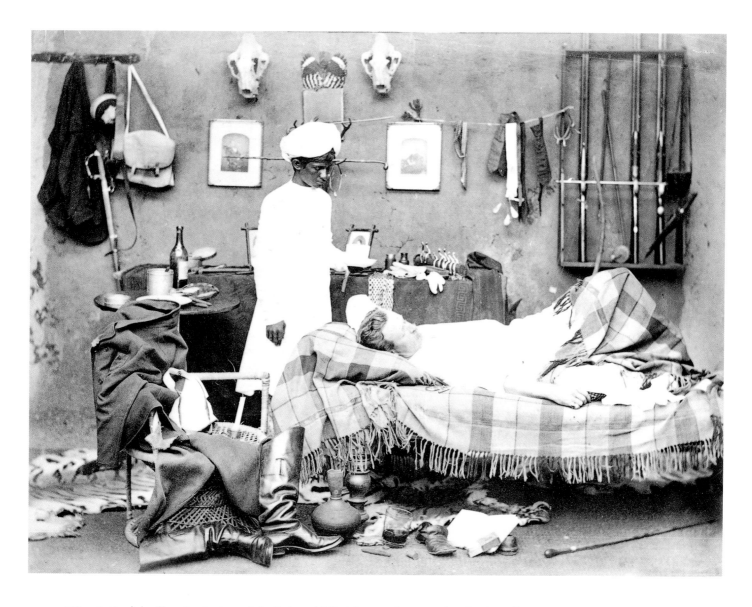

135. *An English officer in the days of the Raj. c. 1870. Photograph. Oriental and India Office Collections, The British Library*

After a hard day's work in unaccustomed heat, the colonial gentry expected to rest, but the servant was never allowed to be far away.
The true gentleman took care to minister to, not abuse, his staff.

bored and saw little reason why he should pass time with those who could not make him laugh and talk, or to whom he could say nothing personal. He enjoyed dining with his friends, and they in their turn gave some of the most lavish dinner parties ever seen.[7] There was the group of friends with whom the king was seen and was visiting as regularly as when he had been prince. Apart from the noble households this included many he met at the London gaming clubs, such as White's, the Turf, and the Marlborough. High society also included a group whose structure was based entirely on birth and tradition, who eschewed the admission of the merely wealthy to their drawing rooms.

Finally, there was a smart set, a mere fragment of the whole, but well satirized in Sandy Wilson's version of Valmouth:

Do you remember Coko Foulkes
Flossie St. Vincent and Bimbo Stookes
Twirly Rogers and Bushy Ames?
They all of them had such expressive names,
And Monkey Trotter in guardsman's rig
Doing a rather suggestive jig.

In *Great Morning* (1948), one of the four volumes of Sir

136. Frank and William James on safari in East Africa. 1885. Glass-plate photograph.
The Edward James Foundation, West Dean, Sussex

Frank and his two brothers were the first Europeans to enter the interior of Somaliland. After inheriting a fortune made in North America,
they explored Africa and published their experiences in "The Unknown Horn of Africa" (1886).

Osbert Sitwell's autobiography, that perceptive writer describes the London season before the Great War when the Edwardian age was enjoying its heyday:

Never had there been such a display of flowers. . . profusion of full-blooded blossoms, of lolling roses and malmaisons, of gilded, musical-comedy baskets of carnations and sweet peas, while huge bunches of orchids, bowls of gardenias and flat trays of stephanotis lent to some houses an air of exoticism. Never had Europe seen such figs, nectarines and strawberries at all seasons, brought from their steamy tents of glass. Champagne bottles stood stacked on the sideboards. . . and to the rich, the show was free.

Yet with the outbreak of war there could be no dance-pirouetting transition from the years of Edward VII to those of George V. Fun, gracious living, a great show of

plate on the mahogany buffet, cigar-smoke-puffed indifference to the poor and the starving at home and in the empire may be the perception of Edwardian life. The truer one was perhaps something near what Price Collier, an American observer, wrote in 1909:[8]

In England. . . when a man has made wealth and leisure for himself, or inherited them from others, he is deemed a renegade if he does not promptly offer them as a willing sacrifice upon the altar of his country's welfare.

When James Bryce (afterward Lord Bryce) was British ambassador to the United States in 1909 he gave support to Collier's view:

The altruistic spirit, now everywhere visible in the field of private, philanthropic work seems likely to

137. Lord and Lady Curzon on a tiger hunt. c. 1902. Photograph. Oriental and India Office Collections, The British Library

George Nathaniel Curzon, Lord (afterwards Marquess) Curzon of Kedleston, and his American-born wife,
the daughter of a Chicago millionaire, became Viceroy (and Vicereine) of India in 1899. Far from his Derbyshire
home at Kedleston, he found that there were tigers, rather than foxes, to hunt.

spread into the field of civic action.

The "richer and educated classes," he noted, had a "warmer feeling of sympathy and a stronger feeling of responsibility" for those less fortunate sections of the community.[9] Society in fifty years had changed at a rapid pace and the king had played his part in that.

The men we loved have all passed on
Like the world we knew, they are dead and gone.

The king's temperament and his rumbustious personality were a wild corrective to the strictures of the nineteenth century. It might well be that all those saddened

at his death, on May 6, 1910—grave titled friends, head dipped over an unlit pipe, and all those of poorer station— knew that he had, amid his careless laughter, brought a touch of greatness before the sharp decline in national and private life.

The great threat to Britain's national security from the German invasion of Belgium led on August 4, 1914, to a declaration of war on Germany, with Britain supported by all the Dominions and India. The cold hard columns of casualty statistics give little indication of what it all meant in human suffering and despair—the death of someone almost every minute. What could Eton and Oxford do in the training of any young man that gave greater immunity than to the grocer's son? All were leveled, all were recalled by the sharp stringency of poems by Wilfred Owen, Siegfried Sassoon, Ivor Gurney, Rupert Brooke, and Isaac Rosenberg. Gurney's poem "To His love" echoes that distraught moment, as the fated telegram came to the silver salver of many a country-house hall:

Cover him, cover him soon!
And with thick-set
Masses of memoried flowers
Hide that red wet
Thing I must somehow forget.

Indeed, Gurney was driven mad, eventually, by the wounding, gassing, and shellshock he had endured in 1917 and spent the last fifteen years of his short life (1890–1937) in various mental hospitals.[10]

The sharp cataclysmic impact of war's rigorous division of men into officers, noncommissioned officers, and "privates," the men in the ranks, confirmed class barriers. Some of these were submerged when war was over by the seeming trivia of life, of which a preoccupation with sport was one. This had become a laudable pursuit in England after about 1850. It encouraged the cult of the amateur, the code of fair play, of no argument with the rules, and of smiling back the salt tears of defeat. Gentlemen had always indulged in hunting, shooting, and horse racing. Now their staffs, discarding the morning coat obligatory to being on duty "above stairs," could show prowess at bare-fist boxing and at cricket.

Some games demanded additional dedication: racquets, real tennis, yachting, and Rugby and Eton fives. They were also exclusive to gentlemen, whereas almost anyone could excel at bowls, football, and wrestling. Sport polarized somewhat into different games, played by those who had enough money and those without. Edward VII, who enjoyed sporting activities, indulged in horse racing and yachting, and in 1909 his colt Minoru won the Derby. The royal patronage led to considerable interest in bloodstock breeding and to interest from America, and elsewhere, in riding to win. With the American jockeys Tod Sloan and Danny Maher holding the title of champion jockey for several years before the First World War, they even defied the traditional English riding stance, instead using a "monkey crouch," sitting almost on the horse's neck.

And watching all of it would be peers such as the Earl of Lonsdale, standing in his phaeton—he had a retinue of yellow cars too—with his long cigar drawing gently on the racetrack air.

Horse racing had long been a reason to gamble. The upper classes could bet off the course on credit; cash on the course was needed from workingmen—and betting was illegal if done by cash elsewhere. In 1902 the House of Lords Select Committee on Betting had recorded the spending on gambling of some five million pounds a year. Even the University Boat Race on the Thames between Oxford and Cambridge attracted attention from the press in 1906 over gambling on the result. This annual contest between two teams had started in 1829 and moved to its present course in 1845. Raced annually over a distance of four and a quarter miles in a little more than seventeen minutes, it tests every stretching sinew. While statistics abound about the heaviest, the lightest, the longest, it is interesting in the upbringing of gentlemen that the 1905 boats contained ten Old Etonians between them.

In India most officers took to playing polo, guiding nimble ponies, mainly with knee pressure, to good positions to make their energetic, near-diagonal swipes. In international polo England was represented usually by cavalry officers, pitting themselves against superior American teams. On the eve of the First World War, however, the English team brought back, for the last time, the prestigious Westchester Cup. Considerable resources were lavished on the regimental teams, but in time polo was taken up privately by many young gentlemen and is still a highlight of weekend sport at Cowdray Park and elsewhere. Again a Prince of Wales has been a leading figure in establishing a trend.[11]

Every age throws up new games that subsequent generations do much to refine and improve. Lawn tennis, invented in Britain and played from 1873, grew in popularity with the famed championship games at Wimbledon from 1877 and those of the Davis Cup, starting in Boston in 1900. Croquet, with English and American variations (plate 128), had become popular on country-house lawns during the 1860s, with the All-England Croquet Club at Wimbledon becoming the "All-England Croquet and Lawn Tennis Club" in 1877. Golf grew gradually into a world sport for men and women, and soon the men at least were

138. *Maxim's flying machine at Baldwyn's Park. 1895. Photograph. Trustees of The Science Museum, London*

On 5 July 1895 a splendid posed group of some 26 gentlemen of the Royal Aeronautical Club were photographed in front of Sir Hiram Maxim's wired and canvas wonder of a flying machine. Sir Hiram, gentleman circumnavigator, is seated in the center.

hitting out, dressed in neat Norfolk jackets with vented back flap pockets, breeches, stockings, and a very English cloth cap. The earliest women's golf was played at first in Scotland, but it spread rapidly to England, and in 1893 the Ladies Golf Union was formed. Lady golfers wore heavy tweed skirts, which reached almost to the grass, with straw boater hats perched precariously on piled-up hair. As for hockey, cricket, rugby, association football, and athletics, they occupied every school and university's game fields, an enthusiastic mix of energy and fun. As such they were largely of alien interest to the conscious aesthetes, a small group, admittedly, but guardians of literature and music, those of high temperament and fashionable

prominence and the friends of Evelyn Waugh, the Sitwells, Harold Acton, Cecil Beaton, or Virginia Woolf.

It is easy to imagine, in an unguarded moment, that the interwar years were one round of wild parties. Evelyn Waugh (1903–1966), after attending Lancing College and Oxford, became a full-time writer in 1928. Two years later his wife left him: he converted to Roman Catholicism, but in the same year, 1930, he wrote his novel *Vile Bodies*. It has much to say of wild parties; but in a fine balance of wit and perception, its conclusion tells of the coming of another world war without answering the question between whom the war is fought.

Waugh's 1930 novel attracted the sharp criticism of

Wyndham Lewis (1882–1957) in his own novel *The Apes of God*, published also in 1930. It is a satire on the Bloomsbury group but was aptly described as a "massacre of the insignificants." Lewis had gone to Rugby School but had then studied at the Slade School of Art, becoming a war artist and a founder of the Vorticist group of artists. In their various ways both Lewis and Waugh railed against the struggles between "civilization" and the "barbarians," with Waugh's magnum opus, *Brideshead Revisited* (1945) largely losing him his literary reputation because many were outraged "at feeling," as he put it, "God introduced into my story." From this point on Waugh attacked the "barbarians," Hopper and Mottram in his *Brideshead*, American culture in *The Loved One* (1948), and Fido Hound and Ludovic in *Officers and Gentlemen* (1955) and *Unconditional Surrender* (1961).

It was possible for gentlemen to travel much further afield in pursuit of pleasure, or, more rarely business, by the phenomenal growth in use of the motorcar, and, to a certain extent, the private aeroplane. The liberal social critic C. F. G. Masterman wrote in 1910:[12]

When every man of a certain income has purchased a motorcar that definite increase of expenditure will be accepted as normal. But life will be no happier and no richer for such an acceptance; it will merely have become more impossible for those who are unequal to the demands of such a standard.

Motorcars came to be symbols of speed and status racing "with incredible velocity and no apparent aim" (as Masterman had it) down the country lanes in England. Even Mr. Toad, in Kenneth Grahame's *The Wind in the Willows* (1908), was as reckless as any, and W.E. Henley's *A Song of Speed* (1903) captured a journey in the Mercedes car of Alfred Harmsworth, owner of the newspaper *The Daily Mail*:

Speed as a chattel:
Speed in your daily
Account and economy
One with your wines
And your books, and your bath—
Speed!

Speed as a rapture:
An integral element
In the new scheme of Life.

As early in its history as January 1906 *The Times* could state: "The motorcar is everywhere and there are few [Parliamentary] candidates who do not appreciate its advantages and invoke its aid."

But intending voters were conveyed at a very decorous pace. The Motor Car Act of 1903 had established the speed limit at twenty miles per hour, as well as requiring registration, numbering, and lights for nighttime use, although one has the feeling that Mr. Harmsworth and many others were already exceeding twenty miles an hour. By the First World War there were over 132,000 car owners, many bent on doing the same.[13] Some cars, such as the Rolls Royce "Silver Ghost," were expensive (costing 1,000 pounds) from the start—yet the Earl of Lonsdale had a fleet of yellow ones in which his shooting parties could be conveyed to the butts, with wicker picnic baskets creaking with the weight of the contents.

In 1900 J. T. C. Moore-Brabazon (later Lord Brabazon of Tara) took off a day from Harrow School to see the start of the 1,000-mile test for 65 cars. He was later to become an addict of both motor racing and flying. For his truancy he had to copy out 1,000 lines of Greek verse, one for each trial mile. But soon he was racing on the Brooklands track and flying from Hendon, with the first pilot's license to be issued. Indeed, in 1903 the Wright brothers had startled many a peer and others such as Brabazon at their morning toast and marmalade when the papers carried news of their flight at Kitty Hawk in North Carolina in a machine heavier than air. H. G. Wells, noting the following flight of Louis Blériot across the English Channel, on July 25, 1909, saw that Britain was no longer an island fortress secure behind the surrounding sea. Land, sea, and now the air were conquered.[14]

Despite these great advances in transport history there were still many who seemed to languish in days gone by, in the age of the horse tram and horse ploughing on their estates. In his diary entry for July 1906, George Sturt, a Farnham wheelwright, recorded that "meadow grass grows better after the scythe than after the mowing machine." Despite the announced horrors each few days from the

139. Edward, Prince of Wales, and Lord Montagu in a Daimler 12 motorcar. 1899. Photograph.
The National Motor Museum, Beaulieu

The prince, cigar in hand, is at the wheel. The chugging car would need to be handled with care, and there was little protection against inclement weather. But it smacked of things to come. Almost as soon as he became king (1901), Edward could witness the machine's improving image and technical advancement.

battlefront, many an elderly peer, his son far away on the Flanders battlefields, would wince at his daughter's swift emancipation. The magazine *Punch*, which had started as an English humorous weekly periodical in 1841 employing the best satirical writers and illustrators, had published a verse in the autumn of 1904:

Time was, not very long ago,
When Mabel's walking skirt
Trailed half-a-yard behind to show
How well she swept the dirt.

But "short and sweet" are in again;
No more the grievance rankles,
For Mabel's now curtailed her train
And shows her dainty ankles.

And lying beneath "Mabel's" bedside table, hidden by a piece of Berlin wool-work, had not his wife found the first two volumes of Havelock Ellis's *Studies in the Psychology of Sex* (1897–1899), which Dean Inge had solemnly buried as being "unwholesome," or D.H. Lawrence's new novel *The Rainbow* (1911), against whose author a charge of obscenity had been brought? Soon she would be trying to join the suffragettes (set up as the women's social and political union in 1903 by Mrs. Emmeline Pankhurst) and agitating for the vote. Of most rich women, Masterman wrote in 1909, "What did they find to do with their time?" Mrs. Pankhurst found them a vocation, well away from the fate of H. G. Wells's heroine, Ann Veronica, in his novel of that name (1909):

"Then I suppose when I have graduated I am
to come home."
"It seems the natural course."
"And do nothing?"
"There are plenty of things a girl can do at home."

There was homemade music on Sir Edward Burne-Jones's new "Orpheus" pianos, the afternoon callers to tea, and. . . well, reading. It was not to be until 1930 that Vita Sackville-West got the feeling right in her novel, *The Edwardians*—a feeling of pride in a heritage, a family, and a house. It was a world of often idle privilege, but at "Chevron" (Vita's family home in Kent of Knole), Sebastian stood on its roof:

Acres of red-brown roof surrounded him, heraldic beasts carved in stone sitting at each corner of the gables. Across the great courtyard the flag floated red and blue and languid from a tower. Down in the garden, on a lawn of brilliant green, he could see the sprinkled figures of his mother's guests, some sitting under the trees, some strolling about; he could hear their laughter and the tap of the croquet mallets.

In the "Indian Summer" of it all, "the house was really as self-contained as a little town":

The carpenter's shop, the painter's shop, the forge, the sawmill, the hot-houses, were there to provide whatever might be needed at a moment's notice.

And like an "Indian Summer," scenes like that would go before din and misery. And when the war was over "society" had ceased almost to have any meaning at all. It has been estimated that in 1919 alone over one million acres of land changed hands in Britain, to be exceeded by four more hectic years of sales and changes of ownership. Combined with the depression in agricultural activity, with death duties, increasing costs of house maintenance, and a paucity of eligible sons to carry on the line, war had been the final enveloping chaos with significant change in its bloody wake.

An army commission had automatically made one a gentleman, whatever the pedigrees recorded, as did a degree at one of the old universities, or taking Holy Orders in the Anglican Church. With the war over there were many ex-officers without money, with no rich relatives to support them or to "export" them elsewhere. Slump and counter-slump jerked England toward economic depression. The prime minister, Lloyd George, had promised a land fit for heroes, but he spent too much money on houses, schemes for roads, and education. The United States alone was owed more than 900 million pounds and as a "great creditor nation it did not wish to cancel the obligation." Yet, serious as the situation was, the country longed for relaxation, to bask unheeding in the "full sunshine of Peace" and to believe that crime, sex, and folly were better ingredients to provide and entertain than religious instruction.

The moneyed and young railed against restrictions in the 1921 Licensing Act. Cocktail drinking was the most reprehensible form of alcoholic abuse, declared the *Practitioner* magazine: Nightclubs proliferated to defeat the act, which stated drinking glasses had to be removed at 12:30 P.M.—all were well attended, whether squalid or expensive, or both.

Recreation was hard work, with late hours, and it was becoming fashionable to invest it all with the laconic disillusion of Noel Coward's songs, or T.S. Eliot's "Love-Song of J. Alfred Prufrock":

For I have known them all already, known them all—
Have known the evenings, mornings, afternoons,
I have measured out my life with coffee-spoons.

For the leisured modern young man what remained but to embrace the "Scarlet Woman" of the Catholic Church, as Evelyn Waugh, G. K. Chesterton, and the Honorable Evan Morgan, the inspirer of the Bright Young People, had done. Even the Prince of Wales, the future Edward VIII for a few days, had taken to dancing at the Kit-Cat night-club, but that was acceptable; at least thirty peers were known to be members.[15]

Whilst these could be complicated topics at a very late breakfast, what was preoccupying the heads of many great households more was the General Strike of 1926, which had demonstrated Britain's dependence on organized labor, particularly the miners. Wicked capitalists, condemned by Karl Marx, were now almost a thing of the past. The newspapers in the early 1920s had made "wicked capitalists" of a number of landowners who drew royalties from mines and rents from the dilapidated houses of the miners. But the agricultural side of estates was hardly helping to support them. Death duties were 50 percent of a property's value. If a family suffered the loss of three heads of the house in rapid succession very little of an estate could remain unsold. Many peers therefore converted their estates to limited liability companies. This was an imaginative and well-advised move from estate to company, from private to public. It undoubtedly helped save some estates from having to demolish houses or to disperse pictures and libraries.

The companies so formed had the power to trade in farming, fishing, mining, oil and shale works, quarrying, forestry, and shooting. The eager quest for oil, so vital in the growth of many of America's great families, had begun in England in 1919. But perhaps too much was left in the hands of the lawyers, and they could but grimace as the Wall Street crash of 1929 splashed black, or more significantly, red, across every banner headline. As Americans had been in the way of taking over the Scottish grouse-moors shoots each year, so "paying" for young Harold's fees at Harrow, income was immediately in threat, with ruin for sporting-gun manufacturers too. Every house in the land tried to keep up with the news, and the greater ones could still take several newspapers to read while eating Mrs. Post's new cereals. The austere front page of *The Times*, at almost any point in 1933, could announce that half the population of Glasgow was unemployed. The accounts of severe deprivation culminated in 1936 and were epitomized in George Orwell's *The Road to Wigan Pier*, the year also of the start of the Spanish Civil War (to which so many idealists felt drawn, and compellingly so) and, in January, of the death of George V.

Diana (Lady Duff) Cooper records in the second volume of her enchanting autobiography, *The Light of Common Day* (1959), how she attended, in 1936, the king's lying-in-state at Westminster, as so many other of her titled friends did:

> Through a secret door one could slide into the centre of the moving masses, and there I would lead, in patriotic and monarchic pride, any foreign friends visiting London. . . . The sentinels at the four corners of the bier were the dead King's four sons. . . . We saw his body laid in the vault at Windsor, and life begin again at Westminster.

Duff Cooper and Diana had stayed, often enough, with the prince, now Edward VIII, at his royal folly near Virginia Water, Fort Belvedere. Here with "His Royal Highness in plus-twenties with vivid azure socks," and "Wallis [Mrs. Simpson] admirably correct and chic," they played golf in the afternoons, but the social life centered around the swimming pool. Tea was at 6:30 P.M., cocktails at 8:30 P.M., and dinner at 10:00 P.M. "The Prince changed," said Diana, "into a Donald tartan dress-kilt with an immense white leather purse in front, and played the pipes round the table after dinner, having first fetched his bonnet." They "reeled" to bed at 2.00 A.M. When she got back to London later in the year, from foreign travels with Duff Cooper, it was to news, on December 10, of the king's abdication and a "world of tears and sighs." On December 11 Edward left England in the destroyer *Fury* after a reign of but 325 days. The peerage of England, shocked to a man, bent loyal to the new king, Edward's brother George, on May 12, 1937, the same day that had been fixed for Edward VIII's coronation. It was left to the American millionaire's son Neil Vanderbilt, who had secured a ticket for the Westminster Abbey ceremony, to mutter a commentary into a pocket transmitter. With the message picked up by his trailer parked a few hundred yards away, his was the only direct transmission to the United States—an amazing scoop as no one but the British Broadcasting Corporation had been allowed to be at the abbey.[16] None of the ermine-robed peers and peeresses, with ample space to conceal a veritable box full of valves and wires, had ever felt constrained to do the same: it was, as *The Times* of the following day remarked, "another example of American initiative before privilege."

At 11:15 A.M. on the morning of September 3, 1939, the prime minister, Neville Chamberlain, saddened, (and misunderstood by posterity) announced that his country was at war with Germany. Total war had thus come to every son sitting in south-facing sitting rooms, looking across the acres of many a Brown or Repton landscape, as it had to those in the parlors of every humble home.

The young, newly commissioned officers or pilots, with many social levels between them erased by the need to fight the common enemy, were eager to be in the fight.[17] What is more to my purpose is to isolate one or two incidents that show how the families themselves reacted to destruction of their patrimony. And where better to begin than in the published diaries of James (Jim) Lees-Milne,[18] who, as first Historic Buildings Secretary to the National Trust, motored to inspect many great houses in the wartime years. First, on June 20, 1942, he visited Culverthorpe in Lincolnshire, "in a deplorable condition owing to the troops stationed in the house all the war":

> The splendid hall has been partitioned into an orderly room and officers' mess with passage in between. The capitals of the columns have been boarded up, and the Wootton panels shrouded under canvas. I noticed a great crack in the Hauduroy painted ceiling over the stairs. Many glass panes are broken and the surrounds of one window are blackened by a projecting stovepipe.

Nevertheless, it all survived, due to the dedication of its owners. On August 24, 1943, Jim Lees-Milne visited Spencer House, overlooking Green Park in London:

> The house suffered most severely from the bad raid in April 1941 when I watched the corner house, which also belonged to Lord Spencer, burn to the ground. Incendiary bombs have destroyed parts of the top floor, and blast has torn away the stucco from many ceilings.

The seventh Earl Spencer had moved away many fine chimneypieces and doorcases to Althorp, his Northamp-tonshire seat, as war loomed. Now part of the protected structure of that house, they could not be returned and have been copied faithfully and to the highest standards in the immaculate restoration (1988–1990) conducted for the house's present owner, Lord Rothschild.

England has a uniqueness in the wide-ranging nature of its class system, with its institutions of hereditary and life peers. But there are "gentlemen" in each part of the world, and all might have agreed that the United States Secretary of State George C. Marshall was one when he initiated the "Marshall Plan" of "food and other essential products" to be sent to Europe in 1943 and set up a special organization to administer it. Country houses and estates limped along as the Welfare State increased in scope and benefit, with the economic sacrifices equalized to the best of the government's ability. With an integrity of character, allied to toughness and sagacity, Prime Minister Clement Attlee and President Harry S. Truman saw that peace evolved and the economy strengthened. But "the affluent society" seemed always to be just around the next corner, even if J. K. Galbraith's influential and widely read book of that title (1958) preached solutions.

In financial terms, the British Treasury, mindful of the Keynesian lesson that economic depression can be controlled by careful manipulation of credit and investment, tried "expansion without inflation." But the credit squeeze of 1959 was unpopular, and in the budget of 1961 Selwyn Lloyd made concessions to surtax-payers (which by the extent of landed assets and income included many owners of great houses), that were vigorously denounced. Galbraith's "affluent society" could not take slow growth and rising prices. Unemployment rose and there seemed no long-term set of principles to guide policy. Improvement, if it came, was slow to succeed.[19]

In 1974, a seminal exhibition, *The Destruction of the Country House*, took place at the Victoria and Albert Museum, London. In a series of essays in the valuable catalogue, Sir Michael Culme Seymour wrote about "The House and the Estate." He noted how a house and its estate are interlocked "in the continuing life they represent," and how they remain an integral part of that scene if at the center of estate and community life." "But divorced from estate and its active agricultural business, it becomes more a museum or an object of the past." The problems could be acute.

As early as 1813 the poet Byron had written, in his "Elegy on Newstead Abbey," about his family house and of its symbolic decline:

Hail to thy pile! more honored in thy fail,
Than modern mansions in their pillared state;
Proudly majestic frowns they vaulted hall,
Scowling defiance on the blasts of fate.

The seeming necessity of ridding a crippled estate of the burden of maintaining a fine house led to at least a dozen of them disappearing each year from 1920 to 1955. National pride was low, and the toll an indictment to the English conscience, comparable to the dissolution of the monasteries in the sixteenth century. Unheeding of consequence, the actions of a mere lifetime could erase a precious institution of some five centuries.

Fortunately there were those who recognized the part houses could play in education, recreation, and increasing leisure. They were the family houses in long family continuity, even if the croquet lawn had succumbed to the earthy hillocks of the humble mole and the tennis court, long since replaced by a rich crop of thrusting weeds. Owners recognized they were stewards for the community, trying to share with others the experience of keeping great treasures in the houses they maintained, often at considerable sacrifice to themselves and their families.

In the autumn of 1990 the Earl of Shelburne, president of the Historic Houses Association noted:[20] "During the 1980s two hundred and fifty listed buildings with supporting agricultural land were put on the market."

The majority of these sales were caused by escalating maintenance costs. A conservative estimate is 100 pounds (175 dollars) per annum for every square foot that needs to be maintained. Lack of financial help will cause owners "either to sell assets or to postpone repairs which, in the long run, will cost more." Tax-exempt maintenance funds are what the "Compleat Gentleman" of the 1990s needs to avoid dispersal of collections and conversion of historic properties away from being family homes.

CHAPTER X

"The Panoply of Death"

All human things are subject to decay,
And when fate summons, monarchs must obey.

"Mac Flecknoe," I.I.
John Dryden, 1682

When I look upon the tombs of the great,
every emotion of envy dies in me . . .

"Spectator," No. 66, 1712
Joseph Addison

As Shakespeare opined in *Henry IV, Part 2* (II, 35), "Death, as the Psalmist saith, is certain to all; all shall die." There were those, wounded in battle, dying painfully and slowly, who might, given any choice, have preferred the swiftness of death by drowning that befell John Ferrers and his son, Sir Humphrey, in 1678, when trying to cross the swollen River Trent. In Roman dress they are stanced dramatically, even poignantly, on Grinling Gibbons's marble monument to them in St. Editha's Church in Tamworth. Some less fortunate seemed to take a long time dying, as if the cadence of their last memorable words was too important to hasten, and some raised disbelief in others that they had gone at all.

On Tuesday, January 30, 1649, Charles I, with some dignity, handed the George, the insignia of the ancient chivalric Order of the Garter, to Bishop Juxon. He instructed him to give it to the Prince of Wales, together with the one word "Remember." A moment later he was executed; when Charles II, to whom the George was given, died himself on February 6, 1685, there were several farewells, on what has been called "an exemplary death-bed, as might have been expected of one who had learnt early to confront the unknown with courage and hope." The king is said in his last moments to have urged the Duke of York (later James II) to "not let poor Nelly starve" and to "be well to Portsmouth" a reference to two of his mistresses,

140. James Wyatt (1747–1813). The Mausoleum, Brocklesby Park, Lincolnshire, 1787–1794.

141. Isaac James (active c. 1570–1610). Tomb of Henry, 1st Lord Norris.
After 1606. Marble. Westminster Abbey

While the effigies are recumbent, the pious, kneeling figures
of two of Lord and Lady Norris's six soldier sons represented in armor make a powerful impression.

Nell Gwynne and Louise de Keroualle, Duchess of Portsmouth. May we regard the concern as more significant than the laconic last words of Philip Dormer Stanhope, fourth Earl of Chesterfield, who died in 1773? Visited by Solomon Dayrolles, his secretary and godson, he weakly urged, "give Dayrolles a chair" and then died. Thomas, second Lord Lyttelton, the so-called "wicked lord" due to his gambling and scoundrel-like ways, attracted more writings about his death than his life. Horace Walpole, Mrs. Delany, Mrs. Montagu, Dr. Johnson, and other chroniclers all related how on the night of November 25, 1779, Lyttelton had a dream in which a woman dressed in white bade him prepare to die. He replied, "I hope not soon, not in two months." She replied, "Yes, in three days." When he had dressed himself that day to go to the House of Lords, he said he thought he did not look as if he was likely to die. Two days later, having particularly enquired of his servant what care had been taken to provide good bread rolls for his breakfast the next morning, he stepped into bed with his waistcoat on, and as his servant was pulling it off, put his hand to his side, sank back, and immediately expired with a groan.

Society had long been as serious about the panoply of death as the solemn occasion required. It was the final conspicuous consumption of a nobleman's wealth.[1] As soon as the news of the death of a peer was announced across the stretching park, by the solemn muffled tolling of the church peal, a messenger went at once to the College of Arms. One of the heralds of the college then set out for the house, ready to preside over the many weeks of preparation that would be needed before the embalmed body could be lowered in its lead coffin into the family vault, beneath the chancel floor. Indeed over all the preparations was the brooding authority of the College of Arms, its heralds ready soon to visit and to take from a grieving son, quietly but firmly, more golden sovereigns than his father had spent on building, as Ben Jonson had it "the proud, ambitious heap" of his house. Those who had known him in life may well have seen him kneel at the altar rail at the time of his betrothal and at the death of his eldest son, lost fighting alongside Henry VIII at Boulogne.

When the third Earl of Derby was laid to rest at Ormskirk Church, on December 4, 1572, there was time to ponder his greatness.[2] He had been one of the peers who petitioned the Pope to grant Henry VIII's divorce in 1532, was Cupbearer at the coronation of Anne Boleyn, and bore the sword without a point (curtana) before his sovereign at the coronations of Edward VI and of Queen Mary. He had acted as a commissioner under Edward VI for the advancement of the Reformation; under Mary he delivered Protestants to be burned at the stake; as an adroit trimmer, he hunted Catholics to the death in the service of Elizabeth. The Stanley motto "Sans changer," was as inappropriate to him as it had been to his grandfather, Thomas, who had commanded seven thousand men at the Battle of Bosworth in 1485 and had placed the crown of the slain Richard III on Henry VII's head. Edward had buried two wives: his third, Mary Cotton, buried him, and with eight more years left to her, a fact of which, like all, she was unaware, she married again, to the sixth Earl of Kent.

The Earl of Derby had died at Lathom House, on his Lancashire estates, two miles from Ormskirk Church. In marshaling the funeral procession, two yeoman conductors were put in the lead. One hundred poor men, secure in the knowledge of receiving at least food, were clothed in the cheapest blacks. The choir, of forty voices, were in their surplices, followed by an esquire on horseback, bearing the late earl's standard. The earl's household retinue of eighty gentleman, his two secretaries, two chaplains,

and fifty knights and esquires preceded the preacher, the Dean of Chester, the three chief officers, and another esquire on horseback carrying the great banner. In all spectacle there is a high point, and the four heralds riding black horses with black trappings and escutcheons trailing the ground represented exactly the high note of earthly authority. Under a deepening sky, the dark ribbon of the ordered funeral procession, lost and rising again in the folds of the park, wound in measured time toward its appointed place.

First came the Lancaster Herald, wearing the earl's coat of arms and carrying his steel helmet, its parcel-gilt surface a sharp point of light in the midst of blackness. Next came Norroy, King of Arms, with the earl's shield of arms—the Garter, or highest order of knighthood, had been bestowed on him by the boy king Edward VI—and wearing a coronet. Clarenceux carried the earl's sword, its pommel downward, and the Garter King of Arms carried another colored coat of arms. They all horse-pranced before the black draped chariot with the coffin, which was drawn by four more horses. They were surrounded by the awesome sight of ten hooded esquires on horseback, with banners bearing the arms of families in alliance with the Stanleys: the dukes of Lancaster, de Bohuns, de Mortimers, earls of Winchester, Peverils, de Braiose, de Beauchamps, de Vescy, earls of Pembroke—merely some of many in the long line back to the creation of the earldom by King Stephen in 1138.

Behind the trundling chariot walked the chief mourner, Henry Stanley, now the thirteenth earl, thinking perhaps of the occasion when his father and mother (a daughter of Thomas Howard, second Duke of Norfolk) had been at his wedding in 1555 in the Royal Chapel in Whitehall. The new earl was attended by two ushers and eight other mourners led by John, Lord Stourton, the twenty-year-old grandson of the third earl, who had both his wardship and marriage controlled by the earl until death had intervened. The end of this great winding procession was made up of five hundred yeomen and all the servants of the various gentlemen taking part.

When Ormskirk Church was reached, its muffled bell tolling insistently, the coffin was removed from the chariot by eight gentlemen who bore it inside. In the center of the festooned black setting was the vast hearse on which

142. *Jasper Hollemans (active 1586–c. 1630). Tomb of Sir George*
(d. 1612) and Lady Fermor (d. 1628). c. 1630.
Stone and marble. Easton Neston, Northamptonshire

This is one of the finest tombs of its kind in England: an array
of pennons denoting lineage spring from a peacock's tail
behind the two effigies.

it was placed. The hearse towered some thirty feet high and was twelve feet long and nine feet wide. The mercers had provided both black taffeta and velvet to drape this casket—a catafalque of dignity with all its heraldic blazoning intelligible only to the heralds. Sonorously, Norroy, King of Arms, declaimed the name and titles of the deceased. The Dean of Chester preached a sermon, in which he extolled the boundless hospitality of his patron, conducted it was said on household expenses of 4,000 pounds a year. William Camden, in his *Annals of Elizabeth* (1615), noted that "with Edward, Earl of Derby's death,

the glory of hospitality seemed to fall asleep." The new earl proffered pieces of gold to each herald, and the chief mourners then passed to him the late earl's arms, sword, target, standard, and banner. With the mourners, down to the level of the yeomen, having made their obeisance to their deceased master, they formed into procession and set out again to Lathom House.

In the silence that remained, the actual burial took place, with two of the heralds, the attendant esquires, gentlemen, yeomen, and chief officers of the late earl present. Ceremonially their service was at an end: they raised and broke their staves of office and cast them down into the open grave, before the shoveled clammy earth closed the void. And then the heralds rode back to the great feast at the house.[3] Months later a tomb with an alabaster effigy was erected in the Derby chapel, but it can no longer be identified there today with complete certainty.

When Bess of Hardwick died on February 13, 1608, she had already ordained that Mary Talbot, Countess of Shrewsbury, her youngest daughter, should have the "pearl bed," the one in which she had slept at Chatsworth in the 1550s with her second husband, Sir William Cavendish. She had lain wasting away in it at Hardwick Hall, covered with Spanish blankets, with a fire warming the room—but hardly the sick patient. Dr. Hunton from Sheffield attended at her eventual death; the body was disemboweled and embalmed by the apothecary in preparation for its lying-in-state at Hardwick while the Garter King of Arms made his preparations. The tomb and vault at All-Hallows, Derby (now All Saints Cathedral), was prepared to receive the small, five-foot, three-inch figure sealed in wax in its lead coffin. While his mother lay-in-state for three months, her son William Cavendish was married on April 10, 1608, to Christian Bruce, the sister of Edward, first Lord Kinloss. As Bess's biographer has noted:[4] "Bess was practical in dying; the future of her dynasty came before her own funeral." Finally, about May 4, 1608, the long procession of hooded mourners, ushers, heralds, the lady chief mourner, Mary, Countess of Shrewsbury, supported by two hooded barons, her servants, and twelve dazed poor from her alms-houses, set out to Derby. The ceremony was according to rules laid down in 1610 in "Vincent's Precedents," a manuscript of instruction to heralds, with a section for "Funeral of a Countess."[5]

The sermon was delivered by the Archbishop of York, Tobias Matthew, formerly Prince-Bishop of Durham, and sometime Public Orator to Queen Elizabeth. He took as his theme Solomon's description of a virtuous woman (Proverbs XIII, 4) as "the crown of her husband," ignoring the acrimonious marriage dispute in which the queen's commissioners had found in Bess's favour against her husband, the Earl Marshal of England. Then she was laid in the vault beneath, and a great monument made by her faithful surveyor Robert Smythson was erected. The effigy had its hands folded up in piety. Her will provided 2,000 pounds for the funeral, which she specified "be not over sumptuous or performed with too much vain and idle charges," instructions more or less ignored by the presiding heralds.

Bess's servants, their jobs now at the disposal of the rightful heirs, had every reason to enjoy the great party, unheeding of what the morrow, or the one after that, might bring. At all such great funerals there was distribution of food left over to the poor. When Edward Manners, third Earl of Rutland, died at the early age of thirty-eight on Good Friday, April 14, 1587, at Puddle Wharf, London, his body had to be moved on a long and tortuous journey north: a month after his death, it was buried at Bottesford in Leicestershire. It is said that four thousand poor people were fed from the remains of the funeral feast. A little before his death the queen had decided to appoint Edward as her Lord Chancellor. He had trained as a lawyer, after attending Cambridge, and had traveled extensively in France. The queen installed him as a Knight of the Garter in 1585, and he also sat as one of twenty-four noblemen at the trial of Mary, Queen of Scots, in October 1586, and was a mourner at her funeral. The astute control he had over his large estates, "modernizing and re-equipping the Rievaulx ironworks" and living, nevertheless, in princely style has been noted elsewhere.[6] An account of his death and funeral survives in the family archives at Belvoir Castle. The earl's canopied tomb at Bottesford, erected in 1591 by the Southwark workshop of Gerard Johnson, shows him in full armor with a ruff protecting his throat. His wife, Isabel, who died in 1606 at Stepney, and was buried there, is nevertheless represented by her own effigy dressed in an ermine-trimmed mantle alongside that of her husband. Edward and Isabel had

143. *Gerard Johnson (active 1567–c. 1616). Tomb of the 4th Earl of Rutland and his wife. 1591. Alabaster. Bottesford, Leicestershire, St. Mary's Church (detail below)*

Gerard Johnson was paid 100 pounds for this fine tomb. It was made (with that of the 3rd earl) in his Southwark yard, sent by ship to Boston, and then by cart to Bottesford.

144. Funeral order, apparently of Thomas Savage of Rock Savage, burned at Mayfield County in England, December 16, 1635. 1682. Woodcut. Taken from Randal Holmes's "Academy of Armory," London, 1682. Museum of Fine Arts, Boston

no male heir; their only daughter, Elizabeth, who was married when only thirteen years old to William Cecil, grandson of Elizabeth's great High Treasurer, kneels at her mother's feet. She bore a child and died at the age of fifteen. The tranquility of "union in death" symbolized in the tomb ignored the fact that Isabel was buried over a hundred miles from her home and that she had to engage in litigation with the fourth earl over the wishes expressed in her husband's will.

Her suit, which was submitted to the arbitration of Sir Francis Walsingham and Lord Burghley, turned on the expenses of the third earl's funeral. The draperies and clothing alone had cost 898 pounds. The new earl, John, her husband's younger brother, insisted that before Isabel received her legacies the funeral costs should be paid from the estate. "Earl John's revenge for this quarrel, which he lost, was to appeal to the Queen to remove Elizabeth from her mother's care, as a royal ward, on the grounds that

she was not a reliable person to rear her daughter." However, in the middle of these angry quarrels the earl became ill, and he died in February 1588. He had held the title but ten months. The main person to profit—apart from legacies the earl made to his three daughters and servants, with 3,000 pounds to pay his debts, all taken from the third earl's estate—was Gerard Johnson, who also erected the fourth earl's tomb (plate 143) at Bottesford in 1591[7] whilst he was attending to the monument to the third earl.

The great solemn spectacle of an elaborate funeral focused minds temporarily on the good or evil of the deceased. A long Latin inscription could disguise the exact truths from those not versed in its reading. But, despite the elaborate embalming, the long passage of time would take its toll on the mortal body. It was only the marble monument that resisted decay and survived to commemorate the deceased person's social position.[8] The separation of body and the soul that religious teaching had long advocated, was commemorated by those monuments and by paintings.[9] Today this is usually undertaken by photographs and tape-recordings.

In 1700 Sir Henry Chauncy set out the "uses" or "ends" of monuments. They served for four purposes:

1. They are Evidence to prove Descents and Pedigrees.
2. To show the time when the party deceased.
3. They are examples to follow the Good, and eschew the Evil.
4. Memorials to set the living in mind of their Mortality.[10]

As John Webster was mindful in *The Duchess of Malfi* (c.1614), there was still "fashion in the grave," even when eyes were "fixed upon the stars" and minds were "wholly bent upon the world." Likewise, John Weever, in his *Antient Funerall Monuments* (1631), was concerned to point out that epitaphs showed love to the deceased, whose "memorie was continued to posterity, friends were comforted, and the Reader put in mind of human frailtie." Thomas Hobbes in *Leviathan* (1651) also reassured when he stated that monuments were not graven images to worship, in contradiction of the Second Commandment, "but a civil honouring of the person, not that is, but that was."

From the art historian's viewpoint, monuments show good representations of costume, whether knights and soldiers in plate and mail armor, ladies in ruffs and loose robes, or children swaddled tight or kneeling in doublets and long skirts. Heraldry played an important role, for from medieval days the use of distinctive bearings had been born on a "coat of arms." The accuracy of this, with any motto or inscription, had been approved by a herald, and was a reliable means of identifying the person represented, particularly in time of heated battle, when a raised blue and white coat of arms to rally to was worth more than a name shouted to the wind. Many tried to enter this lucrative supervisory field, so much so that in 1618 the Garter King of Arms proclaimed that owing to the "sinister" actions of pretenders to the science of heraldry, all carvers, masons, tomb-makers, and herald painters were henceforth to send in copies of their designs to have the arms and epitaphs verified. However, by the middle of the

eighteenth century the heraldic memorial panels had degenerated into the coach-painters' hatchments, which hang, as lozenge-shaped shields, in so many country parish churches.

The sculptors who settled in England, many from Flanders, were usually admitted to the London company of the Masons, and several settled in the Midland counties near good suppliers of alabaster, at Burton and Nottingham. The use of rich marbles and paint of many

145. *John Michael Rysbrack (1694–1770). Tomb of the 1st Duke of Marlborough. 1732. Marble. Blenheim Palace Chapel, Oxfordshire*

No expense was spared for this "dynastic" great monument, commissioned by Sarah, Duchess of Marlborough. It was set up in May 1732. The design was the work of architect William Kent. The family group is in Roman dress, with the duke in armor.

colors characterized the Elizabethan tomb, but by the 1630s black and white marble was in vogue. By this time too, simpler surrounds, rather than the towering four-post superstructures of Elizabeth's reign, were in evidence, and kneeling figures were being replaced by busts. By the 1670s there were many monuments with standing figures in a quasi-baroque manner. The fine Campden monument at Exton by the workshop of Grinling Gibbons (1684–1685) cost 1,000 pounds to erect. It represents a new type of monument, in which two standing figures, on each side of a central urn, are free of any constraining framework around them. Gibbons probably did not charge 1,000 pounds again until 1699–1700, when he made an imposing monument to the first Duke of Beaufort. This was made for erection in the Beaufort Chapel at St. George's Chapel, Windsor. In 1874 it was moved to Badminton, a few yards from the house the first duke had created in the 1660s.[11]

By the early eighteenth century the popularity of the Grand Tour had made study of sculpture a requirement for each young gentleman. Jonathan Richardson and his son issued in 1722 what became a standard guide to those intending to look for sculpture and pictures in Italy, *An Account of the Statues, Bas-Reliefs, Drawings and Pictures in Italy*. The transporting of monuments themselves had several precedents, notably the tomb of the fifth Earl of Exeter and his wife, which the earl had ordered in Rome from Pierre Monnot. The earl died in 1700 in France, and when his body returned to England it was buried near to his family home, Burghley House, in the church of St. Martin at Stamford. Monnot's tomb was sent from Rome and erected in the church in 1704. The earl and his countess are shown reclining on a sarcophagus in Roman costume.

One of the finest tombs of the Palladian years of the 1720s and 1730s is the towering monument by the Flemish sculptor John Michael Rysbrack to John Churchill, first Duke of Marlborough (plate 145). The monument, erected in the chapel at Blenheim Palace shows, on the base, the surrender of French forces to Churchill at the battle of Blenheim and is flanked by winged figures of "Fame" and "History." The monument was erected by Duchess Sarah, a figure of whom looks up at the duke. Their two sons (both of whom died young) are also commemorated. The spiked dragon of "Envy" is pinned down by the weight of the sarcophagus. On May 24, 1732, the duchess had written to Sir Philip Yorke to say that at last the Blenheim chapel was finished. She stated further that more than half the tomb was there ready to set up: "All in Marble Decorations of Figures, Trophies, Medals with their inscriptions and, in short, everything that could do the Duke of Marlborough Honour and Justice."[12]

The duke had died in London on June 16, 1722. The lying in state was arranged at Marlborough House, and with temporary burial at Westminster Abbey, as "Sarah's Chapel" was not yet ready at Blenheim. Her irascible behavior had long delayed work on the house and chapel.[12] It was not etiquette for a widow to attend the funeral, but the duchess sent her black coach, lined with forty-eight yards of black cloth and six yards for harness ("enough," as she said, "to cover my Garden"), and containing the Duke of Montagu as chief mourner. Eight other dukes and a long procession of soldiers and horses followed. The bill for the funeral (5,265 pounds, if household mourning is included) paid also the small sum for seven trumpeters to sound the last call to a heavenly kingdom. The duchess comforted herself with reading Bishop Ezekiel Hopkins' *Death Disarmed of Its Sting* (1682).

Husband and wife were joined together in death in the Blenheim chapel. When Sarah died on October 18, 1744, at Marlborough House, in her eighty-fifth year, she had been witness to six reigns, or part of them. She died immensely rich, but this could only be of use to others. On October 30, 1744, Marlborough's body was brought from Westminster Abbey to lie with Sarah's in the chapel vault at Blenheim. This journey involved a coach-and-six to carry the coffin, bearers, a room hung with mourning, fourteen hatbands, and fourteen pairs of men's black-topped gloves. Of her own "journey" nothing is recorded, and the final ritual ceremony took place without her usual unheeding intervention.

The full impact of neo-classicism on sculpture came late to England. Important decorative influences were imparted in the 1760s by the architects Sir William Chambers and Robert Adam after their Italian journeyings, and those made in Greece by James Stuart and Nicholas Revett. The "inanimate insipidity," words that Sir Joshua Reynolds used to describe "the many thousand antique statues which we have," in his *Discourse on Sculpture* (1780), char-

Vanity of Vanities all is Vanity. Eccle. I, 2.
Duſt thou art, and unto Duſt ſhalt thou return. Gen. III, 19.
Then ſhall the Duſt return to the Earth as it was: and the Spirit ſhall return unto God who gave it. Eccle. XII, 7.
Tremble, ye Women that are at eaſe. Isa. XXXII, 11.
She that liveth in pleaſure, is dead while ſhe liveth. I Tim. V, 6.
O that they were wiſe, that they underſtood this, that they would conſider their latter end! Deut. XXXII, 29.
For what is your life? It is even a vapour that appeareth for a little time, and then vaniſheth away. Jam. IV, 14.
I have ſaid to corruption, Thou art my Father; to the Worm, Thou art my Mother and my Siſter. Job XVII, 14.
Like Sheep they are laid in the Grave, Death ſhall feed on them their Beauty ſhall conſume in the Grave — the Houſe appointed for all living — to be laid in the Balance they are altogether lighter than vanity. Psa. XLIX, 14, Job XXX, 23, Psa. LXII, 9.
Becauſe the Daughters of Zion are haughty, and walk with wanton eyes — the Lord will take away their tinkling ornaments — and inſtead of ſweet ſmell, there ſhall be ſtink. Isa. III, 16, 18, 24.
IN THE MIDST OF LIFE WE ARE IN DEATH! Com. Prayer.
FAVOUR is DECEITFUL, and BEAUTY is VAIN. Pro. XXXI, 30.
One Night, CORINNA was all gaiety in her Spirits, all Finery in her apparel, at a magnificent Ball: The next Night, ſhe lay pale and ſtiff, an extended Corpſe, and ready to be mingled with the mouldering dead. Hervey's Med.
How lov'd, how valu'd once, avails Thee not;
To whom related, or by whom begot.
A heap of Duſt alone remains of Thee:
'Tis all THOU art! and all the PROUD ſhall be!
LIFE how ſhort! ETERNITY how long!
Now get you to my Lady's table, and tell her, let her paint an inch thick, to this complexion ſhe muſt come at laſt. SHAKESPEARE.
MASQUERADE
GAMING

146. *"Life and Death Contrasted, or An Essay on Woman." c. 1760. Line engraving. Colonial Williamsburg Foundation*

Issued by Bowles and Carver, print sellers in St. Paul's Churchyard, London, this satirical print contrasts the variety of women, as exemplified in the rich clothes, with the inevitable reaper. The many biblical texts include the harsh words from I Timothy, verse 6: "She that liveth in pleasure, is dead while she liveth." Gentlemen, of course, were not averse to bearing the consequences of too much dalliance.

147. *Sir Francis Chantrey (1781–1841). Monument to Anna Maria Graves. d. 1819. Waterperry, Oxfordshire*

This poignant representation of the young gentleman kneeling by his dying wife and child is overcharged with emotion; perhaps rightly so, for death is ever the painful divider.

acterized much neo-classical sculpture."[13] It was a combination of "sentiment and the love of clean contour" which led to some fine monuments demonstrating the poignancy of grief (plate 147). The work of Joseph Nollekens (1737–1823), Thomas Banks (1735–1805), John Bacon (1740–1799), and John Flaxman (1755–1826), at the end of the eighteenth century and into the nineteenth, gave patrons considerable choice in deciding on a suitable memorial. It was certainly the area of activity in which Flaxman's "most distinguished sculpture is to be found." His cause was advanced by the monument he sculpted in 1801, to William Murray, first Earl of Mansfield (c. 1793) sited in Westminster Abbey.[14] Its motifs are taken from seventeenth-century papal tombs in St Peter's in Rome. The earl is in his robes as Lord Chief Justice and at the back is a "finely designed figure of a condemned youth," a careful appeal to sentiment and to the impartiality of the law suggested by the figures of Wisdom and Justice.

When William Lowther, first Earl of Lonsdale, died at York House, Twickenham, on March 19, 1844, at the age of eighty-six, the whole complicated process of attending death was again put into solemn action. His remains were encased in three coffins. The inner of lead, the second lined in white satin, and the "outer, or state coffin" manufactured of the best Spanish mahogany, covered with rich Genoa velvet, studded with jet nails, and ornamented and emblazoned with the armorial bearings of the deceased earl. His names and title were inscribed deep on the plate, surmounted by the image of his coronet. The coffin was moved reverently by estate staff sent down to Twickenham, to the London and Birmingham railway terminus at Euston, preparatory to the three-hundred-mile journey north to Lowther. Trains transported it from London to Birmingham and then on to Lancaster. A horse-drawn coach brought it to the "Royal Oak" at Burton for an overnight stay by those accompanying it. Then from

Burton on to Lowther. At Burton the bells were tolled in muffled peal and all shops were closed. At Kendal the town hall flag was at half-mast, and the parish church bells were tolled. With great ceremony of mutes and plumes, outriders, coaches, and mourners, the earl was buried at Lowther, on April 1, 1844. He is commemorated in the church of St. Michael there by a free-standing marble tomb-chest.[15]

There is an even greater recognition of death accorded by the silhouette of a mausoleum. The greatest example is that by Nicholas Hawksmoor at Castle Howard, finished in 1736, the burial place of the Earls of Carlisle. The most elegant of the neo-classical mausoleums is that by James Wyatt at Brocklesby Park, Lincolnshire (plate 140; 1792). It stands on a traditional site of a Roman burial place and its elevation is based on the temples of Vesta at Tivoli and Rome. The main cella stands on a podium surrounded by twelve fluted Roman Doric columns. A cool diffused light illuminates the domed and coffered interior, flecked with occasional color as the sun shines through the stained glass by Francis Eginton in the lantern. At the center stands a marble figure by Joseph Nollekens of Sophia Aufrère, the beloved young wife—she was but thirty-three—of Charles Anderson-Pelham, first Lord Yarborough, who died in 1786. Her coffin was removed to the mausoleum from the church in 1794. The statue is moving to contemplate. It is set on a plinth and above a pavement with a pattern of inlaid marble and brass, surrounded by a brass rail. A privately printed description of the mausoleum, undoubtedly Wyatt's finest small building, was published in 1832.

Let me conclude with words from a poem by Anna Hume from her *Triumphs of Love, Chastitie, and Death*, published at Edinburgh in 1644.[16] It expresses the sadness that all feel at the death of someone loved, albeit the more piercing if that person, as Sophia Aufrère, was too young to die:

The fatall houre of her short life drew neare,
That doubtfull passage which the world doth feare;
Another company, who had not beene
Freed from their earthy burden there were seene,
To try if prayers could appease the wrath,
Or stay th'inexorable hand of death,
That beauteous croude conveen'd to see the end.

Which all nicest taste, each neighbor, every friend
Stood by, when grim death with her hande tooke hold,
And pull'd away one onely haire of gold.

The measured words of the funeral service tell for all, "compleat gentleman" or no, that resolute truth: "There is a time for living, and a time for dying. . . ."

Notes

INTRODUCTION

1. H. M. Colvin and J. Newman, eds., *Of Building: Roger North's Writings on Architecture* (Oxford, 1981), p. 5.

2. Ray A. Kelch, *Newcastle: A Duke without Money* (London, 1974), pp. 200–203.

3. J. V. Beckett, *The Aristocracy in England, 1660–1914* (London, 1986), p. 305.

4. *Ibid.*, pp. 307–309.

5. David Cannadine, *Decline and Fall of the British Aristocracy* (London, 1990).

6. Geoffrey Keynes, ed., *The Poetical Works of Rupert Brooke* (London, 1960). See "1914, III, The Dead."

CHAPTER I

1. Guy Miege, *The Present State of Great Britain*, 1691, reprinted in D. A. Baugh, ed., *Aristocratic Government and Society in Eighteenth-Century England* (New York, 1975), pp. 28–53.

2. *Oxford English Dictionary*. 1964 edition.

3. Beckett, *op. cit.*, pp. 25–26. The arguments about the status of gentlemen may be further pursued in R. Kelso, *The Doctrine of the English Gentlemen in the Sixteenth Century* (Illinois, 1929); H. R. Trevor–Roper, "The Gentry, 1540–1640," *Economic History Review* (supplements), 1, 1953. For an analysis of the subsequent controversy see J. H. Hexter, *Reappraisals in History* (1961); S. R. Letwin, *The Gentleman in Trollope* (1982), chap. 1; Beckett, *op. cit.*, chap. 1.

4. Beckett, *op. cit.*, p. 27 and Appendix; Lawrence Stone, *The Crisis of the Aristocracy, 1558–1641* (Oxford, 1965); John Cannon, "The Isthmus Repaired: the Resurgence of the English Aristocracy, 1660–1760," *Proceedings of the British Academy* 48 (1982).

5. A. S. Turberville, *The House of Lords in the XVIII Century* (Oxford, 1927), pp. 501–513; Turberville, *The House of Lords in the Age of Reform, 1784–1837* (London, 1958), pp. 42–43; Beckett, *op. cit.*, pp. 28–36.

6. Stone, *op. cit.*, chap. 11.

7. John Nichols, *History of the County of Leicester*, vol. 2, pt. 1 (1794), p. 49.

8. Mary Coate, *Social Life in Stuart England* (Westport, Conn. 1921), p. 37.

9. Miriam Slater, *Family Life in the Seventeenth Century: The Verney Family* (London, 1984), p. 118.

10. *Memoirs of the Life of Colonel Hutchinson by His Wife* (London, 1908), p. 60.

11. E. S. Morgan, *The Puritan Family* (New York, 1966); Lloyd de Mause, *The History of Childhood* (New York, 1974); Lawrence Stone, *The Family, Sex and Marriage in England, 1500–1800* (London, 1977).

12. J. F. Cliffe, *The Puritan Gentry* (London, 1984), pp. 69–70.

13. *Ibid.*, p. 13, citing British Library, Harleian, MS, 1598.

14. Thomas Wentworth, Earl of Strafford, *Letters and Dispatches* (London, 1739), p. 16.

15. Slater, *op. cit.*, p. 111.

16. Stone, *Crisis, op. cit.*, p. 306.

17. Dorothea Townsend, ed., *Life and Letters of Endymion Porter* (London, 1897), p. 22.

18. John Locke, *Some Thoughts Concerning Education* (London, 1690), p. 8.

19. *Elizabeth, Lady Falkland, Her Life* (London, 1861), p. 12.

20. P. Ariès, *Centuries of Childhood: A Social History of Family Life* (New York, 1962). Subsequent attitudes to childhood and parentage are noted in M. Gordon, ed., *The American Family in Social-Historical Perspective* (New York, 1978).

21. Gervase Huxley, *Victorian Duke: The Life of Hugh Lupus Grosvenor, First Duke of Westminster* (London, 1967), pp. 4–5.

22. Rosalind K. Marshall, *The Days of Duchess Anne: Life in the Household of the Duchess of Hamilton, 1656–1716* (London, 1973), p. 131.

23. D. G. Allen, "The Social and Cultural Landscape of Seventeenth-Century New England," *New England Begins* (Boston, Museum of Fine Arts, 1982), p. 7.

24. Elisabeth D. Garrett, *At Home: The American Family, 1750–1870* (New York, 1990), pp. 232–234.

25. Rhys Isaac, *The Transformation of Virginia, 1740–1790* (Chapel Hill, N.C., 1982), p. 125.

26. Bernard Holland, *Life of the Duke of Devonshire, 1833–1908* (London, 1911), p. 11.

27. Earl of Ronaldshay, *The Life of Lord Curzon* (London, 1928), vol. 1, pp. 17–19.

28. Merlin Waterson, ed., *The Country House Remembered* (London, 1985), chap. 12.

29. Francis Bacon, *Valerius Terminus, Of the Interpretation of Nature* (London, 1625 edition), chap. 26.

CHAPTER II

1. Kenneth Charlton, *Education in Renaissance England* (London and Toronto, 1965), p. 84.

2. Rosemary O'Day, *Education and Society, 1500–1800* (London and New York, 1982), p. 90.

3. *Ibid.*, p. 90.

4. John Martin Robinson, *The Dukes of Norfolk* (London, 1983), pp. 41–43. For further details of travelers in the Renaissance period see Clare Howard, *English Travellers of the Renaissance* (London, 1914); George B. Parks, *The English Traveler to Italy*, vol. 1: *The Middle Ages to 1525* (Rome, 1954); R. S. Pine-Colffin, *Bibliography of British and American Travel in Italy to 1860* (Florence, 1974), vol. 76.

5. Walter Raleigh, ed., *The Complete Works of George Savile, Marquis of Halifax* (London, 1912), p. 67.

6. J. Axtell, ed., *The Educational Writings of John Locke* (Cambridge, 1968), pp. 354–355; Stone, *Family, op. cit.*, pp. 343–360.

7. Duncan Thomson, *A Virtuous and Noble Education*, (Scottish National Portrait Gallery, Edinburgh, 1971), pp. 7–24, 29; A. L. Sells, *The Paradise of Travellers: The Italian Influence on Englishmen in the Seventeenth Century* (London, 1964); J. W. Stoye, *English Travellers Abroad, 1604–1667* (London, 1952).

8. Christopher Hibbert, *The Grand Tour* (London, 1974), p. 15.

9. Robinson, *op. cit.*, pp. 106–107; David Howarth in *Thomas Howard, Earl of Arundel* (Ashmolean Museum, Oxford, 1985–1986), p. 6.

10. Andrew W. Moore, *Norfolk & The Grand Tour* (Norfolk Museums Service, 1985).

11. *Ibid.*, p. 30.

12. Rose Davis, *The Good Lord Lyttelton* (Bethlehem, Pa., 1939), p. 20.

13. Sir Brinsley Ford, articles on "Six Notable English Patrons in Rome, 1750–1800," *Apollo* 149 (1974); Jenkins, pp. 416–425; Byres, pp. 446–461.

14. E. K. Waterhouse, *Painting in Britain, 1530–1790* (London, 1953), pp. 200–204; Jules Prown, *Copley* (Cambridge, Mass., 1966, 2 vols).

15. W. L. Sachse, *The Colonial American in Britain* (Madison, Wis., 1956), p. 20.

16. A. Koch and W. Peden, eds., *The Life and Selected Writings of Thomas Jefferson* (New York, 1944), pp. 385–387.

17. J. K. Howat, *American Paradise: The World of the Hudson River School* (Metropolitan Museum of Art, New York, 1988), pp. 3, 27–30.

18. Frankin Kelly, et al., *Frederic Edwin Church* (National Gallery of Art, Washington, D.C., 1990), p. 116.

19. Quentin Bell, *Ruskin* (London, 1963), chaps. 1, 2.

20. James Fenimore Cooper, *Notions of the Americans picked up by a travelling bachelor* (New York, 1828; reprinted 1963), vol. 1, p. 144.

21. F. M. L. Thompson, *English Landed Society in the Nineteenth Century* (London, 1963), p. 190.

22. L. T. C. Rolt, *Victorian Engineering* (London, 1970), p. 22.

CHAPTER III

1. William Cecil, Baron Burghley, *Certaine Precepts for the well ordering and carriage of a man's life* (London, 1617). I have used the text in *Practical Wisdom* by Elizabeth Strutt (London, 1824), pp. 11–17.

2. I. Maclean, *The Renaissance Notion of Women* (Cambridge, 1980), chap. 3; L. Jardine, *Still Harping on Daughters: Women and Drama in the Age of Shakespeare* (London and Totowa, N.J., 1983), chap. 4.

3. David Durant, *Bess of Hardwick: Portrait of an Elizabethan Dynasty* (London, 1988), p. 126.

4. *Ibid.*, p. 127.

5. Quoted by Alice T. Friedman, *House and Household in Elizabethan England: Wollaton Hall and the Willoughby Family* (Chicago and London, 1989), p. 57.

6. Stone, *Crisis, op. cit.*, p. 282.

7. Joel Hurstfield, *The Queen's Wards: Wardship and Marriage under Elizabeth I* (London, 1958), p. 62.

8. Stone, *Crisis, op. cit.*, p. 282.

9. *Ibid.*, p. 286.

10. *Ibid.*, p. 289.

11. L. Bonfield, *Marriage Settlements, 1601–1740* (Cambridge, 1983); Beckett, *op. cit.*, pp. 58–62.

12. E. W. Harcourt, ed., *The Harcourt Papers* (London, 14 vols, 1880–1905), vol. 1, pp. 171, 173, 179.

13. Cliffe, *op. cit.*, p. 64.

14. *Ibid.*, pp. 66–67.

15. John Cannon, *Aristocratic Century* (Cambridge, 1984), pp. 74–75.

16. G. H. White, ed., *The Complete Peerage* (London, 1953), vol. 12, p. 633.

17. Cannon, *op. cit.*, p. 76; Defoe's book was edited for the first time by K. D. Bülbring (London, 1890).

18. Robert Halsband, *The Life of Lady Mary Wortley Montagu* (Oxford, 1956), chap. 2.

19. C. T. Gatty, *Mary Davies and the Manor of Ebury* (London, 1921), p. 7.

20. J. V. Beckett and C. Jones, in *Bulletin of the John Rylands Library* (Manchester, 1982), vol. 65, pp. 21–22.

21. Cooper, *op. cit.*, p. 183.

22. Auguste Carlier, *Marriage in the United States* (Boston, 1867), p. 17.

23. Duvergier De Hauranne, *Huit mois en Amérique* (Paris, 1866), vol. 1, p. 37.

24. Samuel P. Day, *Life and Society in America* (London, 1880), vol. 1, p. 42.

25. Anita Leslie, *Lady Randolph Churchill: The Story of Jennie Jerome* (London and New York, 1969); R. G. Martin, *Jennie: The Life of Lady Randolph Churchill* (London and Englewood Cliffs, N.J., 1969–1971).

26. Consuelo Vanderbilt Balsan, *The Glitter and the Gold* (London, 1953), p. 41.

27. Kenneth Rose, *Superior Person: A Portrait of Curzon and His Circle in Late Victorian England* (London and New York, 1969–1970); M. Edwardes, *High Noon of Empire: India under Curzon* (London, 1965); R. Kenin, *Return to Albion, Americans in England, 1760–1940* (New York, 1979), chap. 6.

28. Beckett, *op. cit.*, p. 475.

29. F. M. L. Thompson, *op. cit.*, p. 201.

CHAPTER IV

1. Eric Mercer, *English Art, 1553–1625* (Oxford, 1962), pp. 12–16.

2. A. F. Upton, *Sir Arthur Ingram, c.1565–1642* (London, 1961), p. 22.

3. Geoffrey Beard, *Craftsmen and Interior Decoration in England, 1660–1820* (Edinburgh, 1982), p. 3.

4. D. Lloyd, *State Worthies* (London, 1766), p. 355.

5. Quoted in Sir John Summerson, "The Building of Theobalds, 1564–1585," *Archaeologia* 97 (1959), pp. 107–126; E. St. J. Brooks, *Sir Christopher Hatton* (London, 1943), p. 17.

6. Sir John Summerson, *Architecture in Britain, 1530–1830* (Harmondsworth, 1963), p. 34.

7. Durant, *op. cit.*, p. 193.

8. R. T. Gunther, ed., *The Notebooks of Sir Roger Pratt* (Oxford, 1928, reissued New York, 1979), p. 24.

9. H. J. Habakkuk, "England," in Albert Goodwin, ed., *The European Nobility in the Eighteenth Century* (London and New York, 1953), pp. 1–21.

10. Gladys Scott Thomson, *Letters of a Grandmother, 1732–1734* (London, 1943), p. 17.

11. Eileen Harris and Nicholas Savage, *British Architectural Books and Writers, 1556–1785* (Cambridge, 1990).

12. John Gwynn, *London and Westminster Improved* (London, 1766), p. 32.

13. I have used the edition of Chesterfield's letters to his son issued by his daughter-in-law, Mrs. Eugenia Stanhope (London, 1774; supplement, 1787).

14. William Hogarth, *The Analysis of Beauty*, J. Burke, ed. (Oxford, 1955).

15. B. Sprague Allen, *Tides in English Taste, 1619–1800* (New York, reprinted 1957), vol. 1, p. 110.

16. John Harris, *Sir William Chambers, Knight of the Polar Star* (London, 1970).

17. Geoffrey Beard, *The Work of Robert Adam* (Edinburgh, 1978), with references to a wide literature.

18. Talbot Hamlin, *Greek Revival Architecture in America* (Oxford, 1944).

19. Mark Girouard, *The Victorian Country House* (New Haven, Conn. 1979).

20. William Whellan, *The History and Topography of the Counties of Cumberland and Westmorland* (Pontefract, 1860), p. 22.

21. For an analysis of Kerr's work, see Jill Franklin, *The Gentleman's Country House and Its Plan, 1835–1914* (London, 1981), pp. 39–46.

22. *Ibid.*, p. 27.

23. Girouard, *op. cit.*, pl. 26.

24. Mary Carbery, *Happy World* (London, 1941), p. 99.

25. Diana Cooper, *The Rainbow Comes and Goes* (London, 1958), pp. 36–37.

26. Huxley, *op. cit.*, p. 142.

27. William Cobbett (Peter Porcupine), *Year's Residence in the United States* (London, 1828), p. 16.

28. Mrs. A. J. Graves, *Woman in America* (New York, 1855), p. 32.

29. Clive Aslet, *The American Country House* (New Haven, Conn., 1990), chap. 1.

30. *Ibid.*, p. 10.

31. C. H. C. Baker and M. I. Baker, *The Life and Circumstances of James Brydges, First Duke of Chandos* (Oxford, 1949), p. 141.

CHAPTER V

1. Alan G. R. Smith, *Servant of the Cecils, The Life of Sir Michael Hickes, 1543–1612* (London, 1977).

2. J. Hurstfield, *The Queen's Wards* (London, 1958), pp. 241–259.

3. Stone, *Crisis, op. cit.*, pp. 427, 773.

4. Menna Prestwich, *Cranfield, Politics and Profits under the Early Stuarts* (Oxford, 1966).

5. C. H. C. Baker and M. I. Baker, *op. cit.*, p. 47; Godfrey Davis, "The Seamy Side of Marlborough's War," *Huntington Library Quarterly* 15 (1951), pp. 21–44.

6. J. H. Habakkuk, "Daniel Finch, 2nd Earl of Nottingham, His House and Estate," *Studies in Social History*, ed., J. H. Plumb (London, 1955), p. 93.

7. Kenneth Darwin, "John Aislabie, 1670–1742," *Transactions, Yorkshire Archaeological Society* 38 (1950), pt.147, pp. 318–319.

8. J. H. Plumb, *Sir Robert Walpole* (London, 1960), vol. 2, p. 128.

9. Friedman, *op. cit.*, pp. 24–25.

10. Durant, *op. cit.*, p. 182.

11. Stone, *op. cit.*, p. 355; Gladys Scott Thomson, *Family Background* (London, 1949), chap. 3.

12. N.G. Brett-James, *The Growth of Stuart London* (London, 1935), pp. 169–170; Gladys Scott Thomson, *Life in a Noble Household* (London, 1937), p. 23.

13. P. D. G. Thomas, *The House of Commons in the Eighteenth Century* (London, 1971), p. 125.

14. Sir John Summerson, *Georgian London* (London 1962), chaps. 5, 7, 12, 14.

15. K. J. Allison, "Flock Management in the Sixteenth and Seventeenth Centuries," *Economic History Review* 2nd series, 11, no. 1 (1958); Alan Simpson, *The Wealth of the Gentry* (Cambridge and Chicago, 1961), pp. 181–196.

16. G. E. Mingay, *English Landed Society in the Eighteenth Century* (London, 1963), pp. 179–184.

17. W. Marshall, *On Landed Property* (London, 1804), pp. 28–29.

18. R. A. C. Parker "Coke of Norfolk and the Agricultural Revolution," *Economic History Review* 2nd series, 8 (1956), pp. 159–163.

19. Stone, *Crisis, op. cit.*, p. 193.

20. Durant, *op. cit.*, pp. 152,192.

21. Baker, *op. cit.*, pp. 94, 419.

22. Eric Richards, *The Leviathan of Wealth: The Sutherland Fortune in the Industrial Revolution* (London, 1973), p. 43.

23. Stephen Birmingham, *America's Secret Aristocracy* (Boston, 1987), p. 177; Aslet, *op. cit.*, p. 224.

24. W. R. Prest, *The Inns of Court, 1590–1640* (London, 1972), p. 154.

25. *Ibid.*, p. 119.

26. R. L. Edgeworth, *Essays on Professional Education* (London, 1809), p. 313.

27. D. Duman, *The Judicial Bench in England, 1727–1875* (London 1982), p. 126; W. R. Cornish and G. de N. Clark, *Law and Society in England, 1750–1950* (London, 1989), p. 22.

28. Phillips Bradley, ed., *Democracy in America:* Alexis de Tocqueville (New York, 1956), vol. 1, p. 282; Robert Stevens, *Law School: Legal Education in America from the 1850s to the 1980s* (Chapel Hill, N.C., 1983), p. 6.

29. Sir John Hale "The Defence of the Realm, 1485–1558," *History of the King's Works*, ed., H. M. Colvin (London, 1982), vol. 4, pt. 2, p. 378.

30. Anthony Bruce, *The Purchase System in the British Army, 1660–1871* (London, 1980), p. 25; John Cannon, *Aristocratic Century: The Peerage of Eighteenth Century England* (London, 1984), pp. 117–118; Beckett, *op. cit.*, p. 409.

31. D. A. Baugh, "Naval Administration, 1715–1750," *Navy Records Society* (London, 1977), p. 5.

32. Bruce, *op. cit.*, p. 121.

33. Cannon, *op. cit.*, p. 120.

34. *Ibid.*, pp. 63–64, citing D. R. Hirschberg, "The Government and Church Patronage in England, 1660–1760," *Journal of British Studies* 20 (1980), pp. 109–139. Hirschberg supports the Browne Willis percentage of peers awarding 12 percent of livings.

35. Cannon, *op. cit.*, p. 65.

36. Mingay, *op. cit.*, pp. 126–130.

37. C. W. James, *Chief Justice Coke* (London, 1929), p. 323.

38. Allen, *op. cit.*, p. 3.

CHAPTER VI

1. Geoffrey Beard, *The Work of Christopher Wren* (Edinburgh, 1982), pp. 24–35.

2. H. P. R. Hoare, *Hoare's Bank: A Record* (London, 1955), p. 7.

3. J. Douglas Stewart, *Sir Godfrey Kneller* (National Portrait Gallery, London, 1971), Appendix, pp. iv-xviii; David Piper, *Catalogue of Seventeenth-Century Portraits in the National Portrait Gallery* (London, 1963), p. 47.

4. Robert Halsband, *The Life of Lady Mary Wortley Montagu* (Oxford, 1960), pp. 4, 8.

5. Brian Allen, *Francis Hayman* (Mellon Center, London and New Haven, Conn., 1987), pp. 102–103.

6. There are excellent collections at the British Library (Banks and Heal collections), at the Henry E. Huntington Library, San Marino, Calif. (P. R. Boxes 342–347); the Boston Atheneum, Mass., etc. Sir Ambrose Heal published *London Tradesmen's Cards of the XVIIIth Century* (London, 1925); *The English Goldsmiths, 1200–1800* (Cambridge, 1935); *The Signboards of Old London Shops* (London, 1947); and *The London Furniture Makers, 1660–1840* (London, 1953).

7. Nicholas Taylor, *Monuments of Commerce* (London, 1968), p. 30.

8. M. Aston, "The Bath Region from Late Prehistory to the Middle Ages," *Bath History* 1 (1986), p. 71.

9. Graham Davis, "Entertainments in Georgian Bath: Gambling and Vice," *Bath History* (1986), pp. 1–26.

10. Anon., *A Step to the Bath with a Character of the Place* (London, 1700), p. 7.

11. Davis, *op. cit.*, p. 9.

12. Tim Mowl and Brian Earnshaw, *John Wood: Architect of Obsession* (Bath, 1989).

13. Friedman, *op. cit.*, p. 136.

14. Eric Gee, *The Architecture of York* (York, 1979), pp. 136, 139.

15. Rudolf Wittkower, "Lord Burlington's Work at York," in Margot Wittkower, ed., *Palladio and English Palladianism* (London, 1974), pp. 135–146.

16. Peter Brown, *Pyramids of Pleasure* (York, 1990), p. 11.

17. The building accounts, 1740–1754, are in the Library of the Royal Institute of British Architects, London.

18. The other examples of Kent's "admired" architecture were 44 Berkeley Square, London with its wonderful theatrical staircase (1744) for Lady Isabella Finch; and the Temple of Venus (before 1732) at Stowe, Lord Cobham's seat in Buckinghamshire.

19. Arthur Young, *A Six Weeks' Tour through the Southern Counties of England and Wales* (London, 1768), p. 110.

20. For all Walpole citiations I have used the forty-seven volumes of the Yale edition of his correspondence, W.S. Lewis and others, eds. (New Haven, 1937–1983).

21. J. A. Home, ed., *The Letters and Journals of Lady Mary Coke* (Edinburgh, 1892), vol. 2, p. 115.

22. F. H. W. Sheppard, ed., *Survey of London* (London, 1960), vol. 29, p. 143.

23. Northumberland MSS., Alnwick Castle. I am indebted to the late 10th and present 11th Duke of Northumberland for allowing me access to documents at Alnwick and Syon over many years.

24. See note 20 above.

25. Christoper Simon Sykes, *Private Palaces, Life in the Great London Houses* (London, 1985), p. 307.

26. *Ibid.*, p. 249.

27. Huxley, *op. cit.*, pp. 142–143.

28. Sykes, *op. cit.*, p. 282.

29. Hermione Hobhouse, *Lost London, A Century of Demolition and Decay* (London and Boston, 1971–1972), p. 19.

30. Barbara McLean Ward, "Boston Goldsmiths, 1690–1730," in *The Craftsman in Early America*, ed., Ian M. G. Quimby (New York and London, 1984), p. 135.

31. John Bivins, Jr., "Charleston Rococo Interiors, 1765–1775," *Journal of Early Southern Decorative Arts* 12, no. 2 (1986), p. 2.

32. Graham Hood, *The Governor's Palace, Williamsburg* (Colonial Williamsburg, Va.) 1991.

CHAPTER VII

1. James S. Ackermann, *The Villa: Form and Ideology of Country Houses* (Princeton, N. J., and London, 1990). p. 35; K. D. White, *Country Life in Classical Times* (Ithaca, N. Y., 1977), gives an anthology of ancient writings.

2. Stone, *Crisis, op. cit.*, pp. 289–291.

3. R. H. Tawney, *Business and Politics under James I* (Cambridge, 1958), p. 26; Stone, *Crisis, op. cit.*, p. 295.

4. L. Dickins and M. Stanton, *An Eighteenth Century Correspondence* (London, 1910), p. 230.

5. P. J. Bowden, *The Wool Trade in Tudor and Stuart England* (London, 1962), pp. 5–12.

6. E. J. Evans, *The Contentious Tithe, 1750–1850* (London, 1976), pp. 74–76. The Tithe Commutation Act of 1836 gave the benefit to the clergy of substituting a money payment. Since 1936 this has been collected on their behalf by the Government.

7. Paul Langford, *Public Life and the Propertied Englishman, 1689–1798* (Oxford, 1991), p. 368.

8. *Ibid.*, p. 274, citing B. R. Pollard, *Four Early Pamphlets by William Godwin* (Gainesville, Fla., 1966), pp. 130–131.

9. J. A. Phillips, *Electoral Behaviour in Unreformed England* (Princeton, N.J., 1982), p. 83.

10. Letwin, *op. cit.*, p. 183.

11. J. C. Sainty, *Lists of the Lieutenants of England and Wales, 1660–1974* (London, 1979), p. 72.

12. N. Landau, *The Justices of the Peace, 1679–1760* (Berkeley, Calif., 1984), p. 206.

13. Nicholas Kingsley, *The Country Houses of Gloucestershire* (Cheltenham, 1989), vol. 1, p. 157.

14. Edward Gregg, *Queen Anne* (London, 1980), p. 12.

15. *Victoria County History of Leicestershire*, vol. 3,. p. 271, cited by Thompson, *op. cit.*, p. 150; Raymond Carr, *A History of Foxhunting* (London, 1976), p. 242.

16. Thompson, *op. cit.*, p. 146.

17. J. H. Plumb, *The Commercialization of Leisure in Eighteenth Century England* (Reading, 1972), p. 16; W. Vamplew, *The Turf: A Social and Economic History of Horse-Racing* (London, 1976), p. 199.

18. Robert Rowe, *Adam Silver* (London, 1965), pls. 6–9.

19. Giles Worsley "Aldby Park, Yorkshire," *Country Life* (London, February 13, 1986), p. 376.

20. Beckett, *op. cit.*, p. 358.

21. Mingay, *op. cit.*, p. 152.

22. William Cavendish, Duke of Newcastle, published his book on *haute école, La Méthode Nouvelle pour dresser les Chevaux* in 1657 and built extensive riding schools at Bolsover Castle and Welbeck Abbey. See A. S. Turberville, *Welbeck Abbey and Its Owners* (London, 1938), vol 1.

23. Thompson, *op. cit.*, pp 139–141; P. B. Munsche, *Gentlemen and Poachers, the English Game Laws, 1671–1831* (London, 1981), p. 56.

24. H. M. Colvin, ed., *History of the King's Works*, 1485–1660 (London, 1982), vol. 4. pt. 1, pp. 22, 106.

25. J. Smyth, *Lives of the Berkeleys*, ed. J. Maclean (Gloucester, 1883), vol. 2, p. 363.

26. By act of Victoria, 12–13, c. 92 (1849–1850).

27. J. Dixon Hunt, *Garden and Grove, The Italian Renaissance Garden in the English Imagination, 1600–1750* (London, 1986), p. 105.

28. Stone, *Crisis*, *op. cit.*, p. 697; J. Marshall, *Annals of Tennis* (London, 1878), p. 61.

29. *Westmorland Gazette*, January 9, 1847.

30. A. MacKenzie, *History of the Highland Clearances* (London, 2nd edition, 1914), p. 19.

31. J. Prebble, *The Highland Clearances* (London, 1963), p. 103.

CHAPTER VIII

1. L. O. J. Boynton, ed., "The Hardwick Hall Inventory of 1601," *Furniture History* 7 (1971).

2. Prestwich, *op. cit.*, p. 544.

3. The fascinating account of the life of the Duchess of Hamilton is given in Rosalind K. Marshall, *The Days of Duchess Anne, Life in the Household of the Duchess of Hamilton, 1656–1716* (London, 1973), chap. 4.

4. Baker and Baker, *op. cit.*, pp. 192–194.

5. *Ibid.*, p. 181.

6. Peter Brown, *Pyramids of Pleasure: Eating and Dining in Eighteenth Century England* (York Civic Trust, 1990), p. 11.

7. James Lees-Milne, *Tudor Renaissance* (London, 1951), p. 97.

8. Durant, *op. cit.*, pp. 166–174.

9. Prestwich, *op. cit.*, p. 225.

10. Marshall, *op. cit.*, pp. 86–90.

11. Linda Baumgarten, *Eighteenth-Century Clothing at Williamsburg* (Colonial Williamsburg, Va., 1986), pp. 52–61.

12. Albert Boime, "Sargent in Paris and London," in Patricia Hills, ed., *John Singer Sargent* (New York, 1987), p. 102.

13. Robin Simon, *The Portrait in Britain and America* (Oxford, 1987), p. 107

14. Baumgarten, *op. cit.*, pp. 16–20.

15. Natalie Rothstein, *Silk Designs of the Eighteenth Century in the Collection of the Victoria and Albert Museum* (London, 1990).

16. Oliver Fairclough, *Grand Old Mansion: The Holtes and Their Successors at Aston Hall, 1618–1864* (Birmingham, 1984), p. 77.

17. M. Blundell, ed., *Blundell's Diary and Letter Book, 1702–1728* (Liverpool, 1952), pp. 66–67; Baker, *op. cit.*, p. 424.

18. Halsband, *op. cit.*, pp. 109–112, 255.

19. W. H. G. Armytage, "Scientific Discoveries in the Service of Man," in Alfred Cobban, ed., *The Eighteenth Century: Europe in the Age of Enlightment* (London, 1969), p. 113.

20. Mingay, *op. cit.*, p. 222.

21. *Ibid.*, p. 223.

22. Mark Girouard, *Life in the English Country House* (London, 1978), chap. 7, "The Social House: 1720–1770."

23. Baker and Baker, *op. cit.*, pp. 169–170.

24. J. D. Williams, *The Restoration of Audley End, 1762–1797* (Chelmsford, Essex, 1966), p. 32.

25. Mary Mauchline, *Harewood House* (Newton Abbot, Devon, 1974), p. 93.

26. Christopher Gilbert, *The Life and Work of Thomas Chippendale* (London, 1978), vol 1., p. 59.

27. Augustus Hare, *The Years with Mother* (London, 1896), vol. 1, p. 66.

28. Catherine Gore, *The Diamond and the Pearl* (London 1849), vol. 1, p. 288.

29. Garrett, *op. cit.*, p. 15.

30. Arthur W. Calhoun, *A Social History of the American Family* (New York, 1945), vol. 2, pp. 137–138.

31. The detail of home life in Washington are based on two publications issued by The Octagon, Washington, D.C.: Barbara C. Carson, *Aspiring Appetites* (1990) and their exhibition catalog on "Genteel Dining," *The Taste of Power* (June–October 1990).

32. Garrett, *op. cit.*, p. 252

CHAPTER IX

1. Donald Read, *England, 1868–1914* (London and New York, 1979), pp. 3–4.

2. *Ibid.*, pp. 190–191.

3. Christopher Hibbert, *Edward VII, A Portrait* (London and New York, 1976), pp. 91–97.

4. Beatrice Webb, *My Apprenticeship* (London, 1926), pp. 45–54.

5. Read, *op. cit.*, p. 31.

6. Wilfred Blunt, *My Diaries* (London, 1920), p. 72.

7. Roger Fulford, "The King" in *Edwardian England 1901–1914*, ed., Simon Nowell-Smith (Oxford, 1964), pp. 1–42.

8. Price Collier, *England and the English* (London and New York, 1909), p. 17.

9. James Bryce, *Hindrances to Good Citizenship* (London and New York, 1909), p. 36.

10. M. Hurd, *The Ordeal of Ivor Gurney* (London 1978); B. Bergonzi, *Heroes' Twilight: A Study of the Literature of the Great War* (London, 1965), pp. 20–31.

11. John Arlott, "Sport" in *Edwardian England* (see note 7 above), pp. 449–486.

12. Lucy Masterman, *C.F.G. Masterman* (London, 1939), p. 84.

13. A. Bird, *The Motor Car, 1765–1914* (London, 1960).

14. C. H. Gibbs-Smith, *Aviation, An Historical Survey* (London, 1970); H.G. Wells, *An Englishman Looks at the World* (London, 1914), chaps. 1–3, both cited by Read, *op. cit.* (note 1 above), p. 419.

15. Robert Graves and Alan Hodge, *The Long Weekend: A Social History of Great Britain, 1918–1939* (London, 1941), p. 129.

16. Graves and Hodge, *op. cit.*, p. 368.

17. Paul Addison, *The Road to 1945* (London, 1975): Angus Calder, *The People's War* (London, 1969), both with full bibliographies.

18. James Lees-Milne, *Ancestral Voices* (London, 1975), pp. 68, 231.

19. David Thomson, *England in the Twentieth Century, 1914–1963* (London, 1964), pp. 187–191.

20. *Historic House*, Autumn 1990, p. 5.

CHAPTER X

1. Stone, *Crisis, op. cit.*, p. 572.

2. The funeral of the third Earl of Derby is summarized in Stone, *Crisis, op. cit.*, p. 572, but I have used the fuller account given in A. Collins, *The Peerage of England* (London, 1779), vol. 3, pp. 55–62. See also Alan Simpson, *The Wealth of the Gentry, 1540–1660* (Chicago and Cambridge, 1963), chap. 1, for details of the funeral of Sir Nicholas Bacon in 1579.

3. Durant, *op. cit.*, p. 224.

4. *Ibid.*, p. 225.

5. *Ibid.*, p. 245.

6. Lawrence Stone, *Family and Fortune: Studies in Aristocratic Finance in the Sixteenth and Seventeenth Centuries* (Oxford, 1973), pp. 171–174.

7. *Ibid.*, pp. 175–176.

8. Nigel Llewellyn, *The Art of Death* (London, 1991), VII, 'Two Bodies.'

9. *Ibid.*, p. 47.

10. Sir Henry Chauncy, *Hertfordshire* (London, 1700), p. 19.

11. Geoffrey Beard, *The Work of Grinling Gibbons* (London and Chicago, 1990), chap. 3.

12. David Green, *Blenheim Palace* (London, 1954), p. 172.

13. Margaret Whinney, *Sculpture in Britain, 1530–1830* (London, revised edition, 1988), p. 285.

14. *Ibid.*, p. 346 and pl. 247; the figure of the youth is illustrated by H. D. Molesworth, *Sculpture in England* (London, 1951), pl. 47.

15. *Westmorland Gazette* (Kendal), March 30, 1844.

16. Germaine Greer et al., eds., *Kissing the Rod: An Anthology of Seventeenth-Century Women's Verse* (London, 1988), p. 103.

Index

Fermour, Sir William, 109
Ferrers, Benjamin, *109*
Fielding, Henry, 33, 153
Fithian, Philip Vickers, 97
Fitzgerald, F. Scott, 101
Flagler, Henry M., 112–113
Flaxman, John, *36*, 210
food: overeating, 181; sources of, 172;
    variety of, 172–174, 185
Ford, Edsel, 53
fortifications, 76–78, 115
Fountaine, Sir Andrew, 45
fox hunting, 159, 161–163
Franklin, Benjamin, 49–51, 70
Fraunce, Abraham, 114
Frick, Henry Clay, 113
Frith, William Powell, 53, 131, *146*
Fulbecke, William, 114
Fuller's, London shop, *118*
funerals, 203–*206*, 208, 210–211
funerary monuments, *201–202, 204–205,*
    206–211, *207, 210*

Gainsborough, Thomas, 49, 165, 180
Galbraith, J. K., 198
gambling, 132, *140*, 164, 192
gardens, 89–90
Garrard, George, *96*
Garthwaite, Anna Maria, 176
Gay, John, 126
gentlemen: books about, 8, 10, 12, 14–16;
    definitions, 14–18, 102–103; income of,
    12, 102–119
George, David, Lloyd, 196
George I, 18
George II, 18
George III, 18, 51, 95, 158, 188
George IV, 168
George V, 190, 197
George VI, 197
Gheeraerts, Marcus, the Elder, *104*
Gibbons, Grinling, 88, 208
Gibbs, James, 88–89, 91, 109
Gilbert, Sir Humphrey, 115
Girouard, Mark, 86
Gladstone, William, 33, 188
Godwin, William, 157
Goldsmith, Oliver, 153
Goodwood Park, Surrey, 161
Gore, Mrs. Catherine, 184
Gothic style, 95
Gouge, William, 21
governesses, 32–33
Gower, George, *59, 103*, 174
Grahame, Kenneth, 194
Grand Tour, *40*, 44–49, *46*, 62, 208
Gray, Thomas, 33

Grenville, George, 66–67
Greville, Hon. Ronald, 100–101
Greville, Margaret Helen McEwan,
    100–101
Grimsthorpe, 88
Grosvenor, Lord, 165
Grosvenor, Sir Thomas, 67
Grosvenor House, 141–143, *147*
guns, hunting, *156*
Gurney, Ivor, 192
Gwillym family, *68*
Gwynn, John, 91
Gwynne, Nell, 202
gymnastics, *39*

Hagley Hall, 49, 152, 168
Halifax, George Montagu Dunk, Earl of,
    157
Halifax, George Savile, first Marquis of, 40
Hall, Sydney Prior, *70*
Ham House, 86
Hamilton, Dukes of: Anne, 172; James, 27;
    William Douglas, 172, 175
Hamilton, Gavin, 51
Hamilton, Sir William, 49
Hamilton Palace, Scotland, 172–173
Hampton, Md., 119
Hardwick, Philip, 131
Hardwick Hall, Derbyshire, 79–82, *79–80*,
    87, 106, 170–172, 182
Hare, Augustus, 26, 184
Harewood House, Yorks., 184
Harington, Sir John, 182
Harlow, Henry, 86
Harrison, William, 36
Harrods, *116*, 131–132
Hatton, Sir Christopher, 78
hawking, *150*, 159
Hawkins, Sir John, 115
Hawksmoor, Nicholas, 211
Haydon, Benjamin Robert, 169
Hayman, Francis, 49, *129, 156*
Hayter, Sir George, *142*
health: of children, 19–20; cures, 13,
    180–182; diet and, 181
Henley, W. E., 194
Henry VII, 60, 203
Henry VIII, 34, 36, 60, 78, 115, 159, 167,
    203
heraldry, 16–18, 203, 207
Hickes, Sir Michael, 104
Hobart, Thomas, 45
Hobbes, Thomas, 207
Hogarth, William, 11, *55, 62, 63*, 94, 117,
    153, *159, 173*, 176, 183
Holbein, Hans, the Younger, *7, 151*
Holdenby Hall, Yorks., 78, 80

Holdernesse House, London, 141
Holkham, Norfolk, 88
Holland, Sir John, 21
Hollemans, Jasper, *204*
Holte, Sir Lister, 180
Homer, Winslow, *162*
Honthorst, Gerard van, 19
Hooke, Robert, 86
Hopkins, Mark, 112
Hopkins, Thomas, 125
horses: breeding, 165; racing, 163–165, 192
Howard, Henry, 13
Howard family, 61
Howell, James, 44
Hudson, Thomas, *69*
Hughes, Thomas, 33
Hume, Anna, 211
Hume, David, 181
Humphrey, Laurence, *The Nobles: or of
    Nobilities*, 34
Humphry, Mrs., *Manners for Men*, 178
Hunt, Charles, *149, 155*
Hunt, Richard Morris, 100
Hunt, William Holman, *32, 143*
hunting, *149, 152, 155, 156, 157*, 159–163,
    165–166, 172, *191*; big game, 165–166;
    laws on, 161, 165
Huntingdon, Henry Hastings, fifth Earl, 61
Huntington, Collis P., 112
Huntington, Henry Edward, 113
Huskisson, Robert, *183*
Hutchinson, Thomas, Gov. of
    Massachusetts, 51
Hutchinson, Mrs., 21, 23

imports, 174
Ince Blundell, Lancs., *101*
income, sources of, 11–12, 53, 102–119
Ingram, Sir Arthur, 12, 76, 105
inheritance: laws, 16, 57–60, 116, 197;
    marriage and, 54–75; wealth from,
    111–113
Inns of Court, 113–114
Italian influence, 43–44, 49, 208

James, Henry, 113
James, Isaac, *202*
James I, 105
James II, 200
Jarratt, Devereux, 29–30
Jefferson, Thomas, 29–31, 51–52, 184–185
Jenkins, Thomas, 46–47, 49
Jerome, Jennie, 73
Johnson, Eastman, *179*
Johnson, Gerard, 205, *205*, 206
Johnson, Samuel, 14, 45
Jones, Inigo, 44, 82, 108, 120